Part memoir, part business fable, this book will delight wine aficionados and inspire young professionals with a career model worth following closely. The book tells of a restless young graduate's serendipitous plunge into the world of wine production and marketing, which led her to a CEO position in the famed Napa Valley.

Full of personal anecdotes, the book is an insider's peek into the Napa phenomenon that came into its own even as the author's career blossomed and matured. The writing sparkles with wit and warmth as surely as the wine that was at the heart of the author's career.

Lynn McBride, author of *How to Learn a New Language with a Used Brain* and lifestyle blogger at southernfriedfrench.com

This smart and fun read chronicling a seminal development in California's wine culture makes us nostalgic for a time providing warmer incubators for freewheeling approaches to business.

But wait! the intrepid author Michaela Rodeno tells us. Her engaging tales of recognizing and creating opportunities are also an inspirational manual for encouraging creative leadership, the kind that can still result in enterprises both novel and successful.

Doreen Schmid, co-author of *Oyster Culture*

Michaela Rodeno is a serial entrepreneur. She has three successful wine startups under her slim belt and, as a director of two publicly traded California banks, has helped them open new markets. A Berkeley/Haas graduate, Michaela has rewritten the textbook on entrepreneurism.

And a delightful textbook it is—witty, humble, and full of how-to wisdom about generating a healthy bottom line while having fun with startups in a fiercely competitive and regulated international industry.

Whether you are a large corporation looking beyond your comfort zone, or a bright-eyed MBA bent on starting the next Wall Street darling, this book, like a glass of Napa Valley red, will be good medicine.

Laird Durham, former senior staff consultant, Arthur D. Little

BUBBLES

TO

BOARDROOMS

Serendipitous Stories
From Inside the Wine Business

For Lauren & Matt —
Enjoy these stories over
a good glass of Sangiovese!
Michaela
Nov 2015

MICHAELA KANE RODENO

VILLA RAGAZZI PRESS
Bubbles to Boardrooms
Michaela Kane Rodeno

Cover: Melanie Doherty Design

Information at www.villaragazzipress.com

Published in the United States by Villa Ragazzi Press
ISBN 978-0-9896342-4-3

DEDICATION

This book is dedicated to my husband Gregory,
our daughter Kate, and our son John, and to those with
whom I've had the privilege to work.
Their support and guidance have made all the difference
in a long, happy career.

TABLE OF CONTENTS

ACT I STARTUPS ARE SUCH FUN

The real stories in this book illustrate how much fun work can be, especially for those lucky enough to be part of starting a new enterprise. Every day is a new experience, exhilarating for those who, like the author, thrive on learning and challenges. The early days of Domaine Chandon in Napa Valley, in 1973 the first major French wine investment in the U.S., were a high-performing hoot.

The iconoclastic leadership of my boss, John Wright, coupled with his belief that good minds and youthful energy outweigh experience, achieved remarkable success in record time. Given the freedom and responsibility to make important things happen, well-educated but untested young people routinely produced results that surprised seasoned observers. In the absence of rules and supervision, innovation erupted.

This is not meant to be a complete or even accurate recounting of Domaine Chandon's early history. These are my recollections of events over the 15 years I spent at Domaine Chandon; others may remember differently. It is not meant to be a comprehensive history, but a fond look back at people and events that helped formed me. It was a freewheeling, slightly crazy, wonderful learning experience for many of us.

Without this grand opportunity to have room to run early in my business education, it is much less likely I would have become one of the rare female CEOs in the wine industry. I have tried to pay it forward, as readers will see in the second part of *Bubbles to Boardrooms*, and I hope this book inspires others to do the same.

1 THE LAND OF OPPORTUNITY

Late in 1972 I followed my young lawyer husband Gregory to his new position with a firm named Rutherford & Rutherford in Napa Valley, a siren song to him that left me unmoved. He already loved wine, but in Alameda where I had graduated from high school, Napa was better known as home to a state mental hospital. These were still the early days of Napa's renaissance as a world-class winegrowing powerhouse.

Most agree the modern era for wine in Napa Valley dates from 1966, when Robert Mondavi founded his winery. There were a few dozen wineries then, not hundreds as now. Even so, it was clear that wine was the most interesting thing happening in Napa Valley. Basalt Rock, Kaiser Steel, Mare Island Naval Shipyard, Napa State Hospital…not for me.

Like many young people, I had no idea what to do to earn a living. Although I love learning, teaching French to undergraduates at Davis had shown me that I was not destined to be an academic. As I soon found, having a master's degree in French Literature was more of a handicap than an asset, ironically making me "overqualified" or, more accurately, unemployable.

While waiting and looking for the right job, whatever that might be, I patched together a series of part-time jobs. My advanced degree qualified as a community college teaching credential, enabling me to land a job teaching French for Napa College (later to be rebranded Napa Valley College).

Our small class had a good time, meeting at 8:00 a.m. every weekday for a semester. Liz (Mrs. Louis P.) Martini and Jamie Davies of Schramsberg Vineyards were among my students. We read aloud to one another, practiced ordering in French from restaurant menus, and did our best with the French national anthem "La Marseillaise," a much easier melody to sing than the Star Spangled Banner. We three made the mistake of trying to counsel a bright young student working as a nursing home aide that she had the potential to try for anything she wanted; perhaps feeling badgered, she quit the class.

At the same time I undertook the project of publishing the Napa College catalogue, an organizational challenge that revealed another career I would not pursue.

To increase my contribution to our rent, I started looking for a part-time job as a winery tour guide. I didn't realize how scarce those jobs were, because there weren't many visitors to the Napa Valley in 1972.

I first met Margrit, the future Mrs. Mondavi, when I came to the winery looking for a job. She gently pointed out that I was overqualified to be a tour guide, even had they needed one in those relatively quiet days. At that time, Margrit and one other person easily handled the visitor traffic at Mondavi.

So I must have been lucky to land a job at Beaulieu Vineyard in Rutherford. Longer established than Mondavi and well known for its Cabernets, Beaulieu needed a team of tour guides. I learned much later that I was their first female tour guide, which seems in hindsight a rather low ceiling to break through. At the close of my first week on the job, the avuncular manager Maynard Monaghan must have decided I was trustworthy. He handed me the keys, asked me to lock up, and ambled off to his cottage on the de Pins estate across Highway 29.

Beaulieu was one of the few pre-Prohibition wineries that had kept its doors open by taking advantage of the "sacramental wine" loophole in the Volstead Act. I recall pouring tastes of its various Napa Valley Cabernets for a Catholic priest in black cassock and white collar who was carefully selecting his (very high quality) altar wine. We still have in the cellar a five-gallon jug of non-vintage BV Cabernet clearly labeled "sacramental wine" acquired during my 6-month tenure at Beaulieu. We never got around to opening it for a party, and now we're afraid to.

Gregory and I spent my entire paycheck and more buying 1968–1971 BV Cabernets at the employee price, which I recall as $2.19. (Or was that my hourly wage for working in the dorm cafeteria during my freshman year at UC Davis?) The BV Founder's wines cost employees more, maybe four dollars, with a two-bottle limit that applied to everyone. We still have some of those wines, which have aged beautifully and are pulled out of the cellar only for special occasions.

This was near the end of the long reign of their winemaker André Tchelistcheff—arguably America's most influential post-Prohibition winemaker—and the wines were superb. Maynard, bless him, honored us with a 1946 Georges de la Tour Private Reserve Cabernet from his own cellar for my birth year, and a 1945 Founder's Reserve Pinot Noir to Gregory for his. We were among those privileged to be invited to André's 1973 retirement party, a well-attended sit-down dinner in the cellar. André continued thereafter to work as a consultant for Chateau Ste. Michelle and others well into his 90s.

In the spring of 1973 a headline in the Napa Register (later rebranded the Napa Valley Register) caught my attention: "French Company to Build $5 Million Winery." This was big news in the wine world, since California was then considered a producer of mostly jug wines. France and Germany produced the world's best wines, and it raised eyebrows around the world for a renowned French producer to invest in California.

It was also big news for me. To a French major with no marketable skills other than fluency in that very language, this sounded like opportunity.

Lacking actionable details, I tapped into my husband's legal network to unearth a local contact for this elusive new enterprise. Within two weeks I'd learned that the founding president was John Wright, a former management consultant who was working out of his garage on Mt. Veeder. The connection came through his neighbors, two young attorneys with small children. She was keeping the books for the fledgling wine company, hiking through the woods every few days to pay bills and make hand-written entries in the general ledger.

I commandeered our only vehicle, Gregory's prized Alfa Romeo, and motored up the mountain without an appointment. Walking into the garage at 1743 (an address chosen because it was the year Moët & Chandon was founded) Mt. Veeder Road, I found John Wright working alone at an improvised plywood standup desk and managed to blurt, "I speak French; do you need help?" He was surprised, but kindly gave the idea a few seconds of thought and replied, "Yes, I guess so."

Not long before he died in 2012, John would tell my St. Supéry colleague Lesley Russell that the day I walked through that garage door was the best day of his work life. Mine too.

2 THE FUTURE OF WINE IN AMERICA

Following his return to the family business after WWII, where he was a leader of the Resistance and lost a finger to Nazi torturers, Comte Robert-Jean de Vogüé had devoted himself to developing Moët & Chandon from one of many small champagne houses to France's largest.

In addition to acquiring other champagne houses, including Mercier and Ruinart, as the chairman of Moët & Chandon Robert-Jean built the business in other innovative ways. Given the strict volume and origin constraints imposed by the *appellation contrôlée* of *la Champagne viticole*, he took advantage of growth opportunities by exporting the firm's winemaking expertise in lieu of increasing volume in Champagne. As early as 1960 he sent winemakers to Mendoza, Argentina to consult on producing high quality sparkling wine using local grapes in a new winery funded by Moët. Another important part of Moët's success in distant markets was to hire local management.

Without the prohibitive cost of import duties on champagne, the wines were more affordable, and quality, based on the firm's know-how from Champagne, was superior. This strategy reduced the pressure on *la Champagne's* limited capacity to meet increasing worldwide demand.

Other Moët-sponsored offshore winemaking ventures followed in Brazil and Germany. With an eye for developing markets, after a 1978 visit to California, Robert-Jean had been waiting for the right opportunity to do the same in the U.S. Although the U.S. had consumed only 100,000 cases of champagne annually for years, he was convinced that significant growth was possible.

When John Wright's extensive market study, Wine/America, written for his employer Arthur D. Little and offered to a range of clients, came to the attention of Comte de Vogüé, Robert-Jean immediately requested a meeting. He liked what he had read since it confirmed his conviction that the U.S. was a promising, if underdeveloped wine market. He also liked

John, a kindred entrepreneurial spirit who embraced innovation and risk-taking, and who at 40 was half his age.

Eager to move on the opportunity he had been eyeing for years, Comte de Vogüé offered John Wright the job of starting up a sparkling wine business in the U.S. with Moët's full support. It didn't faze him that John's relevant experience consisted of making home wine from the hybrid grapevines in his back yard in Connecticut and, since transferring to ADL's office in San Francisco, spending weekends with partner Herb McGrew planting a small vineyard named Pickle Canyon on Mt. Veeder, in Napa Valley. John immediately accepted Robert-Jean's irresistible offer, said goodbye to Arthur D. Little, and dived in.

Champagne is France's northernmost, coolest winegrowing region, and its climate has a major impact on the type of wine it is able to produce. John's mission was to produce fine sparkling wine using Moët's expertise, which made the warmer areas of California inappropriate for this project.

In spite of his personal toehold in the Napa Valley, John dutifully evaluated all the other suitably cool winegrowing areas of California before deciding to base the new enterprise in his adopted hometown. In March 1973, M & H Vineyards was incorporated and the grand adventure began with the acquisition of more than 1,000 acres in Carneros, Yountville, and Mt. Veeder.

In June 1973, John Wright and Robert-Jean de Vogüé were featured toasting the chairman of Wine institute on the cover of *Wines & Vines*. The word was out, at least in wine circles. To their credit, California vintners and even Napa Valley sparkling wine producers like Schramsberg's Jack Davies and Hanns Kornell welcomed the new venture. They understood that the imprimatur of France's largest champagne house could only enhance Napa Valley's reputation. If they had any reservations about a foreign invasion, they kept them to themselves.

3 STARTUPS ARE SUCH FUN

With no business experience and only one apparently useful skill, I joined M & H Vineyards in May 1973 as its second full-time employee. Although highly intelligent, analytical, and creative, John Wright had no operational or P&L experience. No longer could he swoop in as a management consultant, share his brilliant insights and advice with the client, and then leave town.

John turned out to be the perfect boss for me. I didn't like being told what to do, and he didn't like giving orders or supervising people. He was a leader, not a manager.

With vineyards to plant, a winery to design and build, wines to make, a marketing strategy to develop, and an organization to build, there was more than enough to keep us fully occupied. It was all important, and we were in a hurry. Ours was a simple arrangement: I did whatever John didn't want to do or hadn't time for. My business card grandly proclaimed me "Assistant to the President," but since there were only two of us, the job defied description.

We were in a hurry to get started, but lacked grape sources and a temporary place to make the first wines. At a cocktail party to introduce the new venture to local vintners, John Wright and Robert-Jean de Vogüé met Katie and Gene Trefethen. In 1973, Trefethen Vineyards grew and sold hundreds of acres of wine grapes in the cool – ideal for sparkling wines -- Oak Knoll part of the valley. Katie told Robert-Jean that Trefethen had grapes available for sale and, like us, wanted to start making wine. A symbiotic partnership was born.

We optimistically offered to equip Trefethen's historic winery building, vacant since the 1950s, in the two months then remaining before the 1973 harvest. This meant paving the dirt floor, shoring up the second floor of a redwood building built in 1886 to support the considerable weight of champagne bottles *en tirage*, air-freighting a Vaslin press from France (which increased the cost of the press by 50%), ordering custom stainless steel tanks and fittings, contracting for grapes from Trefethen and other growers, obtaining permits and licenses, and completing myriad organizational tasks. More experienced wine people would have said "It can't be done!" but John Wright was an early practitioner of the art of the possible and we just did it.

Gregory (left) and Michaela (right) receiving an early Domaine Chandon visitor at Trefethen. The original winery's exterior wall is barely visible at right.

Starting up a company is exhilarating, as any entrepreneur can tell you. With the financial and reputational backing of Moët-Hennessy to mitigate the risks that face most new businesses, we were able to enjoy learning by doing. And we did it mostly without professional help, I being fairly innocent of the usefulness of experts and John, having been a consultant himself, leery of them.

This is how I came to draft the minutes of an early board meeting, armed with my scribbled notes and a mail order pamphlet outlining the Corporations Code. When reasonably sure I had this legal document right,

I mailed it to France to be signed by Moët-Hennessy's officers and directors. By the time it eventually came back from Paris, Champagne, and Cognac with all the required signatures, I had discovered several errors and had to re-do the document. And get the required signatures again. No one seemed to mind. And I, although married to a lawyer, never thought of seeking legal assistance.

The local Bureau of Alcohol, Tobacco & Firearms (BATF) office was housed in the basement of Napa's downtown post office. There were fewer than fifty wineries then, and the two officers seemed happy to have a visitor when I came looking for help. They walked me through the federal permitting requirements, application process, and reporting procedures. The directors of Moët-Hennessy were surprised to learn that the U.S. government wanted their fingerprints, but obliged.

4 EVERY BOARDROOM IS DIFFERENT

My first experience with a board of directors took place in Épernay, seat of many of the great champagne houses including Moët & Chandon, Perrier-Jouët, and Pol Roger. While researching champagne houses and their facilities in late 1974 with John Wright and Bob Mountjoy, the lead architect on the Napa sparkling winery project, we were invited to lunch with Moët-Hennessy's board of directors at the Trianon. Although only three or four board members had any direct involvement in the California venture, they were all eager to hear about it.

Alain Chevalier was the *président-directeur général* (French equivalent of CEO) of Moët-Hennessy, the holding company for Champagne Moët & Chandon and Hennessy Cognac formed when the two merged in the late 1960's. A graduate of the prestigious *École Normale Supérieure*, one of France's *grandes écoles* that produce most of the country's titans of industry and top government officials, Alain was the only non-family member on the board. The directors included Kilian Hennessy, chair, Frédéric Chandon de Briailles, Ghislain de Vogüé, Alain de Pracomtal and other titled and accomplished leaders whose families went back generations in the French wine industry. M. Chevalier ran the board meetings as a highly educated businessman and neutral party; everyone had a voice, and everyone's time was respected. Lunch in the Trianon invariably followed the regular Monday morning board meeting.

The Trianon is an exquisite eighteenth-century townhouse across the Avenue de Champagne used by Moët & Chandon for VIP entertainment. Much like a mini-Versailles, it featured an *orangerie*, tapestries, gilt *boiseries*, a marble staircase, and formal gardens.

There were twenty of us around the polished oval table for an elegant, multi-course luncheon prepared by Moët's chef Joseph Thuet, honored as a *maître cuisinier de France*. I, as one of two women present, had the bad luck to be served first. I was completely unprepared for Italian style service. It takes practice, or at least the opportunity to observe someone else do it, to serve yourself from a platter offered over your left shoulder.

I managed to wrestle a slice of rare filet mignon onto my plate, but when the white-gloved waiter returned with a sauceboat, the silver ladle slipped from my nervous fingers into the sauce. He must have been accustomed to dealing with novices like me. Within seconds he had returned, white gloves spotless, with a clean ladle positioned in the sauceboat as if nothing had happened. Champagne flowed before, during, and after the meal. Now *that's* a board meeting.

From left: Fred Chandon, Alain Chevalier, John Wright, and Edmond Maudiére

Board meetings in Napa were different. John Wright was the president and chairman of the board of M & H Vineyards and, try as Alain might, he seldom could hold John to the agenda. After a thorough discussion, Alain would move to finalize a decision by summarizing the issue and the board's apparent consensus, only to discover that John wasn't finished talking yet.

A few minutes later Alain would try again, and John would ignore his efforts to close the topic. He had more to say. This could happen several times before Alain succeeded, or someone changed the subject. With hindsight, I think John didn't like making decisions —actually, the French call it "taking" decisions—because that would close off other options. With John, there was always a better idea.

Rather than being frustrated, Alain seemed to like this open-ended way of thinking and acting. Like John, he was a man ahead of his time. In the mid-1970s he had written a small, dense book entitled *The Social Balance Sheet* about corporate responsibility, years before the concept reached the U.S. (Corporate social responsibility is still a rare topic on board agendas in both Europe and the U.S., with only a few forward-thinking companies giving it serious attention.) Alain and John admired and liked one another. Domaine Chandon grew and prospered in spite of its unorthodox way of getting things done.

5 LIFE ON THE MOUNTAIN

Robert-Jean de Vogüé and his Moët-Hennessy colleagues found it charming that "heepies" from the Lokoya camp at the top of Mt. Veeder formed a good part of our vineyard crew. The French, as we collectively and affectionately referred to them, enjoyed coming to California. Except, perhaps, the time John Wright decided to go foraging for wild mushrooms.

He had observed a quartet of elderly Italian men from San Francisco disappear into the woods on the former Simmons Ranch on Mt. Veeder in the fall, and return with enough porcini to fill the trunk of their car. He expected everyone to be as delighted as he with such a delicacy. The French directors politely declined the tasty dish served up for lunch by John's wife Renate, who wouldn't eat them either. Only John and I did. That showed how much I trusted him, or how little I as a twenty-something year old knew about the risks of eating wild mushrooms.

The hippies were good foragers, too. The woods on Mt. Veeder are full of deer, which do such damage in vineyards that farmers can easily get a permit to shoot them; the only caveat is that the county requires permitted hunters to turn in the carcasses rather than eat them. One day, one of the hippies found a dead deer and decided that hanging it in a tree for several days would turn it into a fine main course for the next party. It didn't.

Supplying our numerous company parties could be hazardous. As we had not produced any of our own Napa Valley wine to drink, I applied for a federal importer's license and we stocked up on champagne. Gregory and I narrowly avoided a fatal accident when returning from San Francisco one night, my Peugeot 504 loaded with 15 cases of Moët. The extra weight made the car sluggish. When a dead-in-the-water Cadillac suddenly appeared in our headlights athwart the fast lane of I-80, Gregory swerved as hard as he could. We were lucky to escape with only a long gash on the driver's side of the car -- and not a single bottle broken.

John liked to cook, but never from a book. Having done a fair amount of consulting work in Brazil, he loved the mixed grills known as *churrasco* and often made them for our parties. A few years later, in 1980, to provide a better story for a food writer from the Los Angeles Times, he added champagne risotto to the menu and, naturally, tried to cook that on the grill, too. The risotto was a complete failure, unless one happens to enjoy expensive rice soup. Hot coals don't provide enough BTUs for risotto, and using chilled cooking liquid compounds the problem. That didn't stop the Los Angeles Times from immortalizing this occasion with photos, stories, and recipes.

Working conditions on Mt. Veeder were abnormal but entertaining. For two years, headquarters was a room attached to John's garage, its concrete block walls freshly painted lime green to match the new lime green plaid carpeting. Dust, mud, dog hair, and spider webs soon muted those bright colors.

The neighbors who shared our eight-party telephone line were not thrilled at the volume of business calls now overloading the antiquated system; there was always someone who desperately needed to break into our conversations to place a call. It took months for the phone company to run a new line for M & H Vineyards several miles from Napa up the mountain.

The Xerox repairman, in a call to his supervisor, was laughing so hard he could scarcely report what was wrong with our tabletop copier: a mouse had stuffed its warm interior with shredded tissues to make a nest.

Before acquiring the Peugeot, a high-riding car with excellent suspension ideal for bouncing around on unpaved roads and vineyard avenues, I drove Gregory's cherished but temperamental Alfa Romeo from our home in Carneros up the mountain to work. Breaking out of the fog into bright sunlight at 1,200-feet elevation was like arriving in heaven every morning. But when it was time to go home, that car would sometimes refuse to start.

Lacking jumper cables, I once had to recruit some of the vineyard crew to launch me down a steep dirt road to get up enough speed to pop the clutch. It didn't occur to any of us that this might not work. Besides, the Caterpillar D4 was nearby if the Alfa and I needed to be hauled back to the top of the hill. The engine started, and I drove home feeling pleased with myself for knowing something about how cars work.

One December day it snowed on Mt. Veeder. This rare condition caused my trusty Peugeot to lose traction on the steep, winding, unpaved road and slide helplessly backward into a drainage ditch. D4 to the rescue! We all loved that piece of equipment, whose primary business was land clearing and vineyard development. Vineyard manager John Carmer gleefully drove it over his old car in retribution for that clunker's many failures to perform.

Always in search of more fun, one wag had the brilliant idea of having a foot race up the mountain. Four people signed up: John Wright's 15-year old son Gerald; Mike, a beefy, half-crazed photographer and motorcycle maven; 40'ish winemaker Kim Giles, who had the slim body of a marathoner; and my visiting brother Jim, a recent US Naval Academy graduate. I was to lead the way in my Peugeot as they raced several miles up Mt. Veeder.

From left: Jim, Kim, Mike, and Gerald getting ready to race up Mt. Veeder.

Someone yelled "On your mark, get set, Go!" and off we went. I constantly checked the rear view mirror to make sure I wasn't getting too far ahead of the runners. I was expecting my brother, who looked fit, to kick out and take the lead. Sure enough, he did. So I added a little speed to give him running room. He ran faster. I added more speed. Then I noticed that he was looking desperate, and remembered that he was a chain smoker. I slowed the car, he dove into the back seat, gasping, and the race continued without him.

Kim Giles edged out the photographer at the top – that last leg up the unpaved road was more than a mile long and quite steep – but the prize, a case of beer, was awarded to the vineyard manager's girlfriend for streaking the finish line on a bicycle, bare naked.

One of my prouder accomplishments on the mountain was to help extricate a crawler tractor stuck in the mud. In my vestigial Spanish I suggested placing some pieces of wood under the tracks. The crew somehow understood, and soon the tractor was clanking up the improvised ramp and out of the mud.

Another useful bit of knowledge I acquired in the garage was how to keep a toilet from overflowing. This greatly impressed a janitor at the newly opened Palace Hotel in New York a few years later.

Critters, mudslides, heavy farm equipment, hippies, the baby grand piano whose weight should have collapsed the floor of the vineyard manager's tumble-down shack—life on Mt. Veeder added up to quite an adventure.

6 LANGUAGE MATTERS

I appear to be among the few with an advanced degree in French Literature who have been able to make a decent living outside academia. I am always pleased to accept invitations to talk to students about the value of learning foreign languages. As I explained in a keynote speech at the 2009 Women in Leadership conference at UC Berkeley's Haas School of Business (available on YouTube), my ability to speak French provided a serendipitous entrée into a long, happy career in wine.

Some think that studying at UC Davis and Bordeaux must surely have been part of a grand plan to prepare myself for the wine business. I will admit to learning to drink wine, not very good wine, during my junior year abroad at the *Université de Bordeaux*. And Davis is certainly the epicenter of viticulture and enology education in California. So the inference is logical, but it's wrong. My career in wine had little to do with my studies.

As graduation approached, the French department at UC Davis offered me $2,000 a year to work as a teaching assistant while studying for my master's degree. I didn't have any better ideas, and I was interested in staying in Davis for a couple more years to see what might develop with a certain young law student I'd met, so I accepted the opportunity. This stipend was a handsome sum in the late sixties, and the workload was minimal: teaching French 1-2-3 to undergraduates for one hour a day left plenty of time for poolside literature study. The best part was that my future lawyer husband and I would complete our degrees at the same time.

The closest I came to the study of wine at Davis was our friend Tom Ferrell, an enology graduate student who rented a room from Gregory's fellow law student Nick Van Male. Nick was the connection whose recommendation brought Gregory to a law firm in Napa and me to a career in wine.

Tom, who would in time become the winemaker/president of Franciscan Estate, then president of Sterling Vineyards and later Spring Mountain Vineyard, could always be counted on to provide lab experiments for our parties. This was, of course, against state law, but who could countenance pouring perfectly good wine down the drain?

Once we arrived in the Napa Valley, it was all about wine for both of us. Being fluent in French soon proved a surprisingly useful credential, as Domaine Chandon fell out of the sky at just the right time for me in early 1973. For my young lawyer husband, the land use challenges inherent in Napa's 1968 Agricultural Preserve ordinance provided a steady stream of clients.

You might wonder how two degrees in French literature would be helpful to a business in California, where Spanish is the second language of choice. In spite of the high value I place on speaking another language, here I would point to the literature component more than the language fluency. I'd been trained to read and write, and analyze with a critical eye. Given the sad, underfunded state of public education today, this has regrettably become a rare skill. I have often wished there were more literate people available to hire, as clear communication is vital to successful collaboration.

That said, being able to communicate in French is remarkably helpful when working for French owners. No matter how good their English, if the dialogue is in their native tongue they can relax instead of straining to find the right English word. Misunderstandings are minimized, and trust builds. This may seem a small thing, but it's not.

In the early days of Domaine Chandon, my fluency in French put me in the center of the action. From the beginning, Moët-Hennessy had assigned Moët's *chef de caves* Edmond Maudière to consult with Domaine Chandon's Napa winemakers. Edmond was a wonderful character, full of enthusiasm for innovation and always eager to see how far we could take the new venture in terms of wine quality. When I visualize him now, I see and hear his typical wide-eyed, excited "Ooh, ooh, ooh…" about whatever idea we were then testing. But he couldn't speak English in 1973.

Viticultural French is very different from the literary French I had studied. Edmond found a six-language viticultural dictionary to help me translate useful information for our vineyard managers, winemaker, and John Wright, whose French could best be described as creative.

Business French was also new to me, very formal and stilted. Closing a letter with the flowery phrase "In the hope of having news from you soon, we beg you, dear sir, to accept our very best sentiments" seemed rather over-the-top compared to "sincerely yours." And who knew that *bilan* means balance sheet, or *chiffre d'affaires* is top line revenue?

Every culture, every industry—every workplace—has it own vocabulary and unique ways of doing things. These can be learned. Harder to learn, perhaps, is how to best adapt them to the business at hand.

7 THE FIRST FLYING WINEMAKER

Edmond Maudière must have been the first flying winemaker, or traveling winemaking consultant, of which today there are many. Starting in 1973, he made the long trip several times each year from Épernay to Napa Valley to work with Domaine Chandon's winemaking team, led by Dawnine Dyer from 1976–1999.

Architect Jerry Gabriel inspecting the polished, horizontal stainless steel fermenters inspired by similar tanks at Champagne Mercier.

Edmond had been the *chef de caves* at Champagne Mercier for years until its acquisition by Moët & Chandon in the late 1960s. Soon he found himself the designated consulting winemaker for Moët's sparkling wine operations in Argentina, then in Napa Valley, and eventually Brazil and

Australia. Germany, too, had a Moët project but the *sekt* it produced there was less successful than the other, more traditional sparkling wies.

When he first started coming to Napa Valley, Edmond's English was limited. This created a wonderful opportunity for me to learn about winemaking while acting as translator for many technical conversations between Edmond and his California *confrères*. I learned firsthand how sparkling wine is made in the *méthode champenoise* and how different the approach to viticulture had to be.

Base wines for sparkling wine *cuvées* are intentionally designed to have low alcohol and high acid. The second fermentation in the bottle will raise the alcohol slightly, and acid assures the crisp delicacy prized in high quality sparklers. That same acid is also an occupational hazard for *chefs de cave* and sparkling winemakers, who regularly have their teeth re-enameled and should own shares in Sensodyne. It's hard on one's teeth to taste hundreds of samples of early-picked Pinot Noir ranging in color from white to *oeil de perdrix* to nearly rosé, not to mention Chardonnays from many separate vineyard blocks, while assembling several *cuvées* every year.

Edmond had his own scoring system for evaluating a formidable lineup of samples, all similar in delicacy and color and presented in identical small chimney glasses that concentrated their subtle aromas. He would examine the color, an important matter when trying to make white wine from black (a wine term for red) grapes, then the aroma, and finally taste—and spit. He could spit accurately into a bucket from three feet, using the space between his front teeth to good advantage. Rather than use a 100-point system, or even the 20-point UC Davis system, he would quickly note a plus or a minus, and/or push a wine back or pull one slightly forward from the lineup to indicate his preferences. It was simple, efficient, and effective.

Blending is the heart of what makes champagne a great wine and is, in fact, the real reason for Dom Pérignon's place in wine history. Blindness may have sharpened his other senses, especially smell and taste, contributing to his rare skill in distinguishing and assembling wines from many vineyards. Edmond wasn't blind, but he was certainly oblivious to everything around him while tasting, so intent was he on the task at hand. He even managed to repress his sense of fun and enviable *joie de vivre* when creating *cuvées*.

One of our early public relations coups was a 1979 blending session I suggested we hold for the New York Wine Writers Circle. They eagerly accepted. I worked with Circle president Harriet Lembeck to organize the

John Wright and Moët's Edmond Maudière enjoying a working tasting.

concept and logistics, and flew to New York with Edmond for the event. We tasted the base wines, all Pinot Noirs and Chardonnays, and Edmond explained what he looks for when building a sparkling wine *cuvée*. Blending tastings are a bit like finger painting in kindergarten: messy, creative, and fun. All of the writers wanted Edmond to taste and admire his or her own *chef d'oeuvre*, which he did with generosity and tact.

As a licensed pilot, Edmond was always happy for an opportunity to fly small planes and even helicopters. Once, his hard landing of a rented helicopter in nearby Angwin airport put an end to his wife Jacqueline's willingness to fly with him. On another occasion, he took me aloft in Epernay in a tiny, single engine, low-wing plane that he shared with several partners. The airstrip was a bumpy grass field. Riding in the cockpit beside him felt like sitting inside a bubble on dining room chairs perched atop a board.

Did I mention that Edmond's enthusiasm was infectious? He loved the freedom to innovate that he found in California, after decades of working under the precise mandates of Champagne's *appellation contrôlée*. He was free to make the best wine possible in this brave new world.

For all his joyful charm, Edmond occasionally surprised me with his shyness about speaking English. Even after several years of consulting for Domaine Chandon and steadily improving his language skills, he wasn't quite ready for the torture of appearing live on television. I didn't realize this, and booked him into a 6:00 a.m. interview in Palm Beach. The host was too inexperienced to help him through a painful, five-minute segment during which he answered questions monosyllabically, avoiding eye contact and clearly wishing he were somewhere else. That was the first and last television appearance I asked him to do for Domaine Chandon. We returned to his public relations comfort zone: telling stories over a relaxed lunch.

Years later, in 2014, Gregory and I visited Edmond and his wife Jacqueline at their home in Epernay. Still in fine fettle at 88, he had recently been awarded the *Légion d'Honneur* by the French government for his many contributions to improved winemaking in Champagne. And maybe also just a bit for serving as a teenager in the *Résistance* during World War II.

8 BE CAREFUL WHAT YOU PROMISE

In the exuberance of Domaine Chandon's early days, a promise was made that would be collected years later.

In honor of a 1974 visit by Comte Frédéric Chandon de Brialles, whom everyone called Fred, we organized a luncheon for the employees. This small group, consisting mostly of vineyard and cellar workers, was excited to welcome Fred. The gathering was held inside the Trefethen winery, our shared, temporary winemaking facility during the four years when Domaine Chandon was being planned and built.

Fred was, of course, charmed by this very American, very democratic celebration, and rose to make a toast to the future of Domaine Chandon. The first bottles were not even *en tirage* yet, making the launch of our own wines seem unimaginably far off in the future. Raising his flute of Moët & Chandon Brut Impérial, Fred graciously announced to all present, "When we sell the millionth bottle of Napa Valley sparkling wine, you will all be my guests in Champagne!" We already loved Fred, but with that offer his stock blew off the chart.

Time passed. We sold the first Chandon sparkling wines late in 1976, barely in time for the holiday rush. Soon we were opening up select U.S. markets, expanding within three years to nearly complete national distribution. Like other American wineries, we counted sales in cases, not bottles as in France. A million cases is a lot of wine, but a million bottles is doable in fairly short order for a winery originally designed eventually to produce about three million bottles a year. Cumulative sales grew and quietly surpassed the one million bottle mark. No one noticed—except Marcy Thomas. She supervised the bottling line, and she counted in bottles.

In 1982, eight years after our memorable luncheon, Marcy came into my office to ask whether I remembered Fred's promise to take us all to France when we'd sold one million bottles of Chandon sparkling wine. I did. Oh my, I thought to myself, this could get interesting. I assured Marcy that I would find out whether Fred remembered. He did.

34

And that is how I came to shepherd the ten remaining Domaine Chandon veterans present at that fateful luncheon in 1974 on a weeklong adventure to Paris and Champagne as the honored guests of Fred Chandon.

I had no idea what I was getting into.

These were not experienced international travelers. I discovered too late, on arrival at Charles de Gaulle in Paris, that one of the more mature vineyard workers believed, not entirely unreasonably, that his green card was a valid international travel document. French immigration police disagreed and refused him entry.

I came back to the end of the passport control line to investigate, and found my charge sequestered in a spartan, closet-sized room surrounded by hostile airport police. Working hard to rescue him, I tried to explain the documentation problem in my best French. *Les flics* didn't care that a green card was equivalent to a passport between the U.S. and Mexico. I tried again, and again. For my reward an armed policeman whose mood had escalated from surly to angry shoved me out of the room, hard.

Charles de Gaulle remains my least favorite airport in the world, evoking stressful memories of being manhandled every time I go through passport control or even see a uniform. I suppose I should be grateful they didn't shoot me.

Luckily, we had flown to Paris via Heathrow, so the *gendarmes* put our man on the next plane to London instead of all the way home to California. That provided a small window of time to enlist the help of Moët & Chandon London, but it was Sunday and the office was closed. I tried Edmond, only an hour's drive away in Épernay, but he wasn't home. I spent that first night in Paris worrying about my stray lamb, who spoke only Spanish and had never traveled in Europe on his own.

Twenty-four hours later, to my astonishment and relief, our errant colleague rejoined the group in Paris. He had shown remarkable initiative, somehow locating and presenting himself on Monday morning at the offices of Moët London. They managed to arrange his entry through passport control in Paris without a passport, a minor miracle then and certainly impossible today. Maybe he said the magic word: Moët.

The cellar workers were mostly former hippies from the commune at Lokoya, so recreational marijuana was part of their lifestyle. They didn't know, as I did, that in France using any substance that could be considered a drug was a felony, and being caught would result in major legal hassles. My Californian charges weren't concerned. They partied all night. I fretted as the sweet fumes wafted through our small Paris hotel. I didn't sleep. The *gendarmes* did, luckily for us, and we left the next morning for Champagne with no one in hot pursuit.

The "millionth bottle of Chandon" group touring Champagne with Edmond.

We spent the following week in a Mercedes minibus provided by Moët & Chandon, touring *la Champagne vinicole* and being warmly received at all the champagne houses we visited. Edmond took special pride in showing us his home ground.

To close our excellent adventure, Fred invited us to join him for a dinner show at the Lido in Paris, famous for topless chorus girls wearing mostly a few feathers and some glitter. We enjoyed front row seats, a fine meal, and as much Dom Pérignon *en magnum* as anyone could desire. It's likely that Fred's Paris friends are still wondering about his California friends. But this was a man so comfortable in his skin that he had no qualms about doing unorthodox things, including putting ice cubes in his flute of Dom Pérignon on warm days.

Shortly after we returned to California, UC Berkeley invited me to lead an alumni group on a canal barge tour in France in exchange for free passage for my husband and me. I wasn't tempted.

9 A WINE OF OUR OWN

The first vintage, 1973, for the enterprise that would become Domaine Chandon was meant to be experimental. Renaud Poirier, the "golden nose" from Moët & Chandon, flew over post-harvest to taste more than a dozen varietals purposely vinified as base wines. His succinct report to France described them in turn as *"exécrable,"* *"abominable,"* *"inutilisable,"* *"imbuvable"* or, grudgingly, *"pas mal."* There was even a *"bon"* or two.

It pained him to acknowledge that the best choices for making sparkling wine in Napa Valley proved to be Pinot Noir and Chardonnay, as in Champagne. He had apparently expected to get by in less exalted winegrowing regions with less expensive grape varieties. We saved those free-run Chardonnays and Pinot Noirs to build the first Chandon *cuvées* and sold off the Burger, Green Hungarian (Zsa Zsa Gabor was then the "face" of Weibel's Green Hungarian), French Colombard, Chenin Blanc, Pinot Blanc, Ugni Blanc, etc., remarkably still available in old Napa Valley vineyards. Today, hardly any of these grape varieties survive, except for some Pinot Blanc and Chenin Blanc.

Once the first *cuvées* were blended, there remained a tank of rather tasty Chardonnay *premières tailles* without an obvious purpose. This may have been the first "no oak" Chardonnay made in Napa Valley, as we did not use barrels for sparkling wine production. Although we had Moët champagne we'd imported for company parties, we few employees were desperate to have some wine of our own to enjoy. It wasn't hard to persuade the boss to let us bottle some of this Chardonnay, since he, too, wanted to drink it.

Because federal law prohibits removing unlabeled wine from bond, I volunteered to make a label for our first, quasi-commercial bottling. I hadn't done anything like this, but as usual it didn't occur to me to hire someone who knew how. How hard could it be?

I sent off for a copy of the Federal Alcohol Administration Act and attendant regulations. After acquiring a shaky grasp of labeling requirements, I went looking for art supplies. The local stationery store had a fine selection of rub-on transfer letters, a ruler, and some heavy-duty paper. An eraser completed my primitive toolkit.

It didn't take long to decide on a name for our insiders' wine. Musing about the people involved in Moët's groundbreaking project soon lead us to Fred Chandon. We admired Fred as a dashing, cosmopolitan *bon vivant* whose elegant manner was the very definition of charm. Before he married Camilla, the granddaughter of Somerset Maugham, he was often photographed squiring beautiful women to *soirées* in Paris. This inevitably led me to the perfect brand name for our first bottling: Fred's Friends. He had many friends, did he not, including us?

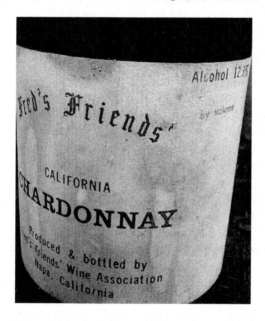

Several sets of ruined rub-on letters later, I had the Fred's Friends label ready for the printer. In 1974 wineries were required to submit a final printed label to the BATF for approval before the labels could be used. It will surprise no one that my submission came back stamped "not approved." I had indicated the wine's alcohol (12.3%) as required, but failed to add the vital qualifier "by volume."

To spare the expense of reprinting the labels, I had a rubber stamp made and hired John Wright's 12-year-old daughter Karin to add "by volume" to 1,200 individual labels so they would conform to regulations. I'm not sure she's forgiven me yet for her first paying job.

Employees and friends quickly claimed the first 100 cases of Fred's Friends Chardonnay. The price, one dollar per bottle, may have had something to do with this. The word spread; people were clamoring for more. Encouraged by this success, we made the giant leap of bottling the remainder of the tank, a daunting 450 cases. This time I got the label right, but selling this much wine would require a more systematic approach.

Our temporary winemaking home at Trefethen was neither open to the public nor set up for sales yet, and we could hardly expect people to make the trek up Mt. Veeder to our headquarters in the garage. We had to find another way to deliver Fred's Friends Chardonnay to its eager fans.

I sent a note to employees and other buyers of the first bottling informing them there would be more Chardonnay available. (We also daringly raised the price to $18/case.) All they need do was mail in an order and a check, indicating which of two proffered 2-hour windows they preferred to pick up the wine in Yountville. At the appointed time, their wine would be brought to the entrance to the Domaine Chandon construction site on a flatbed truck.

The first round buyers apparently shared my note with their friends, and the news spread fast. All 450 cases were sold within a week. People came from all over Napa Valley and from as far as San Jose to stock up on this new find. All the buyers appeared promptly as arranged to pick up their wine, excited and happy to claim their pre-ordered, pre-paid Fred's Friends Chardonnay.

When he learned about our first commercial success in his name, Fred Chandon was delighted.

10 PANACHE

Edmond brought more with him than champagne winemaking expertise. He also brought generations of champagne traditions, including different ways to use press cuts (tailles) that weren't suitable for the best cuvées. One was to bottle a still Chardonnay. The only such wine I had the privilege to try in Champagne was the Saran Nature that Moët named after its château and used for entertaining there. I don't believe Saran Nature was ever sold commercially.

By now you will have recognized the inspiration for our first Fred's Friends Chardonnay.

The other champagne tradition was Pinot Noir based, following Edmond's grandfather's practice of making a barrel of *ratafia de champagne* at harvest every year. None of us had ever heard of this, and Edmond happily explained. *Ratafia* is made by adding high proof alcohol to unfermented Pinot Noir press juice. The high proof effectively prevents any fermentation, and the amount used results in a powerful, *apéritif* style wine with about 18 percent alcohol and the sweetness of grapes.

When Edmond realized how good the Napa Pinot Noirs were—we used to take cups out to the presses to grab sips of free run juice—he decided it would be fun to make *ratafia* in California. The problem was finding suitable high proof. He experimented with cognac, but its flavor was too strong and its alcohol level too low for this purpose. It was illegal to buy high proof in California, but not in Nevada. John Trefethen volunteered to fly his single-engine plane to Reno to pick up the necessary supplies. Mission accomplished, the first batch of *ratafia* was prepared, tasted, and declared worthy of continuing.

The BATF wouldn't let us label our *ratafia* as such because "it *ratafia* is widely understood to come from France" and consumers must not be confused. Thus started a naming contest, which my husband Gregory won by tagging it Panache. The new product eventually sported an Art Nouveau style label like those later designed for Fred's Friends. For a few years we sold these non-sparkling wines only at the winery.

Later, when we began working with Schieffelin nationally in 1981, their president expressed interest in our high octane Panache. The old liquor salesmen still in the sales force then weren't so sure, comparing it to Wild Irish Rose, a sticky-sweet fortified wine usually served in paper bags. In spite of that diversity of opinion, Schieffelin increased sales of Panache to 7,000 cases in a couple of years.

We helped with marketing support. We deluged food writers with Panache recipes, including a rather good BBQ sauce. I stayed up late many a night making buckets of melon balls soaked in Panache—a new take on the classic port-filled charentaise melons favored in France as a first course--for our parties and events. We concocted Panache cocktail recipes. We even had Veronica di Rosa bake and decorate a Panache cake for a media event.

When Plan M for Mitterand (see the chapter entitled Rising Star) came into effect, we had to redirect all sales and marketing resources to building the Chandon sparkling wine volumes. Panache shrank back to a winery-only product.

11 OPENING ANOTHER DOOR

In the early days of the enterprise that would become Domaine Chandon, we were in stealth mode under the name M & H Vineyards (for Moët-Hennessy). Anyone searching for us was just as likely to find the M & H Meat Co. in Vallejo in those pre-Internet times. More than one frustrated reporter resorted to hearsay and guesswork, which resulted in a good deal of misinformation on the new venture.

That it was a newsworthy story was never in doubt. No other major French wine producer had invested in the U.S., much less California, which had yet to develop a reputation for high quality wines. For a group of Moët-Hennessy's stature to take a gamble on Napa Valley in 1973 was a shot heard around the wine world.

It was clear to me that someone needed to provide information not only to the owners in France, but to the media -- if only for the sake of accuracy, as we were still years from opening the winery and offering the first Chandon *cuvées*. That is how I added responsibility for communications to all the other exciting things I was thoroughly enjoying doing as the assistant to the president of a major startup.

It's a tribute to their sleuthing skills that Frank Prial of the *New York Times* and Robert Lawrence Balzer of the *Los Angeles Times* were able to find us on the mountain. Perched on a stool in the garage, impeccable in his signature bow tie and blazer, Balzer regaled John and me with a meandering tale whose punch line was that his aunt was buried next to Agoston Haraszthy in Los Angeles' Forest Lawn Cemetery. (This contradicted the accepted wisdom that Haraszthy had been eaten by alligators in Nicaragua, but Balzer was a gifted *raconteur* with no need to rely on exotic critters for a good yarn.) I don't recall him asking any questions, but he produced an accurate article for the *Los Angeles Times*. Frank Prial did the same for the *New York Times*.

Moving out of the garage on Mt. Veeder in 1975 and into temporary offices at the Vintage 1870 (now V Marketplace) in Yountville was a major change in lifestyle. We were now in a public place, though still hidden in plain sight as M & H Vineyards. In two more years the winery under construction across Highway 29 would be finished.

That same year, I acquired my first assistant. Jane Thomson, 19, had just finished a year of secretarial school in Canada. Her stepfather Alan Ferguson was the president of Molsons, a large Canadian brewer that was a major investor in Robert Mondavi Winery. Alan asked John Wright about employment ideas for Jane. John offered to hire her—to help me. Bright and funny (she liked to call me Mikey the Cookie), Jane was not wired for business. It took me several years to convince her to take that excellent brain to the university where it should have been from the start. She graduated in architecture and now works for the City of Napa.

By 1976, with the winery opening a year way, I realized I wanted a fiefdom of my own in this soon-to-expand enterprise. I knew I would not be happy as an *adjointe* for long, no matter how stimulating the work or how much I admired my boss.

I was already handling communications, and liked it. The problem was how to tell John Wright I wanted to do this without sounding as if I were rejecting him and his challenging workload. I grew progressively silent and grumpy, naively expecting he'd notice and ask what was wrong. Of course that didn't happen.

One day we both lingered in the lab after a long day in our temporary production facility at Trefethen, tasting wines and talking. A little more wine loosened my tongue until at last I was able to say aloud what I wanted: to be responsible for public relations rather than continue as assistant to the president. John was surprised, but agreed. He may not have been aware of my hopes and dreams but he was not one to stand in anyone's way.

12 MASTERS OF PUBLIC RELATIONS

Not long after, a young Jancis Robinson arrived in Napa, striking in her cloud of frizzy blonde hair topped by an outsize, floppy black hat and dressed in flowing black robes. She was wearing her signature red eyeglasses even in the mid 1970s. Having gotten wind of Moët doing something in California, perhaps from the reporting by Prial and Balzer, she wanted to know more.

I dutifully gave her a hardhat tour of the winery construction site, explained our plans to make high quality sparkling wine, and took her out for a sandwich. It wasn't until reading her memoir 23 years later that I learned her early reporting in the U.K. on our Napa Valley venture was the breakthrough in what became a magnificent career as a wine writer.

To prepare for opening Domaine Chandon, I then spent the month of June 1976 in Champagne studying Moët's high-powered public relations and visitor programs. It was wonderful to see their teams in action, and to experience the VIP hospitality Moët offered.

An efficient staff kept a handwritten information card on every guest Moët entertained. When the phone rang, without even putting the call on hold one of the team would pull that person's card from a nearby wall of wooden file cabinets. A quick glance provided all the information needed to greet the caller like an old friend. These accessible records also enabled seamless chats about past visits, what the British peer or German wholesaler would like to do this time, and how are little Sophie and Thomas? Witnessing this was surely the genesis of my appreciation for consumer databases.

There were many ways visitors could be received at Moët & Chandon. At the most basic level, a tasting of two or three champagnes was offered. But most of the visitors were not tourists; they were members of the wine trade, VIPs, and journalists – from all over the world, as Moët champagne was exported internationally. Those visitors were royally received for luncheons in the Trianon, overnight stays at the Château de Saran or the Royal Champagne, private visits to the living museum of Dom Pérignon's life and work in Hautvillers and, of course, a VIP tour of the extensive cellars including a stop to admire Napoleon's hat.

The author with Dom Pérignon's wax effigy in Moët's living museum in Hautvillers, 1976. It looks remarkably like Edmond Maudière.

I wasn't able to borrow Napoleon's hat for Domaine Chandon's planned mini-museum, but I did get an ancient oaken horizontal press, some 18th century hand blown flutes, and a collection of stunningly sensuous Mucha menu cards made by the artist for Moët & Chandon's entertaining use. The latter treasures inspired menu covers for the restaurant, invitation cards for events, and much nicer labels for Fred's Friends. Eventually Panache would also get a Mucha-inspired label. Moët's generous support for Domaine Chandon was gratefully received.

If a VIP guest failed to show up for a typically elaborate luncheon at the Trianon, where chef Joseph Thuet presided over a fine kitchen, the *châtelaine* would invite me to be an *estomac* to fill in. I was once pulled out of the employee cafeteria line for this tough duty. After the guests had departed and the Comtesse de Maigret and I were finishing our cognac, I was privileged to witness her scolding, in a most elegant way, two young British *stagiaires* who had aroused the concierge at 2:00 a.m. to unlock the door for them after a long night of drinking. Bad form, that.

My quarters were shifted several times during that month. I started in splendor at the Trianon, where a maid brought me café and croissants on a tray every morning. To make space for a visiting sales manager I was moved to the Château de Saran, where I not only slept in *grand luxe* but also dined with the baron and baroness on host duty and that evening's VIP guests. It was remarkable to watch them entertain – in several languages -- a mixed group of U.S. distributors, British MPs, Austrian wholesalers, and French captains of industry.

After a few days at Saran, I was shifted to the Royal Champagne, a Michelin one-star restaurant and *auberge* overlooking the vineyards owned by Moët and used for overflow entertaining. This time it was my turn to awake the concierge early in the morning after a long, convivial dinner in the home of a Moët colleague. As I recall, the women were intrigued by my lifestyle: I had an advanced degree, was married but had no children, worked full time, and sewed my own clothes. I don't think they had many opportunities to meet Americans.

Then the Royal Champagne needed its very comfortable room for a paying guest so I was shifted to a vast, nearly unfurnished nineteenth-century house up the street from Moët's headquarters on the Avenue de Champagne. It would have made an excellent haunted house for Halloween. Usually inhabited by transient *stagiaires*, my new abode was vacant at that time. There was no one to help if I was unable to open the garden gate with its heavy iron key. I felt lucky not to blow up the whole place, striking matches to ignite the gas water heater mounted on the wall over the bathtub.

There is something fascinating about bottling lines. In champagne making, they get to do multiple operations where still winemakers only do one. There are two alcoholic fermentations, the first in tank and the second in bottles. Later come three passes through the bottling line: the first for *tirage*, the second for disgorging, and the last for labeling.

It was while I was enjoying being mesmerized by labeling operations – front label, back label, and *collerette*, not to mention a long, pleated foil capsule—that I noticed a large cabinet full of stacks of different export labels. Naturally, I brought home several samples to plagiarize if the need arose. One reason why champagne bottles were not labeled when disgorged is that exporting to dozens of countries, each with different labeling requirements, meant it was more efficient to label as orders were received. We didn't have to do that at Domaine Chandon since we had one major market, the U.S. and just a little export to Canada. International was Moët's territory.

One day I was in Reims to see the oldest of the champagne houses, Ruinart, which was founded in 1729 and became part of the Moët-Hennessy group. Its caves are beautiful underground chalk quarries that produced paving blocks for Roman roads. Naturally, after the visit I invited for lunch by Ruinart's public relations person.

Everyone I met seemed eager to introduce me to the fine points of French cuisine and, of course, champagne. My host, a charming marquis only a bit older than me, ordered up a bottle of Ruinart Blanc de Blancs, and *foie gras* as a *premier plat*.

French people are brought up to clean their plates. His *foie gras* soon disappeared. The large slab on my plate didn't. It was so rich I could barely nibble at it, washing each small bite down with blessedly palate-cleansing champagne. My host waited patiently, keeping up the conversation while I worked my way through this formidable first course. We both knew the server wouldn't bring the *entrée* until I'd finished every morsel. Two hours later, or so it felt, we moved on to the main course. It was the longest lunch of my life.

To this day I leave the joys of *foie gras* to others.

13 MARKETING AND MBAs

I found that I enjoyed the company of journalists and writers, and was easily able to put myself in their shoes. They needed story ideas, and I was able to offer both ideas and the facts to develop the stories. Many are still actively writing about wine, including Hugh Johnson, Jancis Robinson, Mary Ewing-Mulligan, Charlie Olken, Patrick Fegan, Barbara Ensrud, L. Pierce Carson, Larry Walker, and Dan Berger. Some have added tweeting and blogging to their activities. Others have retired, like Gerald Boyd and Gerald Asher, or been lost to us: Robert Lawrence Balzer died in 2011 at age 92, and Frank Prial in 2012.

Marketing events, starting with the opening of the winery in April 1977, also fell to me. Once we had sparkling wine ready to sell, it was time to add market visits, media tours, and offsite consumer events to my portfolio. Traveling with champagne consultant Edmond Maudière, winemaker Dawnine Dyer, or Philippe Jeanty, who took over as *chef de cuisine* one year after Domaine Chandon's restaurant opened, kept all of us fully occupied. The story of the first collective Napa vintner tour is a chapter on its own, as is the genesis of the Chandon Club. Advertising and packaging development were added to my duties. It was all fun.

At the same time, I finally succumbed to pressure from my husband to get an MBA. He knew I would have less time for him but he believed the sacrifice was worth it. I, too, knew it was the right thing to do if I was to be taken seriously in the business world. Many employers wouldn't help develop or promote young women because they expected motherhood to end careers. John Wright was too forward thinking for that, but I didn't want to take any chances. Besides, I had a lot to learn. The problem was that I'd finished a master's degree only a few years earlier. I was not eager to leave the exciting real world to return to academic theorizing.

Having assiduously avoided math while an undergraduate, I needed to complete five of the six prerequisites for UC Berkeley's MBA program before I could apply. It was a pleasant surprise to discover that calculus was easy. Berkeley's evening program was a good fit, financially and geographically, though it would take three years to complete the degree while holding a full-time job.

This MBA program was much more than getting my ticket punched. I learned time management from juggling my day job with Domaine Chandon and commuting an hour to and from evening classes in Berkeley or San Francisco; I learned a holistic view of business, which took me beyond the marketing world; I learned analytics (Berkeley was known as a quant school); I learned how lucky I was that Macs would soon make mainframe computers with their arcane language irrelevant to my work; and I had a wonderful living laboratory in Domaine Chandon to apply what I was learning in class. Surrounded by young bankers aspiring to more exciting careers, I was a celebrity because I already had a dream job.

One of my professors, a lawyer who was teaching part time at Berkeley, came to visit me at Chandon after I graduated. He told me that he had decided to give me an A in the class if I would only stop asking him questions he couldn't answer. I wasn't trying to stump him, I asked because really wanted to know. The A was not my objective, but I got it anyway.

Shortly after I completed the degree from Berkeley (now Haas School of Business) in 1980, John Wright promoted me to Vice President/Marketing. This is the same person who'd snorted, "What do you want an MBA for?" when I asked him for the required letter of recommendation from my employer. At the celebration of John's life in February 2012, I learned that the man I had worked with for 15 years and thought I knew well had an MBA from Wharton.

14 BUT WHAT ARE YOU GOING TO CALL IT?

When M & H Vineyards started early in 1973, there were only two producers of *méthode champenoise* sparkling wine in Napa Valley: Schramsberg, an historic winery resurrected by Jack and Jamie Davies in 1965, and Hanns Kornell, who signed his correspondence "Champagne Master to America." The former innovatively (for California) used classic Chardonnay and Pinot Noir grapes, the latter purchased Riesling and Chenin Blanc still wines to blend. Both labeled their wines "champagne," legal under U.S. law when qualified geographically, to indicate quality.

The alternative class and type designation permitted under federal regulations, "sparkling wine," was used primarily to identify less expensive charmat and transfer process bubbly.

As the scion of Moët & Chandon, France's largest champagne house, Domaine Chandon could not label its wine "champagne" without causing the growers in Champagne to riot or, worse, stop providing Moët the only grapes it could legally bottle as champagne under French law. Champagne is one of the most fiercely protected appellations on the planet, although the *champenois* had failed to defend it legally until too late in the U.S.

It was because of this that when journalists got wind of the young Napa Valley operation that would become Domaine Chandon, the first question was always "But what are you going to call it?" It was inconceivable that Moët would allow its Napa Valley product to be labeled champagne, but it was just as inconceivable that, given its pedigree, it would be burdened with a down-market designation like sparkling wine.

John Wright and I consistently responded to all inquiries that the Napa Valley wine would be labeled "sparkling wine," but no one believed us, especially the journalists who were hoping to uncover a controversy. "Yeah, but what are you *really* going to call it?" they'd say.

This brouhaha about nomenclature was a stroke of unintended marketing genius. The media never seemed to tire of the topic, and the debate kept interest in the new venture at a high level. I suspect there were people taking bets on both sides.

When Chandon Napa Valley Brut was released in April 1977, the answer was apparent to all. Its front label carried the truthful legal description "Napa Valley Sparkling Wine" and ... some additional truthful information. Across the bottom, in two-point type, was the statement "This cuvée was produced in the California cellars of Domaine Chandon under the supervision of Champagne Moët & Chandon, Épernay, France." Also noted on the front label was *"méthode champenoise."*

One wonders how those bets paid off.

The *champenois* are surely gratified that most high quality producers of sparkling wine in the U.S. have voluntarily come around to respecting their appellation, many years after we elected not to label our wine "champagne."

Mother Nature then presented an unexpected opportunity to expand the product line.

Although purposely picked slightly unripe at 18–19 degrees Brix, even the Pinot Noirs from the cool Carneros region released their skin's dark color into the juice more easily than in *la Champagne viticole*. This regularly produced juice of a pale bronze color that occurs naturally only in the greatest, i.e., warmest, vintages in the northerly vineyards in Champagne.

In the opinion of Dr. Ralph Kunkee, a UC Davis enology professor who joined us for a tasting in the lab at Trefethen in 1974, the lovely tint of our Napa Pinot Noirs was not acceptable for sparkling wine: the wine wasn't white enough. We all, including Edmond, thought color was less important than the fact that the wines were delicious. Besides, those delicate colors ranging from *pelure d'oignon* to *oeil de perdrix* would have been highly prized in Champagne as the mark of a great vintage.

We decided to use the paler lots of Pinot Noir (blended with Chardonnay) for the originally intended *cuvée* to be called Napa Valley Brut, and create an innovative, one hundred percent Pinot Noir *cuvée* using the more colored lots. Not a rosé (that's a different production method and a different color range), this *cuvée* had noticeable color, more fruit, and firmer body, and was also finished brut. Chandon Blanc de Noirs became an immediate hit with American consumers, perhaps because of its uniquely beautiful color.

15 OUR LOWEST INCOME COMMUNITY

In 1973, when John Wright purchased 350 acres adjacent to the Veterans Home on the west side of Highway 29 as the site for the future Domaine Chandon, Yountville was a sleepy, somewhat rundown rural village.

Forty years later, based on Michelin stars per capita, Yountville had become and probably still is the gastronomic epicenter of the United States. The French Laundry, Redd, Bouchon and *étoile* restaurants earned more stars than any other city in America. Of course, Yountville's population remains small and the restaurant scene is at a disproportionately high level, so New York needn't get its knickers in a twist.

Back then, atop a hill on the winery site across the highway from Yountville stood a large, empty, redwood water tank, hoops sagging and staves leaning. In the pre-Highway 29 days, water pumped from a bountiful well on the property into that tank had supplied the town via gravity flow.

One night in 1974, in plain view of anyone who cared to look in that direction, a bold person or persons dismantled the water tank and sneaked off with the lumber. Yountvillans blamed the new French owners for tearing down this cherished landmark, but the fact is, those valuable three-inch thick, twenty-foot long, knot-free redwood planks probably built someone with a larcenous heart a very nice house in Marin County. Domaine Chandon raised a new water tank for vineyard irrigation use on the same hilltop, where it remains today in full view of the Town of Yountville. The locals were pleased.

There was more going on in Yountville in 1974. The building that would soon house The Diner and ultimately Ad Hoc restaurant was still operating as the Greyhound bus station. The entire population of 3,000 souls consisted of half townies, many of them farm workers, and half residents of the Veterans Home. There were numerous bars in town to accommodate the veterans' need for socializing; each had a naked light bulb mounted over the front door that the bartender could use to signal for a taxi when a wobbly vet needed transportation back home.

The Diner was a welcome culinary development in Yountville. Owned and operated by a group of the nicest hippies you could hope to meet, it offered well-prepared, fresh food at reasonable prices. Partner Nickie Zeller, later the owner of Pearl restaurant in Napa, never forgot to hold the garbanzo beans from my otherwise favorite green salad–with a smile. Julia Child once famously enjoyed a "Humdinger" hamburger there.

The Yountville Saloon was so rustic one could get splinters. I think they served buffalo and beer. Our crew once had a raucous party there in honor of a visit by Fred Chandon and Alain Chevalier.

Sally Schmitt's welcoming Chutney Kitchen inside the Vintage 1870 was a warm, friendly place offering homemade soups, salads, various dishes involving chutney, and more. We had parties there, too. Vintage 1870, now V Marketplace, offered upscale shopping for Yountville's infrequent visitors under the management of Sally's husband Don, a banker turned entrepreneur.

Between the tiny, dilapidated shacks that constituted the housing supply, the bars, and the Veterans Home residents, Yountville was an odd contrast to the multi-million dollar winery going up nearby.

In 1975, the imminent expansion of the team obliged us to leave John Wright's garage and move into offices above Groezingers Wine Merchants (now Napa Style) in the Vintage 1870. Manager Phil Faight happily signed Domaine Chandon's first fair trade contract, a legal requirement at the time, making Groezingers the winery's first retail account in 1977. This location was also more convenient for hardhat tours of the winery construction site across the highway. I finally had a real desk, a WWII gray metal military hand-me-down from Kaiser Shipyards, on loan from Gene Trefethen.

That's where we were when the *Los Angeles Times* decided to do an investigative report on the lowest income community in California. Yountville made its first headlines. If the *Times* had waited only a while, there would have been no story, as things were changing rapidly.

When Domaine Chandon opened in 1977, its offerings included the first *haute cuisine* restaurant in the Napa Valley. About the same time, Don and Sally Schmitt started renovating an old brick building on Washington Street for a new restaurant to be named The French Laundry after one of the building's historic uses. It had also been a brothel (oh, those veterans). I toured the building during construction and observed a narrow upstairs hallway with 10 to 12 tiny numbered rooms; if that had been a hotel, it wasn't designed for long stays.

The French Laundry opened in 1978, with Sally presiding over the kitchen and offering a different *prix fixe* menu (no substitutions needed, it was delicious) every night. Don was in charge of the wines. In two years Yountville had gone from not much happening to a whole lot happening.

By 2012, Yountville had become a wealthy community thanks to the sales and occupancy taxes generated by its numerous hotels and restaurants. They provided a whopping 66% of the town's municipal budget.

16 FINE DINING, FINALLY

In the 1970s, Napa vintners had to entertain VIPs in their homes or wineries because there were no local restaurants offering cuisine to match the quality of the wines. Among Margrit Mondavi's many duties in the early days was to cook a simple but tasty chicken lunch for visiting distributor groups. Apart from the Great Chefs cooking school founded in 1972 by Michael James and Billy Cross, there wasn't anything publicly available for *becs fins* in the Napa Valley. And then Domaine Chandon happened.

Driven by the need to convince Americans that sparkling wine could be enjoyed anytime–not just on New Year's Eve or at weddings–the decision was taken to incorporate a fine dining restaurant into the plans for the new winery. This idea quickly ran into an obstacle in the form of the 1968 Agricultural Land Preservation (commonly known as the Ag Preserve) zoning regulations, which preclude any commercial uses (except wineries) in nearly all of the winegrowing areas of Napa Valley. Restaurants, hotels, shops, more than one residence per legal 40-acre parcel, all are *verboten* in the Ag Preserve.

To this day all those who appreciate Napa Valley's natural beauty and fine wines are grateful the Ag Preserve has protected its vineyards from the rampant development that forever transformed the once bucolic Santa Clara Valley into San Jose.

Domaine Chandon's winery site adjacent to the Veterans Home in Yountville was zoned Ag Watershed, an even more restrictive zone than Ag Preserve. How to accomplish our goal of including a fine dining restaurant in the winery project?

Since commercial uses including restaurants are allowed within city limits, one early thought was to offer to annex the winery to the City of Yountville, as its contiguous neighbor, the Veterans Home, was in the city limits. Paradoxically, given the potential for increased sales tax collections and in spite of the property's 2,000 gallon/minute well that in the past had provided a healthy supply of water to Yountville, the city fathers declined.

That left one option: to ask Napa County for a variance, a notoriously difficult exception to obtain. Dealing with government bodies was one of the things that John Wright didn't want to do, so the task fell to me. Perhaps he thought that being young and female I'd have better luck with county officials.

Armed with an exorbitantly expensive $25,000 Environmental Impact Report (EIR) that would cost $250,000 today, architectural renderings, and a well-developed rationale for the winery and its hoped-for restaurant, I presented our case to the various official panels involved.

The first was the California Environmental Quality Act (CEQA) committee. The lone vintner on the panel, Louis P. Martini, chuckled quietly as I earnestly explained the carefully designed wastewater treatment ponds would be neither noisome nor bother the veterans next door. He quietly remarked that "all ponds stink," and let it go at that. The other committee members listened attentively, asked some questions, and agreed that the plans posed no environmental problems that could not be mitigated. Next stop: the county Planning Commission.

Napa County's Planning Department was responsible for making recommendations to the Planning Commission on projects applying for use permits. While wineries are an allowed use in the Ag Watershed zone, we expected opposition to the restaurant part of our application. To our surprise, Planning Director Jim Hickey was remarkably helpful. One can only imagine that the fear of setting a potentially troublesome precedent was more than offset by the prospect of having a high quality restaurant in the Napa Valley.

His creative solution to the regulatory problem was to carve out a small island within the 350-acre winery parcel precisely matching the footprint of the restaurant and rezone it to Planned Development, a zone that allows restaurants. The rest would remain Ag Watershed.

The Planning Commission members were suspicious. They seemed to think we the applicants were trying to pull a fast one, and during the public hearing I was grilled extensively about our *real* plans. I took their mistrust personally, but in the end the commissioners approved the plan as presented. The Board of Supervisors blessed their decision, and we had our use permit.

When it opened in June 1977, the restaurant at Domaine Chandon was an immediate hit. The handwritten menu, in French, was elegantly simple and the cuisine refined. My back page note was a bit pompous, a fine example of name dropping: *Domaine Chandon's chef de cuisine, Udo Nechutnys, echoes the legendary Fernand Point in noting that "la grande cuisine ne doit pas attendre le client; c'est le client qui doit attendre la grand cuisine." Chef Nechutnys' mentor, Paul Bocuse, does not disagree."* Roughly translated, fine cuisine waits not for the client; it's the client who must wait for fine cuisine.

Looking at these prices, one is tempted to research what a dollar in 1977 would be worth today.

Soupe de poisson *Paul Bocuse*	3.00
Consommé en gelée aux piments	2.50
Terrine de canard	4.50
Assiette gourmande	5.00
Barquettes de coquilles St. Jacques *F. Point*	4.50
"Huré" de saumon au citron et au poivre vert	4.50
Saumon à l'oseille *frères Troisgros*	6.00
Panaché de poissons	7.50
Barbue au champagne	7.50
Carré d'agneau rôti (*pour deux*)	17.50
Caneton au Chambertin	8.75
Poularde aux morilles	8.25
Côte de boeuf à la bordelaise (*pour deux*)	20.00
Salade verte à l'huile de noix ou à l'huile d'olive	2.00
Fromages	2.50
Le grande dessert et les pâtisseries	4.50

"Très fin" was the admiring comment we heard often from French visitors. Sipping sparkling wine from graceful *flûtes* instead of shallow *coupes* was new to most Americans, and they enjoyed it. Reservations became a competitive sport, with the restaurant's phone lines ringing constantly and would-be diners trying to pull strings to get a table. The restaurant's success proved that fine food and fine wine, even fine wine with bubbles, belong together on the table.

John Wright wanted to name the new restaurant *Le Bouchon d'Or* but I dissuaded him on the grounds that it was more important to establish the winery's name (Domaine Chandon) and brand (Chandon); the restaurant played a supporting, though important, rôle in the principal mission of making sparkling wine. Years later, changes were made. The restaurant finally got a name of its own: *étoile*, after Domaine Chandon's *tête de cuvée* and playing on the iconic symbolism of stars in the world of champagne. The winery, now well established, is simply called Chandon, like the brand.

It is ironic that until recently Napa wineries were not permitted to offer food with their wine tastings. This natural combination was considered an abuse of the Ag Preserve's limitations on non-agricultural uses. During the debate over the more restrictive Winery Definition Ordinance in 1990 there was even talk of prohibiting sales of wine-related merchandise in tasting rooms. Some of us wondered about the logic that it was perfectly OK to grow and make wine, but selling it...well, that was not.

The inevitable result of such thinking became clear before the new rules were finalized, so visitors can still buy souvenirs like corkscrews, wineglasses, logo wear, and books in winery sales rooms–along with wine. Thoughtful officials eventually recognized that small bites of food make wine tasting safer and more productive (coincidentally increasing sales tax collections), so in the twenty-first century the regulations were amended to allow food pairings in Napa Valley's winery tasting rooms.

Until December 31, 2014, when Chandon abruptly announced that *étoile* would close, it was still the only winery in Napa County's Ag Preserve with a restaurant open to the public. The announcement came as a shock to many, including me, but upon reflection I realized that its purpose had been accomplished. The restaurant had been a wildly successful, mostly self-funded marketing program that had changed public attitudes about when and how to enjoy sparkling wine, and had attracted many people to the winery who might not otherwise have come. Although repurposing the restaurant space to expand visitor programs makes sense, strategically and financially, we will miss those memorable experiences.

Wineries still do plenty of private entertaining, of course, in spite of the numerous fine restaurants now available in Napa Valley. Many have their own produce gardens and in-house chefs; some raise goats, cattle, and chickens (even guinea fowl, like my friend Julie Johnson at Tres Sabores). Napa is also blessed with a corps of outstanding caterers. Food and wine inevitably find one another.

17 HOW TO BUILD A WINERY

As we didn't know what we didn't know in the heady early days, we were constantly coming up with inventive solutions to issues as they arose. This is one of my favorites.

Bob Mountjoy and Jerry Gabriel, the lead architects from ROMA Design Group in San Francisco on the winery project, were determined that the complex should blend into its oak-studded hillside environment. Neither owners nor architects wanted an imitation *château* dominating the landscape. For this reason, Domaine Chandon is nearly invisible from Highway 29, nestled into its site in natural tones of rust and gray.

That site was riddled with rocks, large and small. Archaeologists identified one as a large bedrock mortar used by the Wappos, Napa Valley's earliest inhabitants, to grind acorns. It was left undisturbed.

The rest of those rocks were calling to ROMA, both for their natural beauty and appropriateness to the site, and perhaps because they were "free" building materials. Bob and Jerry wanted the winery walls to be faced with this native stone. That presented a big problem: how to gather and transport tons of rocks to the construction area from the hillsides where they were randomly scattered over 350 acres? Most of the terrain was too steep to operate machinery safely.

I thought of a mule team, but in those pre-Google days I was unable to locate one. Then, as ideas do, mine evolved. I remembered that René di Rosa kept a pet Percheron at Winery Lake.

Percherons are French draft horses, bred to pull heavy loads. A beautiful grey, Dapples was friendly and docile as draft horses tend to be, and seemed to enjoy his peaceful life sharing a pasture with two pet longhorn steers. He was a good candidate for our project, but only five years old and untrained.

We knew René well, as his Winery Lake vineyards were providing Chardonnay and Pinot Noir grapes to Domaine Chandon, and we often had the pleasure of being invited to the legendary parties in his art-filled baronial home in Carneros.

When I asked if we could borrow Dapples to haul rocks for the winery walls, René was delighted. He had visions of Dapples in harness, probably with colorful ribbons woven into his mane and tail, pulling a buckboard full of guests to a picnic in Winery Lake's olive grove where every tree had a nameplate. René's art collection, including the olive grove, was eclectic, and often humorous.

Dana, a lanky teenage member of the Teicheira clan who was then working in the cellar for Domaine Chandon, volunteered that he knew a 17-year-old girl who had once trained a saddle horse. With those qualifications, the two of them were appointed to transform Dapples the pet into a working draft horse. Dapples seemed to enjoy the lessons. He readily accepted a halter, and even a bit and bridle. He agreeably allowed us to ride him bareback.

The author enjoying a trot on Dapples.

Sourcing tack in his size was a challenge. An antique horse collar appeared from a forgotten corner of someone's barn. Dapples took to it and the rough harness we commissioned from an old-timer in Calistoga like a natural. The winery's mechanic built a stone boat from memory, having grown up on a farm in the Midwest. It wasn't until the stone boat was hitched to Dapples' harness that all hell broke loose.

Horses, even big strong ones, are timorous by nature. Dapples stood 18 hands at the shoulder, weighed close to a ton and had hooves as big as pie plates, but he was terrified by that noisy monster scraping along the ground just outside his range of vision and much too close to his heels. He bolted, the empty wooden stone boat bouncing and clattering behind him, driving him to gallop ever faster. We never would have caught him if he hadn't worn himself out.

The same awful scene was repeated with every attempt to harness him to the stone boat until we tried loading it first. A big pile of rocks did the trick. We harnessed trembling Dapples to the rock-laden stone boat and waited for the explosion. He leaned into his collar and pulled. The load skidded along the rough ground with ease; it was just heavy enough to prevent Dapples from running away.

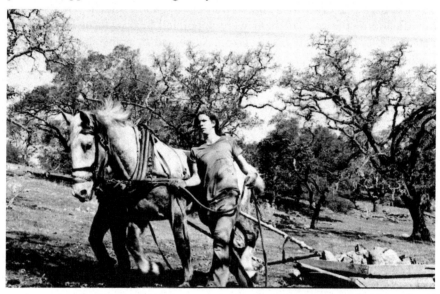

Dapples hauling rocks out of the hills on a stoneboat,
guided by Dana and a helper.

It took months of collecting and loading rocks by hand onto the stone boat to amass enough for the winery walls. (If you have visited Domaine Chandon you will appreciate the magnitude of this project.) Dapples finished the job looking very athletic, and seemingly content.

René welcomed him home, already planning his first horse-drawn Winery Lake picnic, but with lighter loads Dapples proved unreliable. In fact, just the sight of a harness got him excited, and huge excited horses make people nervous. Rather than risk his guests' lives, René wisely retired young Dapples to a life of leisure with his longhorn buddies in a pasture studded with colorful modern sculptures.

18 THE GRAND OPENING

After two years in the garage, and nearly two more working in temporary quarters in Vintage 1870, it was time to start planning for the grand opening of Domaine Chandon. This would be another first for me. I'd never planned a public event, much less a grand opening.

While construction had been moving smoothly, the estimated timeline for completion was still a few months away. A grand opening couldn't be planned and executed at the last minute, so a date had to be chosen in spite of the risk of delays. And delays there were.

As April 23, 1977, crept closer, everyone was feeling the pressure. Construction was moving at a frantic pace to meet the deadline set months previously. The weekend was to be filled with events: a dedication ceremony for local dignitaries and vintners followed by a sumptuous lunch; a press luncheon for 60 leading journalists and wine writers; and a dinner for 400 San Francisco socialites to benefit their favorite hospital. The plan was to open the winery to the public immediately after these events, on April 25.

Thanks to the construction crew staying late on April 22 to pave the long entrance road to the winery and clean up debris, the plan worked with only minor hitches. Thanks also to Moët & Chandon for sending chef Joseph Thuet to guide and support the newly formed restaurant team. The restaurant was not scheduled to open to the public until June, so they were working under challenging conditions to provide the necessary high-level cuisine for the opening events. Further kudos to Moët-Hennessy for taking out a 4-page, 4-color spread in Time magazine to introduce Domaine Chandon,

The dedication ceremony consisted of John Wright and Moët-Hennessy's Alain Chevalier christening the building yacht-style with jeroboams of champagne. John's broke on the first try, but Alain's bounced off the stone wall twice before shattering. Everyone raised their flutes of Chandon Napa Valley Brut and cheered.

Alain Chevalier breaking a jerobaom of Moët against the stone wall
of Domaine Chandon in 1977, with John Wright flinching away from
the flying glass. André Tchelistcheff is behind them wearing
dark glasses, and John Trefethen salutes in the left background.

As people were leaving, I came across one of the guests stuffing flutes
into a grocery bag with the clear intent of absconding with them – flutes
were still uncommon then. It wasn't easy to persuade him to desist, but he
finally accepted that I knew they were not his and surrendered them.

Organizing the press luncheon nearly turned my hair white; the reasons
why deserve a chapter to themselves. It follows, entitled The Big Hat.

The four hundred socialites arrived in buses from San Francisco for a
gala dinner in the not-yet-equipped bottling room. Most of the men had
pocket flasks to enliven the trek, and were quite jolly. They dined well,
danced the night away to a 20-piece orchestra, and left with happy
memories. By this time the restaurant team, which had been working
heroically for long days, gratefully went home to rest.

The winery opened to the public as scheduled on April 27. We were all slightly disappointed that the long-anticipated avalanche of visitors did not materialize. Perhaps ROMA had done too good a job of blending the winery into its environment? Soon, however, press reports from the opening got out and people started to come. When the restaurant opened, the avalanche started.

19 THE BIG HAT

I was a charter subscriber to *Ms.* magazine in 1972, which explains why I have never forgiven Paul Bocuse.

Months earlier before the planned April 1977 opening of Domaine Chandon, our guardian angels at Moët & Chandon had decided to call in some favors from famed French chef Paul Bocuse (three Michelin stars!) to lend international excitement to the winery's opening and to call attention to its soon-to-open restaurant. Bocuse had already sent over one of his *protégés*, Udo Nechutnys, to be Domaine Chandon's first chef, along with a young *chef saucier* named Philippe Jeanty who had trained under Moët's own chef Joseph Thuet. Then we learned from Moët that the great man himself had agreed to make an appearance at our grand opening.

I set to work planning a media luncheon to introduce sixty journalists to the first Chandon sparkling wines, and featuring a menu to be devised and prepared by Paul Bocuse. As the date drew near and I still had not received any communication from our *grande toque* as to when he would arrive in Napa Valley or what his menu plan was, I was getting nervous. His name was on the invitation. What if he didn't show up?

Three days before our inaugural media luncheon, a friend and southern California cookbook author, Rita Leinwand, called to tell me that Bocuse was in Los Angeles. Reassured that he was only 400 miles away, I dared hope that he would appear in Yountville in time for our event. I still had no direct word from him about his plans or the menu.

The day before the luncheon, a black stretch limousine—a rare sight in those days—pulled up in front of the winery and out piled chef Roger Vergé of the Moulin de Mougins (three more Michelin stars!) and Paul Bocuse with his entourage: his *chef de cuisine*, several minions and his PR person, Yanou Collart. Yanou promptly draped herself over the hood of the limo to pose for photos surrounded by this impressive *brigade*, while Bocuse lit into me for not having sent a driver to meet them at the airport in San Francisco. Today I would have permitted myself a few sarcastic remarks about my inability to read his mind. Being young and inexperienced and needing this event to work, I quietly seethed.

Having vented to his satisfaction, chef Bocuse abruptly decided to forgive me, which he demonstrated by pinching my bottom. He probably winked at me, too, but I was too indignant to notice. I don't care that his *boeuf à la ficelle* was a big hit with the journalists the next day, or even that his presence at the opening was helpful to the launch of Domaine Chandon. The offended me never misses an opportunity to reveal this great chef's condescension, lack of consideration, and ego. *Il m'a fessée!*

20 STAGIAIRES

In France, student interns are viewed differently than in the U.S. They are considered trainees, and are given a meaningful experience with the company during their internship. If all goes well, they can expect a job offer after graduation. In the U.S., internships typically amount to a summer job with little hope for a learning experience or future engagement.

As an American subsidiary of a large French company, every year Domaine Chandon received requests from French students wanting to do a *stage*. Many of them came through Moët-Hennessy managers and their friends, whose sons and daughters were interested in working for a while in California. Others came from students without such connections. At best we could accommodate one or two *stagiaires* each year during high demand season in the visitors center or for crush, so priority went to those with Moët connections.

One of the complications of accepting *stagiaires* in the U.S. is that they as non-citizens cannot easily get a work permit. (Today there are some student programs that can make reciprocal arrangements for appropriate visas, but then most students arrived as visitors.) Since it is considered a social obligation for French companies to accept *stagiaires*, we in California could hardly refuse on the basis that work permits were impossible. So we provided room and board in lieu of wages.

One early *stagiaire* who had no apparent Moët connections later played a starring role in a John McPhee book. Luc Massy was a young Swiss from a winemaking family in the Vaud. After working crush for us at Trefethen in 1976, he returned home to finish his studies and join his father making Chasselas wines at the family's Clos du Boux.

He also completed the compulsory military basic training required of male Swiss citizens, followed by a month of annual reserve duty every year until age 30 (34 for officers). Being promoted in the Swiss army is highly regarded by Swiss corporations, but Luc didn't want to rise in rank because the longer commitment would interfere with Clos du Boux operations, and found subtle ways to get demoted as necessary.

Luc Massy, a crush intern at Domaine Chandon in the 1970s
who later became famous for his service in the Swiss army.

In 1983, author John McPhee was working on a book about Swiss neutrality, and chose Luc's squad of reservists to follow for a week while it reconnoitered the area's extensive but well concealed defense systems. In *La Place de la Concorde Suisse*, published in 1984, McPhee noted that "Switzerland does not have an army, Switzerland is an army." McPhee also wrote about the lighter side of military service with a vintner in charge. The week was more like a camping trip than military maneuvers. For lunch, Luc would uncork his own Chasselas with – what else? a Swiss army knife – and share it with his platoon and McPhee over bread and cheese.

Another early *stagiaire* was James Forbes, a well-connected young Scot who met the love of his life at Domaine Chandon. But that's another chapter.

21 TALENT TRUMPS EXPERIENCE

I wasn't the only amateur on board this new enterprise.

Early on John Wright enlisted vineyard consulting help from Will Nord, a Napa College "ag" instructor. Will soon departed academia to join the team, and hired two recent UCLA graduates to help him develop hundreds of acres of vineyard—neither of them with any farming or vineyard experience on their brief résumés. That didn't matter to John; he always preferred talent and energy to experience. Besides, Will was a teacher.

Perhaps because Zach Berkowitz and Ernie Weir arrived at the same time, belonged to the same fraternity at UCLA, and were both tall, dark, bearded, and handsome, forever after we confused them for one another. It became a running joke they accepted with good grace: they had T-shirts printed announcing in large block letters "I am not Zach" and "I am not Ernie" in which they posed for photographs. They did a fine job managing the vineyards, with Zach focused on the extensive and challenging Carneros vineyard and grapevine nursery, and Ernie in charge of the vines at Mt. Veeder and Yountville.

Today Ernie owns and operates his own vineyards and winery, Hagafen, and Zach is a sought-after vineyard management consultant.

Another recent graduate also got a critical assignment from John Wright. Chip Bouril had just completed a degree in architecture before arriving at Mt. Veeder. His work experience consisted of volunteering at Arcosanti, the Paolo Soleri experimental town project in Arizona. When the time came to start construction on Domaine Chandon, John appointed Chip to be the owner's representative on this multi-million dollar project. The architects who designed the winery were astonished to have such an inexperienced liaison to work with, but assented. All went well: no one was hurt, the buildings were finished on time, and the walls are still standing.

Kim Giles, a self-taught winemaker, was working at nearby Mt. Veeder Winery for the Bernsteins in 1973. John hired him to work with consulting

Moët winemaker Edmond Maudière on the first M & H Vineyards crush at Trefethen.

Kim also made a swan song 1973 Zinfandel at Mt. Veeder Winery from the final harvest of the ancient vines on the former Simmons Ranch before they were ripped out to become Domaine Chandon's new Mt. Veeder vineyards. One of his winemaking duties was to be the weighmaster: Kim stood on a bathroom scale holding a lug box containing about 40 pounds of handpicked grapes, then subtracted the tare (himself and the empty box) to get the precise "tonnage" of grapes. Repeat for every box picked. With yields at a miniscule quarter ton per acre, the wine proved incredibly dark and dense, and took many years to reach drinkability. We still have a few bottles, our reward for helping pick the grapes.

Dawnine Dyer, armed with a UC Santa Cruz degree in Biology, arrived in 1975 to work in the lab under winemaker Sergio Traverso. When Sergio left soon thereafter, Dawnine was promoted to winemaker. She and I were amused by the frequency with which people mistook us for one another, a repeat of the Zach and Ernie show. All we had in common was being close in age, tall, and female–and working for Domaine Chandon, where we were both promoted to Vice President in 1980. This confusion persists; someone who knows me well surprised us both recently by mistakenly calling me Dawnine.

Philippe Jeanty was 21 years old when he arrived from France to be the inaugural *chef saucier* of Domaine Chandon's restaurant. He had been working in kitchens in Champagne since the age of 14, so he was not inexperienced–but after a year he was put in charge as *chef de cuisine* at the ripe age of 22 when Udo left.

Sally McFadden was a tour guide when I invited her into Domaine Chandon's marketing department to manage public relations. Although she could point to no experience in the field, she had the innate ability and qualities needed to do the job. She was a natural.

This partial list of gifted amateurs who helped build Domaine Chandon wouldn't be complete without the biggest amateur of all, John Wright. Our fearless leader's penchant for hiring brains, energy, and talent rather than experience worked well for all but the rare newcomer who didn't thrive on chaos. Without guidelines or supervision, and given opportunities to learn and take on challenges, the level of engagement at Domaine Chandon was high.

As the winery neared completion and staff necessarily expanded, there ensued a certain amount of turmoil caused by our leader's aversion to organizational structure. Some weren't sure where their responsibilities stopped and someone else's began. And everyone wanted to report directly to John, which proved unworkable. It was getting chaotic.

Feeling the pressure, John thought of his old friends Barry Stein and Rosabeth Moss Kanter. Their Boston consulting firm, Goodmeasure, specialized in organizational behavior, a field in which Harvard professor Rosabeth was expert. Barry and Rosabeth spent several days in Yountville debriefing us individually and then conveying what they'd learned to John in private. Just having the opportunity to express our concerns in confidence solved most of the problem. I've always admired John's courage for risking exposing his shortcomings, and for accepting Goodmeasure's advice. We were glad when he invited them back to help us through strategic planning.

John disliked making final decisions. He wanted to maintain flexibility at all times, because there was always the possibility of a better idea. This showed up in many ways, from his appreciation for innovation to a strong aversion to bureaucracy, silos, and employee handbooks. One of his favorite jokes was an org chart in the form of an inverted pyramid, with the janitor on top and management teetering on its point at the bottom. Nonetheless, he did make decisions, big ones, because his job required it.

Domaine Chandon's vice presidents in 1987. From left: Ed Hamler, Dawnine Dyer, Ed Farver, the author, and Will Nord

He invariably returned early from vacations, eager to return to the work he found so stimulating. When he and Renate took a month-long cruise to Buenos Aires I was convinced he'd jump ship after two days and swim back to the winery. He had brought along his Apple computer, and surprised us all by enjoying the cruise. After selling the computer in

Buenos Aires, he sailed home without a thought of work. He returned a different person, relaxed and less willing to dive back into the fray.

That is how Domaine Chandon's vice presidents came together to form a high-functioning management team. We didn't like John's proposal to appoint a COO to liberate him from day-to-day details and decisions, because we wanted to continue to report to him directly.

The five of us suggested that we function as a management cooperative and take on more of his workload ourselves in lieu of hiring a COO. John accepted, and everyone, including the company, benefited.

22 YOUNG LOVE

With so many young people involved, it was inevitable that romance would bloom at newly opened Domaine Chandon. The Immigration & Naturalization Service did its best to slow the course of nature, but ultimately failed.

Philippe Jeanty arrived from Champagne in 1977 to be the winery restaurant's first *chef saucier*. In spite of a taxing work schedule, he was lonely and soon invited his girlfriend Véronique to join him in Napa Valley. She obtained a standard six-month tourist visa and got on a plane.

I had become the default expert in immigration issues because of my do-it-yourself efforts to obtain a green card for Philippe, a lengthy process that usually involves attorneys. We had a good case. He had unique skills—cooking with and for champagne—that couldn't be found in the American workforce. I felt only slightly guilty that he and I were ushered into the INS manager's office in front of a large waiting room full of careworn applicants, apparently because our case was unusual and, no surprise, the INS manager liked wine.

One day Philippe came to me, wanting to know how to extend Véronique's stay in the United States. I realized it wouldn't be easy, since she didn't have any of the special skills required for a work visa.

Consulting with the INS office in San Francisco provided a possible solution. If they were to get married, Véronique could stay in the country legally based on Philippe's pending green card application. This was promising, since it implied his application was headed for eventual INS approval. So I asked the young lovers if marriage appealed to them. They'd been together already for three years, so that wasn't much of a stretch.

The next problem was obtaining the written consent of her parents. She was underage, and her parents were divorced and living in France. Sorting that out took several weeks of airmail letters flying back and forth. By the time all the paperwork was complete, time was running out.

It was the day before Thanksgiving. Véronique's tourist visa would expire the following Monday. With the visa clock now ticking loudly, I realized that the documentation derby had caused me to overlook one significant detail: a wedding ceremony. My calls to the local judges weren't answered: they'd left for a long weekend of fishing. One last, desperate thought came to mind. Maybe the priest in Yountville would perform the ceremony. Philippe and Véronique assented, so I "cold called" him.

Father Canny was kind enough not to hang up on me as I recounted this long tale. I was relieved and grateful when he invited us to come to the rectory on Friday to talk. Having been raised a Catholic, I knew it would be virtually impossible for him to marry two total strangers—one of them underage—at the request of another total stranger.

On Friday morning I arrived in jeans and a sweater hoping to convince the good father to bend the rules to prevent Véronique's potential deportation. Philippe and Véronique didn't help the negotiations by showing up dressed for a wedding, with Chef Udo's wife Mei along as a witness and bearing a bridal bouquet.

For an hour we listened to all the reasons why it was not possible to marry two young French people who were not members of the parish and whom the priest had never even met, much less counseled on the seriousness of marriage vows. He had me convinced, and I was about to apologize and thank him for his time when he abruptly stood and said, "Let's go next door to the church and do this." I served as the shabbily attired best man.

Father Canny, an Irish immigrant, later told me that he had endured five years of bureaucratic nightmares courtesy of the INS and could not bear to inflict such pain on anyone else.

* * *

James Forbes was the Scottish *stagiaire* who'd shown me around the caves and tasted champagnes with me at Moët & Chandon in 1976. Naturally, we talked about the exciting enterprise taking shape in Napa Valley. Young James felt the pull of adventure.

His uncle, Patrick Forbes, had visited Domaine Chandon while it was under construction in 1975. As the managing director of Moët & Chandon London and author of the definitive book on champagne, *Champagne: the Wine, the Land, and the People*, he was struck by Moët's wisdom in leaving the new venture "free to grow and flourish with a style and business flair that are wholly American." Perhaps that added to James' interest. He asked uncle Patrick to help him get an internship in Napa Valley. Patrick was not encouraging, but agreed to inquire.

The letter came to me. Not only would I never turn down a request from Patrick Forbes, whom I had met during his 1975 visit to Napa Valley and whose book was like a bible for me, I had been equally charmed by his nephew. It was easy to say yes. James arrived in 1977 as a *stagiaire* in Domaine Chandon's visitor center. That's where he met a beautiful American named Kerry, who was a tour guide at the time.

Smitten, James would wait several years for Kerry to be available. They were married in the Highlands, where they recently celebrated their twenty-fifth anniversary, and reside happily in the Napa Valley with neither help nor hindrance from the INS.

There are many other romantic stories in Domaine Chandon's history, but none needed my help.

23 ENGAGING WITH CONSUMERS

In the late 1970s the U.S. market was not ready for *méthode champenoise* sparkling wine, and barely ready for Napa Valley. Whoever chose Schramsberg Napa Valley Champagne for the historic 1972 toast in Beijing between President Nixon and Premier Chou En-lai put Schramsberg on the map. Likewise, Stag's Leap Wine Cellars Cabernet Sauvignon and Chateau Montelena Chardonnay were the beneficiaries of the famous "Tasting of Paris" in 1976.

Domaine Chandon enjoyed no such windfall. We would have to work to make our place in the market.

We did have a great story: Moët & Chandon taking the risk of lending its name to a Napa Valley winery and backing that up with millions of francs and years of patient waiting for a return on its investment. These were people whose families had been in the fine wine business since 1743, and they knew how long it would take.

Complicating the task was the American attitude toward bubbly in general. Champagne, sparkling wine, spumante, fizz, bubbles, whatever it was called, was a drink considered appropriate only for specific, and far too few, occasions: birthdays (for the lucky ones), New Year's Eve, and wedding toasts. Most people did not even consider it wine. It was in a category of its own, famous but little understood.

Fortunately for Domaine Chandon, Americans are a curious people, uninhibited by tradition and intrigued by learning. Champagne history and sparkling wine production offer many good stories that we used to generate a following, first at the winery and later out in the market. There were other audiences for our stories, such as the wine trade in its many forms, but I was always focused on the people who would ultimately buy and drink the wine: consumers.

We could explain *la méthode champenoise,* from growing and vinifying base wines through press cuts, blending, *tirage,* aging, riddling, disgorging, and dosage. We could explain the real significance of Dom Pérignon's work, and it wasn't just because he may have been the first to seal bottles with cork instead of oily rags. We could suggest ways to enjoy these festive wines without waiting for a special occasion. Explain the difference between a *tête de cuvée* and a non-vintage brut. Why flutes are better than saucer-like coupes. How the wine ages, if desired. The difference between brut and extra dry. Opening a bottle safely, and without losing half the contents. Reminding people that bubbly is, in fact, wine. It was a long list. We made good progress, but habits and beliefs are slow to change.

The entrenched special occasion use pattern for sparkling wine is what drove us to include a restaurant in the plans for Domaine Chandon. We wanted people to enjoy sparkling wine before, during, and after meals. Every day at the winery we showed visitors how to do it, in the hope they would take this lovely habit home with them. Many did, as you will see in the chapter on the Chandon Club.

There were only 45 wineries in Napa Valley receiving visitors in a new guide book reviewed by Sunset magazine in October 1977. We needed lots of visitors to listen to our story, and even in those days there was competition for them.

In their efforts to attract scarce visitors, Napa Valley wineries traditionally offered free tastings. This was the norm when Domaine Chandon was being readied for its grand opening, but John Wright knew that we couldn't afford it. The extraordinarily high excise taxes on sparkling wines make free samples very expensive, leading John to another first: charging a tasting fee. Amazingly, state law proved helpful. The only way wineries could legally sell wine for consumption on the premises was to have a *bona fide* restaurant. So it was possible, at least for Domaine Chandon, but was it a good idea?

Fearful of losing potential visitors, who I understood to be of great importance to our success, I protested. In two days I pounded out a fervent 10-page white paper explaining how charging tasting fees would destroy our barely launched visitor program.

The economic argument prevailed, and experience soon proved me wrong. The $2.50 tasting fee did not deter visitors, perhaps because we offered an enhanced experience compared to the usual tasting bar staffed by sometimes gruff retirees.

Our visitors were seated in a beautiful setting to enjoy a flute of sparkling wine with a slice of baguette smeared with flavored cream cheese while they enjoyed learning about the *méthode champenoise* and Champagne history. Our tasting room hosts were friendly and enjoyed their work. It was a pleasant place. Visitors liked it, and told their friends.

Tasting fees rapidly spread to nearly all other wineries, and have greatly outpaced inflation since 1977.

24 BUILDING RELATIONSHIPS

I come from a family of word people, with emphasis on the written word. Having gotten over a youthful case of shyness, I believe in communicating. That is probably what pulled me in the direction of public relations and then marketing at Domaine Chandon. It also helped me understand the value of keeping colleagues, bosses, owners, and boards of directors informed.

Interlocutors have varying interests and needs. The media need good story ideas and the facts to develop them. The retail and distribution side of the wine trade has showed little interest in words, preferring scores to descriptions, but that may be changing. Consumers enjoy learning about wine, and being involved. Bosses and shareholders generally don't like to be surprised.

Inspired by the extensive visitor data on file at Moët & Chandon, I started collecting names and addresses as soon as Domaine Chandon opened its doors in 1977. As a gentle reminder of good times, and to maintain the relationships inaugurated during these winery visits, I began writing a "breezy" quarterly newsletter that I thought of as a letter from home. People wrote back, sharing their own stories of memorable moments with their friends and Chandon sparkling wine. The mailing list grew.

As my marketing responsibilities mushroomed, it became harder to find time to write. Given the importance of staying in touch with Domaine Chandon's best friends, the newsletter was always a high priority for me. The solution appeared, as often happens, when one is not trying to find it.

I recalled enjoying the annual one-page *Pickle Canyon Eagle* produced by John Wright's bird-watching, Jungian psychiatrist, former New Yorker, vineyard partner Herb McGrew. His writing style and mine were similar. If he were to take over the Domaine Chandon newsletter, perhaps no one would notice the change of voice.

To my delight, McGrew readily agreed in spite of his full-time practice at Napa State Hospital. The transition was smooth, subsequent editions were similarly breezy, and I was free to focus on other priorities. Almost. It turned out that his work required some editing. This too, is a family trait; I'm not the only Kane born with a blue pencil in my hand. My mother was mortified when I confessed to passing along to McGrew some of her I-can't-help-myself edits on a published Domaine Chandon newsletter. That I had edited. I was mortified, too.

There were many readers of those Domaine Chandon newsletters, including members of the press. Sometimes the latter even printed excerpts. This one, picked up by the St. Helena Star from a Jerry Mead newsletter, is priceless.

> Chandon's vineyard manager was discussing the quality
> of the harvest with a reporter from the St. Helena Star, and said,
> "the crop looks pretty good this year," but the *Star's* typesetter
> decided to print the story differently. "The crap looks pretty good
> this year," announced the *Star*, raising some eyebrows and
> reddening one innocent vineyard manager's face.

McGrew wrote newsletters for me for 25 years, first at Domaine Chandon and later at St. Supéry. I didn't learn until well into our partnership that he had long harbored aspirations to be a writer, so my invitation had fallen on fertile ground. When he finally decided to give up writing newsletters, I didn't try to talk him out of it; I could only be grateful for his contributions. As a measure of how good McGrew's writing is, the first article he submitted over the transom to *Gourmet* magazine was promptly published. No rejection slips for him!

Those decades of newsletters maintained and strengthened relationships while providing a stylistic continuum that helped build distinctive personalities for the two wineries I helped build. Over time the method of delivery evolved dramatically. From black and white printed, folded, hand-addressed and stamped mailers, through computerized records and outsourced mailing services, and currently to e-communications embellished with color photos, links to websites, and other techie bells and whistles, we've come a long way.

Tools for marketing communications have become blessedly cheap, unfortunately for the U.S. Postal Service and the recipients of the resulting e-deluge. Handwritten notes may yet be the most effective way to show people you value the relationship.

25 ROAD TRIP

You couldn't ask for a more supportive parent company than Moët-Hennessy.

In 1978, Domaine Chandon's second year in the public eye, Moët offered us the use of its corporate jet for a month of marketing activity in the U.S. Their French pilot, too. They even paid for fuel, landing fees, maintenance, and an American copilot. The plane, a Dassault Mystère 10 (known in the U.S. as a Falcon 10) carried eight passengers. It was not designed for tall or wide people, and it was blisteringly fast.

Latent fighter pilot fantasies ran rampant. This was going to be better than an impromptu aerial tour of Mt. Veeder in the Bell Jet Ranger that had ferried our Moët leaders to a 1975 meeting on the mountain. Chip and I persuaded the pilot to take us up while that august threesome had lunch

Fred Chandon, Alain Chevalier, Edmond Maudière, and John Wright arriving in style on Mt. Veeder in 1975.

'

in John Wright's home. I don't think foraged mushrooms were on the menu that day.

How best to use Moët's wonderful gift? My first thought was to provide journalists a memorable experience—and with luck get some ink—by flying them to the new winery for a visit. The Moët pilot picked up his American copilot in Teterboro, N.J. and headed west with Comte Ghislain de Vogüé acting as steward and host to a planeload of New York journalists.

It only took a week of flying to and from various major markets to bring every wine writer I knew of to visit Domaine Chandon. We sparkling wined and dined them, had them blend their own *cuvées*, showed them the sights of the Napa Valley, took them to the mud baths in Calistoga, put them up in the winery's condo at Silverado—whose acquisition was justified by Edmond's bimonthly visits and the dearth of hotels in the valley in those days—then flew them home, sated, perhaps exhausted, with plenty of story ideas.

I will never forget the French pilot's reaction after being sandwiched into a long line of heavies on approach at LAX. *"Fantastique!!"* he exclaimed, climbing bug-eyed out of the cockpit, thrilled and slightly stunned by the experience. I had ridden the empty plane down to pick up Robert Lawrence Balzer and other southern California writers, and was equally thrilled at the way that nimble little jet leapt off the runway at takeoff.

That left three more weeks to put our gift jet to productive use in the U.S. Pressure sometimes leads to innovation, which is what happened. We decided to fill the plane with neighbors and hit the road together, another first. Napa vintners have a longstanding, deserved reputation for sharing advice, equipment, and even grape sources, but in 1978 they hadn't yet started traveling together to promote Napa Valley wines.

The vintners we invited were eager to accept. Michael Mondavi, Jack Cakebread, Francis Mahoney of Carneros Creek, Louis Martini and Mike Martini, Jerry Luper of Chateau Montelena, John Trefethen, Tom Burgess, and, of course, Edmond—those last three, all pilots, couldn't resist any kind of flying—committed for all or part of a seven-city tour of the U.S.

With permission, I had the Moët logo painted on the jet's fuselage near the hatch in case some enterprising news photographer wanted to capture the visiting vintners' arrival. None did, but somewhere in Domaine Chandon's archives there may still be a photo of the entire group, including me, in front of the jet at the Napa airport. The photo on the following page was given given to me by Jerry Luper in 2014, proving my story.

Chateau Montelena winemaker Jerry Luper and Mike Martini
with the Moët jet at the Napa airport in 1978.

The unanticipated challenge in organizing this foray lay in the middle
tier of our country's three-tier distribution system. None of the vintners
had distributors in common (in those days there were many more
distributors) so it became my task to convince six competing distributors
in each of seven cities to cooperate. It couldn't have been more difficult.
Although we were supporting their wineries' own sales while promoting
Napa Valley, it required a strongly worded request from each vintner to his
distributor just to get the correct vintages to the designated trade and
consumer tasting venues in a timely manner. They all balked at helping
promote the trade tasting to their own on and off premise accounts.

Each distributor seemed to perceive this cooperative venture as a zero-
sum game where anything done to support its own vintner's brand would
have the undesired effect of also helping the other brands. There's a cliché
about cutting off noses that nicely fits this mindset.

I managed to get the word out through flyers provided to key retail
locations in each city—imagine stacks of flyers organized by city covering
the office floor at Domaine Chandon -- and sent news of the upcoming
events to the wine media. Their interest and support produced the hoped
for attendance at these events.

Patrick Fegan's article in the *Chicago Tribune* featuring a huge photo
of Francis Mahoney helped turn out 700 eager consumers who nearly
broke down the hotel's ballroom doors when we weren't quite ready to

open the event on time. The welcome in Boston, Dallas, Seattle, Portland, New York, and Washington, D.C., was almost as gratifying. Being first with the concept surely helped, but it's also possible the five-dollar price of admission, charged only to facilitate planning, was too good a deal. I can't recall or imagine how we collected the money in advance in those low-tech days. Even the typically blasé trade turned out for this first-ever visit from a group of Napa Valley vintners.

Louis Martini was a big man, and tall, but he never complained about having to sit hunched over for the duration of those flights. Louis did ask his equally big and tall winemaker son Michael to substitute for him a couple of times, perhaps so he could go to a chiropractor.

The Moët jet returned to France after that hectic month. The flying vintners went home to rest, but the powerful impact of that successful shared experience soon drew us back together. We agreed that the program should not be allowed to end just because we no longer had a private jet at our disposal. Besides, I'd learned a lot about matrixes and wanted to use that knowledge.

For the next two years, our small group continued to travel around the country at its own expense, putting on trade and consumer tastings in the name of Napa Valley. Commercial flights were nowhere near as much fun, even in those pre-TSA days. Jack Cakebread took to calling us The Flying Circus, but I never liked that name and didn't use it for our tour materials. I should have thought of a better one.

After a while we resolved that participation in this successful promotion should be open to all the vintners, and approached the Napa Valley Vintners Association board of directors. For reasons I will never understand, our offer to hand over a turnkey, proven program was declined by the leadership. One of the directors went so far as to accuse us of working to promote the Napa Valley solely for self-aggrandizement.

The vintners association has made great progress since then, with annual group market visits of up to 100 wineries a familiar example of Napa Valley cooperative wine marketing. An effective and efficient way to reach out to the trade and consumers, going on the road together has become common practice for vintner associations from all over the world.

26 MEMORABLE EVENTS

Perhaps because of its import license or its own direct sales force selling to Bay Area restaurants and wine shops, or maybe only its French connections, in 1978 Domaine Chandon became the northern California importer for one of Burgundy's brightest jewels: Domaine de la Romanée Conti.

The following year, owners Aubert de Villaine and Lalou Bize-Leroy assigned exclusive national distribution for DRC and Leroy wines to a newly formed national importer-distributor, Wilson Daniels. Jack Daniels and his partner Win Wilson promptly bought all the previous importers' inventory and started a long, successful journey with these fine burgundies, still represented by Wilson Daniels today.

In 1981, Win and Jack decided to organize a black tie dinner at Domaine Chandon for burgundy lovers. It was held in conjunction with the first Napa Valley Wine Auction, which many of the guests had flown in to attend. Marvin Shanken, Ed Jonna, René di Rosa, and others who appreciated fine burgundies were among the 60 guests. The dinner sold out quickly at $250 a plate, with the proceeds going to Renate Wright's favorite local charity, COPE. Three years into his tenure as *chef de cuisine*, 25-year old Philippe Jeanty outdid himself with a multi-course meal that did justice to the DRC, Leroy, and Chandon wines served that hot June night.

Of course the air conditioning chose that evening to malfunction. Gavin Gracey, restaurant manager, remembers the mostly male guests quickly shedding their dinner jackets and ties.

On the other end of the sartorial spectrum, someone (not me) thought it would be a brilliant idea for Domaine Chandon to organize a 10K race through the vineyards surrounding the winery in Yountville. While not without some small hills, the terrain offered little of the rigor of the long-ago race up Mt. Veeder. As the boss himself and several employees wanted to compete, I sighed resignedly and called Chip's girlfriend Penny Proteau's brother Mark, a serious runner, for advice. Although our Run in the Vineyard was billed as "semi-serious," most registrants turned up ready to race in running shorts and shoes.

We discovered too late that the more serious among them expected us, the organizers, to keep track of their finish time and place. My advisor was ready for them with wooden tongue depressors to hand out as each runner crossed the finish line. All I remember after that is an impatient crowd of sweaty people who were not pleased at how long it took to announce the results. The flowing sparkling wine that followed improved their mood. Artist Veronica di Rosa immortalized the start of the race down the Veterans Home driveway in a watercolor that still graces our home.

After we stopped doing the Run in the Vineyard because there were more serious local 10-K runs happening, we continued to support others' athleticism by showering the winners of San Francisco's Bay to Breakers with jeroboams of sparkling wine (corks safely popped, not sabered). They were invariably surprised to find the wine delicious when we offered the winners a taste from the big bottles.

27 RULES, AND MORE RULES

I thought of the wine business as highly regulated, thanks to the government's interest in collecting excise taxes—that is, until I joined the board of a bank. Banks are even more highly regulated, again no doubt because that's where the money is.

The excesses of Prohibition inspired many of the rules governing the wine business. While the Federal Alcohol Administration Act of 1935 aimed primarily to protect the public from poisonous products and misleading advertising, it handed off control of wine distribution and sales to the individual states. This engendered reams of regulations, with each state creating and enforcing its unique set of rules and collecting its own taxes on alcohol. They remain in effect long after the last rumrunners and gangsters whose activities they originally targeted, because entire systems have formed around them that have proven resistant to an evolving industry and market.

As a result, it's nearly impossible to conduct normal wine business without technically breaking the rules in some minor way. All parties, including the regulators, aren't bothered unless and until someone steps over the line by doing something egregiously anti-competitive. Then the chronically understaffed regulators receive a complaint, typically anonymous, which they are obliged to investigate.

For example, most wineries and retailers roundly ignored the rules against direct shipping to out-of-state consumers, until distributors complained. A distributor-instigated sting operation made examples of two well-known California wineries shipping wine to their east coast mailing list customers in the 1980s, raising all wineries' awareness that those rules might be enforced with fines and a reputational black eye. Thankfully, the rules on direct shipping to consumers have changed and continue to evolve rapidly—but we've got a way to go before America becomes as open a market for wine as it is for other consumer products.

One of the least harmful forms of rule breaking was the generally winked-at practice of wineries generously supporting charitable fundraising with donated wine for auctions and tastings. While very recent legislation has finally fixed this problem after repeated pleas for help from nonprofits, in the early days it forced wineries either to take the risk or withdraw their in-kind support from worthy causes. Like volunteer fire departments.

Volunteer fire departments provide protection in the rural areas of Napa County. They always need money for equipment and operating expenses, so fundraising is crucial to their ability to protect the public. When the Dry Creek-Lokoya volunteer fire department approached me at Domaine Chandon for help, of course I said yes.

We were well into planning their first Home Winemakers fundraiser in 1982 when it was brought to my attention that selling tickets, questionably conflated with selling wine that would be consumed at the event, was not legal for non-commercial wines—especially at a commercial winery. (In fact, commercial wineries were licensed to sell only their own wines, unless they also operated a *bona fide* restaurant—a use not permitted in agriculturally zoned Napa County. Catch 22.) Balancing the good (raising money for community fire protection) against the harm (breaking meaningless rules), I decided to take the risk.

It didn't hurt that the highly respected presiding judge of Napa County's Superior Court, Tom Kongsgaard, was a participating home winemaker and supporter of volunteer firemen. My fallback plan, if we were raided, was to throw myself on the mercy of the court.

That first event was a big success, and the Home Winemakers Classic became a much-loved annual event at Domaine Chandon and subsequently at St. Supéry. The quality of the homemade wines improved noticeably over the years, as competition among the winemakers intensified in a good-natured way. Auction proceeds rose steadily.

Eventually, our elected officials succeeded in changing the law to reflect reality and community needs, and nonprofits were allowed to sell tickets and donated wines at fundraisers.

28 RISING STAR

By 1982, things were going well for Domaine Chandon and the wine market in general in the U.S., so with his typical optimism John Wright proposed Plan M (for Mitterand) to the Moët-Hennessy board of directors. Plan M called for a significant increase in production and sales.

The directors, concerned about what the newly elected, first socialist president of France might do to businesses, agreed to support the required investment. Ironically, we now remember late 1982 as the trough of one of many recessions affecting the U.S. economy. In a longterm business like fine wine, recessions are viewed as passing problems to manage through rather than deal breakers.

For a youthful company, ten years felt like a long time and many accomplishments. We giddily decided to celebrate Domaine Chandon's 10th anniversary in 1983 with a big party, and to publish a book commemorating all that had transpired since 1973. Although I like to write, I realized that there was no time to learn how to write and publish a book. Our New York PR consultant, Judy Ostrow, suggested freelance writer Jaime Laughridge and the project was launched.

I shared with Jamie a list of people who might provide useful information for the book, causing her to spend a hectic two weeks in California and on the telephone interviewing John Wright, Comte de Vogüé, Fred Chandon, Alain Chevalier, Edmond Maudière, all the winery employees, consultants, distributors, vintners, neighbors and friends, journalists…everyone who might have something to say about the first ten years of Domaine Chandon's existence. After we'd talked about her draft outline, she went home to New York to start writing.

I asked artist Veronica di Rosa if she'd be interested in illustrating the book with her charming water colors. She and René had been to many of our parties on the mountain, and knew us well. She was happy to accept, took the outline, and began sketching ideas. When Jaime's first draft arrived, I gave a copy to Veronica for inspiration and started a rough edit. Although I was born with a blue pencil in hand (thanks, Mom), I had never edited anyone's work but my own and McGrew's newsletter copy. When I realized that I was laboriously rewriting her draft in my own voice, I stopped. I finally understood that an editor's job is to improve a writer's work, not change it into her own. Editing went much faster after that. As I recall, there was little that I deleted, except the story about cellar workers smoking pot on their lunch hour inside one of the empty, sanitized, horizontal tanks that Edmond was so proud of.

The next step was to lay out the book, which required commandeering the entire floor of the winery office to spread out the chapters and

Rising Star

DOMAINE CHANDON: A DECADE OF SPARKLE

paintings. We moved the pieces around until all fell into place, added front pages and a primer for serving sparkling wine at the end, and send it off to the publisher.

Rising Star is still available for sale at what is now named simply Chandon, like the wines. If you're enjoying this book, you'll enjoy it too.

29 M.F.K. FISHER

I felt fortunate to be included as a guest when the women's tasting group I would eventually join went to visit author M.F.K. Fisher in 1983 at her home on the Bouverie Ranch in Glen Ellen. Her longtime friend Romie Gould, whose husband Paco had authored one of the earliest winery newsletters, Bottles & Bins, for Charles Krug, had made the arrangements.

Exceptionally, all fourteen members of the group turned out. Even I knew how special this opportunity was, having been turned on to M.F.K. Fisher's work by Jamie Davies. How could anyone resist a story entitled *How to Cook a Wolf*?

Mary Frances greeted us as we entered her two-room house, clear blue eyes missing nothing. We respectfully gathered in a semi-circle in her living room while she held forth on wine—and food. Her speech was as engaging as her writing. Being the junior guest I sat quietly, watching and listening. I noted a subtle flicker in Mary Frances' eyes when the occasional silly question was put. I thought she was terrific.

When I told John Wright about having met M.F.K. Fisher, he asked if I could introduce an old friend of his. Elaine Tait was then the food editor of the *Philadelphia Inquirer*. I never would have dared request a second visit to Glen Ellen for myself, although I was eager for more, but doing so on behalf of someone else, someone with real food writing credentials, gave me the required license.

So I wrote her a note, and Mary Frances graciously agreed to receive us. We three enjoyed a glorious afternoon, talking and laughing and tasting an early Fetzer packaging experiment. We gleefully pronounced the Chardonnay in a 6 oz. pull-tab can an aluminum-flavored failure. After that, I was invited to visit often, and I did, as evidenced by a growing collection of books she autographed for me.

Mary Frances had a great sense of fun and loved company—especially if men were involved. When I brought Herb McGrew to visit one time, I noticed that she had her highly arched eyebrows and red lipstick carefully applied for the occasion. My husband Gregory got the same treatment.

She loved parties, and bubbles, too. And she was a firm francophile, having lived and written books in France. She devoted the entire month of July every year to celebrating her birthday, which gave me the fine idea of inviting her Napa Valley friends to a birthday luncheon in her honor at Domaine Chandon. This went on for several years, until Parkinson's disease finally kept her housebound.

She was a wonderful correspondent, always prompt to reply. I've kept all her typewritten notes.

30 COLLATERAL DAMAGE

In the late 1970s and early 1980s, America was waking up to wine. Baby Boomers who had been introduced to wine while backpacking through Europe in the 1960s were beginning to earn enough to indulge in the occasional bottle of something special. They also had a thirst for knowledge.

Napa Valley tasting rooms started to experience a boom in visitors, an apt descriptor referring to the large cohort of Baby Boomers drinking most of the wine then. Wine festivals blossomed around the country, and vintners traveled to share their best bottles and their stories. Domaine Chandon's pedigree earned it many opportunities. Like most of our team, I was invited to speak about sparkling wine, champagne, and the Napa Valley, and pour our Chandon *cuvées* for eager crowds around the country.

The downside to marketing sparkling wine is collateral damage. All of my good shoes were ruined showing VIPs through Domaine Chandon's cellars, whose floors always seemed to have been hosed down immediately before our arrival.

This also happened at public tastings, where I would usually be standing in stocking feet in an icy puddle sloshed from the chilling bins under the tasting table. The pain of frozen feet was less than the discomfort of wearing unaccustomed heels, discarded early in the event and soon to be ruined.

One winter afternoon I was entertaining a wine writer from Santa Clara in my office. We sipped Chandon and talked until after dark. Then it started to rain. She decided it was time to leave, we said goodbye, and she exited the building. Within minutes she was back, having accidentally driven her older model, large American car forward off the paving instead of backing out, leaving its undercarriage hung up on a ledge and the car teetering between the parking lot and the vineyard eighteen inches below. The D4 was miles away on Mt. Veeder, and everyone else had already gone home. So we headed back inside to call for a tow truck, only to find that the office door had locked behind me. It was a dark, cold hike in pounding rain to the nearest telephone, located a mile away in the guard station at the entrance to the Veterans Home. That was the end of a pair of Gucci shoes acquired on a trip to Italy.

Pouring sparkling wine at tastings has other hazards. Opening chilled bottles filled with high-pressure bubbly is a dangerous business. As you remove the *muselet* holding the cork in place, its wire can rip your numb hands. If you permit your mind to wander for a second as you open the bottle, you risk putting someone's eye out with a jet-propelled cork. Sometimes you even drop a heavy bottle on your bare, equally numb, foot. It's easy to make a mistake when you're working as fast as you can to pour tastes for hundreds of eager consumers, while answering questions or even just trying to make sure they know what's in the glass.

A bit of marketing showmanship that should have a cautionary sticker "do not try this at home" is sabering champagne bottles. There's a technique that usually works, but it's risky even for the experts. Robert Gourdin, whose job was to travel the country building huge pyramids of champagne coupes to fill with Moët cascading from sabered jeroboams, was a mass of scars from flying glass. Jean Troisgros, a three-star chef visiting Napa in the late 1970's to lead classes for the Great Chefs of France cooking school, sabered a magnum of Chandon for a group of students. He carefully aimed the bottle away from us, but I – standing *behind* the group – was startled to see a large shard of flying glass land near my feet.

When I was eight months pregnant with our first child, I flew to Los Angeles to work the market (that means calling on accounts) with one of the senior executives of Young's Market Co., Domaine Chandon's distributor. Web Hansen was nearly twice my age and had a bad limp, but he ran me ragged all day. I can't remember whether I was foolish enough to wear heels, and I have no idea whether we succeeded in selling any Chandon (sales has never been my strong point). My back hurt for a week.

There's at least one good reason why airlines won't let women fly in their ninth month, and it's not concern about an unscheduked in-flight delivery; it is simply not possible to get comfortable in those cramped seats.

31 MACS RULE

In the early 1980s, Domaine Chandon's mainframe computer was designed for financial reporting purposes, not marketing. Prior to the invention of desktop publishing and accessible databases, operations as simple as maintaining the integrity of a database in a country where 25% of the population moved annually, or printing mailing labels, required outsourcing and/or lengthy bargaining for time with the IT genie controlling the mainframe.

My hand-picked public relations director for Domaine Chandon, Sally McFadden, was frustrated with the mainframe's limitations for marketing purposes. Then, through her roadie husband, she met musician Herbie Hancock's technical consultant, Bryan Bell.

Bryan was already doing tech consulting with Apple products. Since Domaine Chandon's president John Wright was an early adopter, when Sally introduced me to Bryan in 1985 I instantly agreed to give him a chance. I'd had enough experience with mainframes at Berkeley while working on my MBA to know that a more user-friendly system would be welcome.

If Bryan could find ways for us to get at our data easily and make the marketing workflow smoother and faster, we would have an incredible resource for strengthening our relationship with consumers who had already knew and liked Domaine Chandon.

Burly and bearded, Bryan looked a bit sinister. In reality, he has a sunny disposition, is always looking for ways to save money for his clients, and has a great sense of humor. He is the one who perceptively told me that our two-year old daughter Kate would make a fine queen for a small country, thus reinforcing the nickname already bestowed on this willful child by a favorite babysitter: The Queen of Always.

Bryan is a genuine computer wiz, especially good at workarounds. He began by finding a way to get Domaine Chandon's 100,000+ mailing list out of the mainframe and onto Filemaker software so it could be easily updated and sorted on a Mac by the marketing staff. Next came desktop publishing, allowing Sally to lay out the Chandon Club newsletters in-house. With Filemaker and an inkjet printer we could produce mailing labels in hours, instead of the seven to ten days the task took each quarter when outsourced to a fulfillment house.

We embraced technology.

32 MARKET INTELLIGENCE

John Wright, or Juan Correcto as the restaurant staff liked to call the boss, had wandered into his dream job by proposing and creating a highly professional, data-rich study entitled "Wine/America" in 1972. It attracted the attention of several large wine producers, including Moët & Chandon, in part because it was based on reliable data and in part because the future for fine wine in the U.S. looked rosy.

But how some things have changed in forty years! For example, in 1972 John concluded "the current relationship between grape and wine prices in California clearly favors vineyards over winemaking on a return-on-investment basis."

As a Napa Valley grapegrower myself, I can attest that the value-add is in wine, not grapes. This, however, remains unchanged since the study was completed: "The wine industry is, and will remain, a highly fragmented business in terms of suppliers and specific products."

My first personal experience with market research was in the form of focus groups for Domaine Chandon. These took place a few years after champagne houses Mumm and Piper-Heidsieck, after several years of waiting and watching, had followed Moët's 1973 lead to California. (Roederer and Taittinger were to arrive soon after.)

Our primary interest lay in finding out whether American wine consumers were aware of and valued the champagne pedigrees of Chandon and its similarly well-bred competitors Piper-Sonoma and Mumm Napa Valley. To that end, screeners intercepted mall shoppers who, if they professed to be regular drinkers of champagne and sparkling wine, were invited to participate in a focus group. The group's task was to arrange bottles of French and California bubbly from these and other producers in order of perceived quality. No other information was provided.

It was a surprise—and a disappointment—to observe that our consumer panel's notion of quality seemed to relate only to the amount of gold foil on the labels. Appellation of origin (Champagne, Napa, Sonoma) made no difference.

I had expected them to group the bottles by brand, with Domaine Chandon alongside Moët & Chandon, Piper Sonoma with Piper-Heidsieck, and Mumm Napa Valley paired with Mumm Cordon Rouge. Obvious as it seemed, that didn't happen. I concluded that focus groups were an unreliable resource on which to base marketing decisions.

I sat in on focus groups conducted by Schieffelin in New York and Florida for Moët & Chandon that reinforced my already low opinion of market research based on small samples. Sitting behind the one-way mirror, I witnessed a parade of self-reported champagne consumers whose opinions were worthless. Whoever had done the screening for this group had missed some cues.

One woman who appeared to be a welfare recipient proclaimed from memory, unaided, that Dom Pérignon was her favorite brand of champagne and she enjoyed it weekly. Another apparently had said yes to all screening questions solely to collect the participation fee of twenty-five dollars, as he had nothing at all to say about champagne.

Fortunately, today we have better access to qualitative and quantitative market research through organizations like Wine Market Council.

Sales and financial data are even more difficult to come by in the wine industry because most companies are closely held.

Reports published on pricing, sales volume, and trends are usually based on such broad categories that they are of limited usefulness to all but the largest brand owners. Smaller wineries have to find other ways to learn what's going on in restaurants, retail stores, and distribution that might affect their businesses.

After Moët-Hennessy acquired its longstanding U.S. importer-distributor, Schieffelin & Co., in 1981, Domaine Chandon's contacts with its distributors and trade customers became indirect at best. Schieffelin reported our sales data, but not the color or the dialogues that reveal opportunities or problems.

So when one of Domaine Chandon's tour guides, Rhonda Savitch, came to me with a proposal for a brand ambassador outreach program, I immediately saw the opportunity. The brand ambassador team would have legitimate reasons to travel throughout the country promoting Chandon sparkling wines to trade and consumers, and would also bring back valuable intelligence that was otherwise difficult of access.

I found money in the marketing budget, and Rhonda enlisted three fellow tour guides to join the team. This program was successful for years, strengthening our market knowledge and reinforcing trade and consumer relationships.

33 THE CHANDON CLUB

John Wright was a veritable fountain of ideas. It was probably in self-defense that I took on triage duties, neglecting the impossible ones and working to develop those I believed to be useful and, more importantly, feasible. John seldom mentioned the same idea more than once, so this method worked well. I planted a few in his brain myself, and enjoyed watching them bloom a few days later.

It took a while for me to grasp that ideas John mentioned more than once were important, and not just to him. So many flew by that the first time he proposed something, I barely noticed. A second mention would begin to catch my attention, reminding me that it sounded faintly familiar. A third mention meant that John liked this idea enough to return to it again, so I thought perhaps it was time to think about it. This method worked well, too.

One of his thrice-mentioned ideas was to create a club.

In the mid-1980s, there was no such thing as a wine club. Many small wineries had mailing lists, and a handful such as Stony Hill sold everything they produced on allocation to loyal consumers. But relationship marketing (as opposed to transactional marketing) was in its early stages of development, with American Airlines having launched its innovative AAdvantage loyalty program only in 1981.

I wasn't sure what John meant by a winery "club," and he didn't either. So I started thinking about what a club might be, and what it might do for Domaine Chandon. I had been collecting names and addresses for a visitor database from the moment Domaine Chandon opened. We stayed in touch with visitors through the quarterly newsletter, and often received personal replies that I was delighted to answer. Some people in our database demonstrated a personal attachment to Domaine Chandon, usually started by a wonderful time visiting the winery.

Perhaps those fans could become the nucleus of a wine club. But why would they want to join? What benefit would they derive from membership? What would such a club do for the winery?

Being the interested recipient of incoming fan mail provided the critical insight: these people wanted nothing so much as to be part of Domaine Chandon. On the inside. A member of our tribe. I believed we could do that, provided we took care to maintain the personal relationship they valued. But would that be enough?

Lynn Myers, a journalism scholar on loan from Stanford, our public relations director Sally McFadden, and I brainstormed a list of potential club membership benefits in preparation for testing the reaction of 100 randomly selected visitors from around the country. Most of our ideas were for winery-centric benefits that required being present in Napa Valley, e.g., early access to prized restaurant reservations, complimentary tastings, special tours, etc. When we started making the calls, we learned two things.

First, everyone loved the idea of being part of an exclusive group of Domaine Chandon fans. Second, while they appreciated the proposed winery-based perks, those living more than two hours driving distance away didn't get to the Napa Valley very often; they wanted us to bring Domaine Chandon to them.

And so the Chandon Club was born, in 1983. To maintain the aura of exclusivity, we mailed invitations to the entire database explaining the concept and perks. Although membership was free, an affirmative response was required. We issued a personalized membership card to the thousands who accepted. It was clear that we could never let leak the size of the Chandon Club, or risk disillusioning the winery's growing multitude of close personal friends.

As requested, we took the Domaine Chandon experience on the road. At first we did reception-style events, offering no more than an interesting venue, substantial hors d'oeuvres, plenty of sparkling wine, and someone from the winery to act as host. We charged a minimal attendance fee to assist with planning; there was no intent to make a profit from the events. Fred and Camilla Chandon obligingly took turns hosting, as did Ghislain de Vogüé, and most of the winery's management team.

After a very happy, hungry mob of 750 Chandon Club members in Dallas began lying in wait to ambush waiters leaving the kitchen bearing full trays of hors d'oeuvres, we grew concerned about the format. Lots of bubbles and not enough food could have undesirable consequences. We started adding an educational component to each event to slow the sparkling wine consumption.

I stumbled onto the welcome news that the *New York Times* had an outreach program whereby they offered columnists and editors as guest speakers for no charge, or for a small donation to a favored charity. Thus columnist Anna Quindlen became the main attraction at an event held in

New York's Puck Building for 400 Chandon Club members. The *Times'* crossword puzzle editor gave a fascinating chalk talk to our Boston club members on how to build a puzzle. Each event had its own personality, and all were well attended. Members brought guests and friends.

The club grew to a membership of 100,000 within three years.

With the Chandon Club now our biggest marketing program, it seemed a good idea to test the return on the resources going into it. I decided to do a survey. As usual, this was something I hadn't done before so I didn't know what I shouldn't or couldn't do. I wrote a dense, four-page questionnaire, asking about demographics, hobbies, travel, reading habits, food preferences, wine consumption of all types by occasion, type, frequency – you name it, I asked it.

I ran the draft questionnaire by Domaine Chandon's New York-based advertising agency, which thought the idea was daft. They believed that no consumer alive would answer such a lengthy questionnaire without an incentive. I disagreed. "You don't understand. These people are the winery's best friends, and they love communicating with us."

But I added a preamble to the survey (see Appendix D), advising Chandon Club members that our ad agency didn't believe they would fill out the questionnaire without an incentive, and I had told our agency they didn't know our Chandon Club members. It was almost a double-dog dare. We received 6,000 hand-written questionnaires by return mail, each requiring a minimum investment of 30 minutes to complete.

Six percent of a large sample was a high response rate at a time when direct-mail solicitors were thrilled to get a one percent return, but it did create another problem. How would we collate and analyze all that data?

John Wright, ever at the front of developing trends, was entranced with a recently acquired Apple II. His was the first and so far the only personal computer at Domaine Chandon. By good fortune, he had studied statistics in college. As the only trained and equipped candidate, he had the pleasure of teaching someone who could type to enter the data from 6,000 questionnaires into his Apple II. He spent the following month analyzing the numbers. The results were eye-popping.

With total U.S. per capita wine consumption hovering at about 12 bottles per year, Chandon Club members were enjoying 24 bottles of Chandon sparkling wine every year. Plus another 24 bottles of still wine. We knew we had a statistically significant sample, and these were impressive numbers. Our pure relationship marketing—we were not selling wine directly to consumers except in the tasting room— was generating tremendous brand *pull* in a country where direct sales out-of-state were mostly still illegal.

Our sole attempt to sell anything by mail to Chandon Club members provided further proof of a tendency to impetuosity. We sent off a one-page flyer offering miscellaneous Chandon Club logo merchandise such as sweatshirts, aprons, bandanas, bottle stoppers, cork pliers, and flutes to the membership. None of us had expected or prepared for an overwhelming response, and it took weeks to fill the orders. We didn't do that again for a long time.

Whatever we were spending on the Chandon Club—primarily for events and mailing programs—was more than worth the expense in terms of loyal fans. Not only were they wonderful customers, Chandon Club members proved to be extraordinarily enthusiastic ambassadors for the winery. They shared their personal wine kingdom with friends, neighbors, colleagues, and relatives. Domaine Chandon benefited, as did they.

34 GATHERING CLOUDS

In the mid-1980s there were things going on at Domaine Chandon about which neither John Wright nor I were happy, much of it related to being obliged to surrender our autonomy when Moët-Hennessy acquired Schieffelin & Co. in 1981. While it seemed logical (the French have never gotten over Descartes) to have their New York importer and their Napa Valley winery work together in the U.S., this combination proved suboptimal for several reasons:

- It was expensive: taking Chandon sparkling wine to market through a national distributor added a fourth layer to an already costly three-tier system.

- The split responsibilities made accountability difficult. We agreed that Domaine Chandon would retain control over marketing, and Schieffelin would handle national sales. (As an importer Schieffelin would normally manage both for its offshore suppliers.) Though we all tried to make it work, this was difficult for entities each accustomed to relative autonomy.

- It created a barrier between Domaine Chandon and its champions in France. The top management of Moët-Hennessy, especially Fred Chandon and Alain Chevalier, had long shielded Domaine Chandon from others in France too eager to be involved in the Napa adventure. New York created an inadvertent barrier between the winery and its guardian angels in Paris.

- The two American companies had very different cultures. It was not just suits vs. boots, or right coast vs. left coast. The fundamental problem was that we shared neither goals nor values and had wildly different management styles.

John and I liked and worked well with Schieffelin's management and marketing teams, but many among the more mature members of its sales force disdained Chandon sparkling wines. In that, they weren't alone. On the east coast, the trade and consumers thought of French wines as the only real wine. Most still identified California with jug wines. Napa Valley had barely started rebuilding its historic reputation for fine wine after the damage done by phylloxera, Prohibition, the Depression, wars, and other disasters.

Schieffelin's seasoned liquor salesmen were already disgruntled at having to learn how to sell wine into an evolving marketplace. They understood Moët and especially Dom Pérignon as moneymakers, but this new ersatz "champagne" produced in California by Moët's red-haired stepchild was a step too far for them.

I spent much of the 1980s flying back and forth to Schieffelin's Manhattan headquarters for meetings that were cordial and well intentioned but seldom produced the desired results. Neither John nor I could see an end to this. It was especially frustrating because we had been successful working independently prior to Schieffelin's acquisition.

Of course, there was more to this than I knew at the time: a battle for control at the top was brewing in Paris.

35 TIME FOR CHANGE

Other French wine producers showed great interest in following Moët & Chandon to the Napa Valley, especially the champagne houses. They seemed torn between expecting, perhaps hoping, we'd fail -- and wanting to join us. The result was a constant stream of vinous visitors from France and I, being the only francophone at Domaine Chandon besides chef Jeanty (busy in the kitchen), was the designated greeter in the early days.

That is how, starting in the late 1970s, I met Claude Taittinger, Jean-Claude Boisset, Lucien Peyraud, Henri Maire, and a young Robert Skalli, among many others. Like so many before him, Robert fell in love with the Napa Valley. When he returned to the south of France he told his family that he was determined to "do something" here.

Robert came from several generations of French wine and grain growers who had been colonists in Algeria. In 1961 the Algerians rose up to take back their country, and the Skallis were fortunate to move their businesses safely across the Mediterranean to France. Over time, their wine and pasta enterprises grew large, supplying French consumers with quality products. Their later-divested pasta brands, Lustucru and Rivoire & Carret, are still household names in France.

When Francis Skalli died in a plane crash in 1964, Robert was too young to take over his father's rôle as leader of the family's wine business. He did this after graduating from university, but first began the world travels that help young people explore how wine is made and sold in other parts of the world before settling down in the family business.

That first taste brought Robert Skalli back regularly to the Napa Valley, although his desire to learn more was hampered by not speaking English well. I, along with French speakers Margrit Mondavi and Bernard Portet, became his informal information sources and sounding board on opportunities in the Napa Valley. Margrit spoke six languages and was responsible for public relations at Robert Mondavi Winery, and Bernard grew up at Chateau Lafite in Bordeaux where his father had been the *régisseur*. He was the founding winemaker of Clos du Val winery in Napa.

It didn't take long for the first of the visiting French vintners to invest in their own California wine ventures: Robert Skalli's family bought the unplanted Dollarhide Ranch in 1982 and a winery site in Rutherford from the Boisset family in 1986. Taittinger invested in Domaine Carneros in 1987, and Boisset acquired several operating wineries in Napa and Sonoma starting shortly thereafter and continuing today. Champagne houses Piper-Heidsieck and Mumm also built wineries in California, but they had dallied enough to give Domaine Chandon a significant head start in the sparkling wine market.

Domaine Chandon the startup was a wonderful place, full of fun, innovation, and opportunity. This environment marked me for life, putting me in the camp of those who welcome change and dislike the constraints of organization charts. Our children Kate and John were born toward the end of my 15 years in sparkling wine. The Domainiacs, as we alumni call ourselves, were my extended family. That's why it came as a shock when Robert Skalli offered me a job during one of his periodic visits to Napa Valley.

I liked Robert Skalli. I thought his vineyard project at Dollarhide Ranch was fascinating and, although much larger, it was only four miles away from our family's vineyard in the northeastern hills of the Napa Valley appellation.

Robert had asked me for help in identifying candidates to develop a marketing platform for his nascent operation, and I had made some inquiries on his behalf. I already had enough experience with headhunter calls to know that when someone asks whether you know anyone who might be suitable for a certain job, they're often indirectly asking if you would consider it for yourself.

With that notion tickling the back of my mind, I met with Robert in December 1986 in his trailer headquarters, located in a sea of mud at Dollarhide. I was on maternity leave and brought along our one-month-old son. As I laid out the handful of people who'd been recommended to me as candidates for his job, Robert's expression varied from nonplussed to amused. Then he popped the question.

Even though I was half expecting it, the invitation to join his new enterprise stunned me. I could find nothing to say. Robert wisely gave me a tight deadline—he was returning to France in two days—and I spent those days in a dither, reviewing my situation, what the future held for me at Domaine Chandon, and whether I wanted to make a parallel move to run marketing for the budding Skalli operation. The temptation of another startup was powerful.

Emotionally bound to my Domaine Chandon family, I found the solution by asking my boss a question. Would he replace me with another

VP of Marketing if I left, or would he hand off marketing to Schieffelin? John tipped the balance by stating without hesitation that the work I was doing was necessary and important and if I left he would definitely need to find a replacement. So I stayed.

But the seed had been planted, and the thought of someday leaving this place where I had grown up began to percolate. As a friend memorably said at my Domaine Chandon farewell party in the fall of 1988, "Everyone needs to be repotted once in a while."

ACT II BECOMING A CEO

After fifteen years of learning the wine business on the job and working with a most unusual leader at Domaine Chandon, as recounted in Act I, it was time for the next phase of my career.

Serendipity again played a part. I was offered and accepted the challenge of being the first CEO of another startup enterprise that would become known as St. Supéry Vineyards & Winery. This was my opportunity to apply what I had learned at Domaine Chandon, while adjusting to every new experience that a startup inevitably brings. I am grateful once again to have a boss, Robert Skalli, who gave me running room. Brand-building, innovation, and adaptability were the hallmarks of my twenty-one years leading St. Supéry.

These recollections of my progress as a CEO may prove useful to others who are or who aspire to be leaders. They stuck in my head because they taught me valuable lessons. The stories range from hilarious to inspiring, from somber to uplifting. I hope they will encourage more leaders to open the door to human potential by giving people with promise a chance to test the limits of possibility.

36 HOW I GOT THE JOB

Throughout the 1980s while I was Vice President/Marketing at Domaine Chandon, I maintained contact with Robert Skalli, whose revolutionary, rapidly developing, varietal wine program in Languedoc occupied most of his time. On his periodic visits to Napa Valley, he met individually with me, Clos du Val founder Bernard Portet, and Margrit Mondavi, francophones all, to test ideas for his dream project in Napa Valley and to keep abreast of local developments.

The most notable of these developments was the delimitation of the Napa Valley AVA (American Viticultural Area) in 1981, which was a factor in Robert's decision to purchase the Dollarhide Ranch in 1982. There were a number of French investments in the U.S. that year, not an entirely irrational response to the election of France's first socialist president, François Mitterand.

I believe our encouragement to build his winery where it would be more accessible to visitors than Dollarhide (on the east side of Howell Mountain and used strictly for grape growing) probably influenced Robert's second Napa Valley purchase in 1986, of a 35-acre Rutherford vineyard on Highway 29 from the Boisset family.

I also volunteered to help him vet management candidates when the time came to staff up his burgeoning California enterprise.

In mid-1988, a year and a half after I turned down Robert's unexpected invitation to take charge of marketing and sales for his new venture, the seed of change he'd planted in my mind was sprouting a stem and leaves. I was finally mentally prepared to move on from my alma mater, Domaine Chandon.

I found myself writing a letter to Robert acknowledging the fine team he had assembled, and letting him know that I admired his young enterprise and would be honored to help if the opportunity arose.

I didn't know this, but after six years Robert was tiring of the long trip from France every other month to manage the development in Napa Valley, while simultaneously building his Languedoc varietal wine project. There was important work remaining to be done in California, with the first plantings starting to bear fruit and the winery in Rutherford under construction. He had just engaged the San Francisco office of executive recruiting firm Heidrick & Struggles to find a leader for the nascent Napa Valley operation when he received my letter.

Robert persuaded the other family shareholders, whom I'd never met, that I would be a fine candidate. For their comfort he asked me to interview with Heidrick. It was clear he wanted me to have the job, and I was excited by the prospect of another startup, with me as the leader this time.

I thought it only fair to let Robert know how I would operate if I joined the company, so I wrote him a second letter outlining my management philosophy. In retrospect, that sounds incredibly pompous, but my intention was to prevent any misunderstandings. I expected that if my way of doing things was not to his liking, he could rescind the offer and find someone better suited.

He never replied, and to this day I don't know whether he even read my second letter. He probably did and was too kind to let me know how amusing he found it.

And that's how I came to Skalli Corporation as its first general manager at the end of 1988, after fifteen years of growing and learning at Domaine Chandon. To avoid confusion with the hospitality industry, and possibly influenced by my Berkeley/Haas experience, I recommended that the title be changed to CEO.

Six months into my new job, Robert showed me the Heidrick report on my two-hour interview with them at SFO (I had been, as usual, en route to a meeting with Schieffelin in New York). The recruiter wrote, in essence, that Ms. Rodeno seemed to be a good person and an experienced marketer, but there was nothing to indicate that she would make a good CEO.

37 NEW BOSS, NEW WORLD

Shortly after I accepted the position as first CEO of the Napa Valley enterprise that would become St. Supéry, my new boss Robert Skalli invited me to France to meet the other family shareholders and visit their French operating companies.

Robert, his cousin Claude, and I started our tour in Marseille, where their uncle Albert Skalli presided over Grands Moulins Maurel. This was a six-story semolina mill processing thousands of tons of durum wheat annually to supply the ten pasta factories also owned by the Skalli family. I had never seen anything like it.

Using technology decades old, on the bottom floor machines ground the wheat, which was then blown up to the top floor through pneumatic pipes. There the coarse flour began its descent through a series of increasingly fine sifting devices, passing to the floor below whatever wasn't fine enough to be sifted out at that level. Particles that were still too coarse after six levels of sifting were ground again, and blown back to the top floor to repeat the downward journey.

My favorite part of this simple, yet complex operation was a large room on the fourth floor. It was filled with a forest of sealed wooden boxes approximately 2'x2'x8' suspended vertically from the ceiling on flexible wooden wands. The boxes were vibrated constantly to shake the semolina down through their increasingly fine interior screens. Wandering through the narrow aisles in this quivering maze was a weird and wonderful experience.

From the semolina mill we proceeded to one of the nearby Skalli pasta factories. This was an industrial operation, where gigantic extruders and other mysterious machines of magnitude churned away to produce different types of hard pasta in volume. Semolina dust caked all the machinery. It was impressive, but not as intriguing as the semolina mill.

When Albert asked me which part of the tour I had preferred, I suspected there was one right answer and gave it careful thought before replying that the semolina mill had been fascinating. His big smile told me I'd passed the test.

That same day after lunch I was treated to a thorough presentation on all the pasta products by the vice president of marketing. The large conference room was filled with the owners and management team, and I was the guest of honor.

I learned that Rivoire & Carret was a long-established and very successful brand of hard pasta, and the Skallis took care to maintain its leadership position in the French market. They also owned Lustucru, another brand beloved of French school children for its high quality egg pasta and related products.

They even had a daring plan to replace the white flour used in classic French *baguettes* with semolina. Taking advantage of France's national pride in its literature, they cleverly named their iconoclastic baguette "Pagnol" after Marcel Pagnol, author of *The Baker's Wife (La Femme du Boulanger)*. They even opened special *boulangeries* to bring the new baguettes to market. It was a delicious product, more flavorful and moist than the traditional baguette. They made a good run at changing a national icon, but if there's anything the French love, it is tradition.

The Skallis teased me for years about my nodding off, overcome by jetlag, in the middle of the excellent presentation put on for my benefit.

Then we headed west to the Languedoc to see the Skallis' wine operations. The ultra-modern headquarters, visitor center, and bottling facilities of Fortant de France, all stylish steel, glass, and granite, along with several large warehouses, were situated alongside one of the canals in Sète.

An Impressionist painter must surely have captured this picturesque town bordering the Mediterranean, with its canals, bridges, and colorful fishing boats. We all had rooms overlooking another canal in the center of Sète in the nineteenth-century Grand Hotel, whose four-story, palm-filled atrium we regrettably had no time to enjoy.

After visiting the pristine, high-speed bottling line and tasting numerous blends and finished wines, we headed into the countryside to visit some of the growers supplying Fortant. Robert Skalli had provided cash incentives and long-term contracts to encourage them to rip out their old-fashioned generic vines in favor of grape varieties familiar to American consumers like Sauvignon Blanc, Chardonnay, Cabernet Sauvignon, and Merlot. He also rewarded them for producing high quality fruit, another innovation in this area.

He'd accomplished all this in the Languedoc while simultaneously developing hundreds of acres of vineyards at Dollarhide, planning and starting construction on a winery, and managing the distant Napa Valley enterprise for six years.

38 UNE VRAIE PARISIENNE

Robert Skalli's wife Florence had asked me what I would like to do while stopping over in Paris on that same first trip to France after joining the family's new Napa Valley enterprise.

Une vraie parisienne, Florence knew everything there was to see and do in her city, and enjoyed sharing with visitors. I instantly replied, "Please take me shopping." This turned out to be one of Florence's favorite sports, as French women are known for being always beautifully dressed, coiffed, manicured, and shod.

While I was in the south of France visiting pasta factories, vineyards, caves, and semolina mills, unknown to me Florence was laying out a battle plan for our shopping expedition. She had determined which boutiques offered clothing that would suit my taste, needs, and budget. The year-end *soldes* would be in progress when I returned to Paris, so she personally visited several of the targeted shops, tried on items she thought would work for me, and asked the shopkeeper to hold them until my arrival a week later. She must have been a good client because, remarkably, they did.

On the appointed day, Florence picked me up at my hotel in her Volkswagen Golf and we roared off to the first stop on her list. She double-parked in front of the shop, abandoning the Golf to its fate while we ran inside. With each item I tried on Florence would look at me critically, order me to buy it or shake her head, and we'd leave for the next stop. Sometimes she found a legal parking place, and I marveled at her ability to muscle this small car with no power steering into a space with scant inches to spare.

This went on for the entire day. I spent more money than I'd spent on clothes in my life, but all the purchases were classics that have paid for themselves many times over. I never would have done it without Florence, and I'm grateful to her for making me considerably more stylish than I would have been without her keen eye and *savoir faire*.

On the way back, laden with chic shopping bags, we stopped off to visit Robert's mother. We had to unpack everything so Madame Skalli senior could admire each piece, a necessary ritual to celebrate a successful campaign. She even provided me with an old suitcase, as I travel with only a carry-on and hadn't even thought about how I was going to get all my loot home.

I wore one of my purchases, a Georges Rech white linen suit, at St. Supéry's opening festivities in 1989. Another GR favorite was the tailored

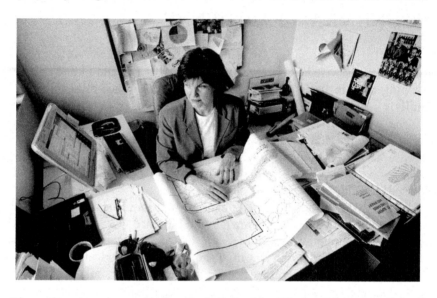

The author at work wearing her Paris "television" jacket. Note the original version of the Turrentine Wheel of Wine Fortune on the bulletin board behind her.

fuschia jacket that proved an excellent choice for photo shoots and television appearances. I still wear it when I want to look businesslike and exude energy.

Nearly ten years later, when I was chairing the 1998 Auction Napa Valley, Florence again took me shopping in Paris. She believed this assignment required that I be a "star," however temporarily. I returned to Napa Valley with a turquoise silk suit that provided plenty of visual oomph, but no shoes.

Florence had apparently taken a good look at my feet, because after I left Paris she found a pair of shoes she liked, and had her husband/my boss hand deliver them to me on his next trip to California. She never even asked my size, and they fit perfectly. Only *une vraie parisienne* could pull that off.

39 A FORMIDABLE TASK

I felt as if Robert Skalli had handed me the keys to an aircraft carrier with orders to turn it around, fast. Translation: monetize this multi-million dollar vineyard and winery investment we the shareholders have been funding since 1982, and do it as quickly as possible. There were challenges, surprises, and speed bumps ahead.

Developing vineyards and building production capacity is the foundation of a new, vertically integrated wine business, but these are only the first investments—with more to come.

There were also inventories to build from a growing production of red wines that would not be ready to go to market for three years. There was a brand to be built, requiring marketing investments, and a visitor program to increase awareness and drive demand. We would need a sales team to transform the ironically illiquid inventory back into dollars. All this was going to take time, like an aircraft carrier making a wide, slow arc as she turns.

The new winery was built to match the vineyards' ultimate output, instead of the usual, capital-conserving practice of starting small and expanding as needed to accommodate growth. Although this full-grown approach was a deliberate decision and offered some benefits, notably a visitor program purposely designed to allow guests to safely get close to the action in the cellar, it also meant that we had more production capacity than needed for the early years.

A post-construction decision to barrel ferment instead of tank ferment Chardonnay used some of the excess square footage, but there remained ample available fermentation, bottling, and case storage space for the near future.

The first crush had just taken place when I arrived in November 1988, and much of the tonnage processed was custom work for other wineries that were short on capacity and/or growth capital. Providing custom services was then a new concept for me and many others in the Napa Valley, but it was an established practice in the south of France. In those early days St. Supéry made Raymond Vineyards' entire production of

California Chardonnay from crush through bottling, along with the overflow from Cakebread Cellars until they were able to consolidate winemaking operations in a single location several years later.

There were additional custom bottling clients to keep our high-speed line and its crew fully employed. In those days, all but the largest wineries' bottling lines lay idle except for a month or two each year. Mobile bottlers and winemaking facilities entirely dedicated to custom services had yet to be invented, so custom services was a solution that worked for St. Supéry and for its clients. Our bottling line ran steadily for ten months of the year, stopping only during harvest so the bottling crew could help with crush. All this custom work provided welcome cash flow while we built up Cabernet inventories and worked on developing a base of customers to buy St. Supéry wines.

Another boon to cash flow is an early-release wine like Sauvignon Blanc, a varietal that showed excellent potential in St. Supéry's vineyards. Although we quickly discovered that even the best Sauvignon Blanc was a tough sell—many Americans didn't appreciate the grape's naturally assertive flavors and crisp acidity, preferring smooth, even sweet, noticeably oaky Chardonnay—we weren't discouraged.

The rule of thumb for the time needed to make a profit in the era when BATF regulations required bricks-and-mortar wineries to safeguard excise taxes, was ten years from the time you had something to sell. For St. Supéry, that meant we could expect to break even in 1999. The Skallis were not pleased. Having invested millions in their California venture since 1982, they wanted to start counting the ten years from then. They pushed us to do better than the norm.

We were careful with expenses, and focused on building a strong St. Supéry brand for the long term. In the meantime we found alternative uses for excess fruit or wine in alternative channels where St. Supéry's brand positioning would not be affected: grape sales, bulk wine sales, airline sales (a specialty market if there ever was one), kosher wines, and a new, lower-priced brand named Bonverre.

The result was that we made our first profit three years ahead of the rule of thumb, in 1996. That was a welcome turning point, but the big job was far from over.

40 EVERYONE REPORTS TO SOMEONE

Those who work for themselves have the toughest boss of all, which is probably why I never started a business on my own. Or maybe it was the lack of capital and a good idea. I spent forty years working with and for and learning from others, including in the context of boards of directors.

The board of Skalli Corporation, dba St. Supéry Vineyards & Winery, was very different from the board of Moët-Hennessy. Instead of nearly 300 years of producing luxurious champagne and cognac, the Skalli family owned high volume wine and cereal businesses started three generations earlier in Algeria and, once safely moved to France in the early 1960s, greatly expanded.

By its nature, an estate Napa Valley winery is not generally a low margin, high volume business. For the Skallis this type of wine was new territory, but they are astute businessmen and understood the patience required for long-term brand building.

As the CEO of the winery and the only non-family member of the board of directors, I was responsible for keeping the shareholders informed. One of many lessons I learned at Domaine Chandon was the importance of keeping your board and shareholders engaged. Bad things can happen if they lose interest in the business.

Since the Skallis were far from passive shareholders, keeping them engaged was not difficult. I thought of this part of my job as "shareholder relations." I made a point of communicating regularly with my boss, Robert Skalli, the wine expert in the family and one of two major shareholders.

Every month St. Supéry's management team submitted a detailed report to me on their departmental activities, including quantitative and qualitative information. I assembled these into a comprehensive report, carefully edited to ensure the shareholders would not misunderstand this English language document. Speaking French helped me spot any transliterations and *faux amis* likely to cause confusion.

I organized the quarterly board meeting agenda and materials. Anywhere from just one (Robert) to five shareholders would fly in from France for board meetings at the winery. They would typically arrive on Sunday afternoon and leave on Wednesday. Early in my St. Supéry tenure, I would be so anxious about being adequately prepared during the weeks leading up to one of our board meetings that my skin would break out like a teenager's.

It was important to me that St. Supéry's management team participate in these meetings. It was also important to Robert Skalli that he and I have time for private discussions. The solution was to meet him and any other shareholders in attendance for dinner prior to the meetings and often for a pre-meeting breakfast. For the duration of their visit, I was on call—but I was used to being on call 24/7.

The agenda always started with a vineyard tour, as none of us ever tired of the beauty of Dollarhide. These vineyard tours had their favored spots.

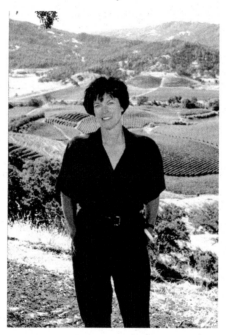

The author at risk of tumbling backward down a steep slope at scenic Dollarhide for photographer Andrée Abbecassis.

At the top of one steep hill is a weathered picnic bench, a sure indicator that others had also appreciated the spectacular view of the contoured vineyards below. The photo above was taken there.

While going up the hill wasn't difficult, turning around in the tight space at the top was terrifying. I usually let our vineyard manager turn my Jeep around before starting the descent. I stood on my brakes all the way down that hill, in low gear and four-wheel drive, certain we were all goners if they failed.

Five years of driving up and down that vertiginous hill went by before our vineyard manager finally took a turn driving my Jeep Cherokee full of shareholders. On safely arriving at the bottom, he handed over my keys and said "Never take this car up that hill again."

Later we started doing the Dollarhide tours on individual all terrain vehicles (ATVs) instead of in trucks. For the Skallis, those ATVs were just plain fun. The board's visits to Dollarhide turned into good-natured races through the vineyard avenues.

When the board meeting resumed in the winery's conference room, the Skallis typically ignored the agenda and jumped immediately to whatever interested them most. Financial results, always, and anything new or creative were sure to grab their attention. I would have given up on organizing agendas had they not been useful for guiding the management team's preparation for the meetings.

French people never skip lunch and, unlike Americans, they do not discuss business during a meal. This further compressed our useful meeting time. We were lucky to address the boring bits, like legal or compensation issues, in the final moments before the shareholders had to return to the airport in San Francisco. Before leaving, they always made time for a quick stop in the winery's retail shop for tchotchkes and logo wear before flying home to Paris. They would never accept gifts from the winery, abhorring the idea of commingling business and personal expenses.

At least half of our quarterly board meetings were held in Napa Valley. Some were held in Paris for the convenience of the shareholders who lived there; others were held in Marseille for the same reason. The turnout of cousins increased noticeably at the Paris meetings.

The board meetings in France were conducted entirely in French. In Napa I tried to keep the dialogue in English for the benefit of my management team, who participated in all but confidential personnel discussions. Thinking and speaking in English required some effort for the shareholders, and they would often lapse into French. When that happened, I would try to provide a running translation for my team, but as the conversation went on I, too, would slip into French without noticing.

During a working tasting early in my tenure as CEO, the directors got into an intense discussion in French about St. Supéry's new vintages. After thirty minutes of this, our suffering winemaker was anxious to know what they were saying about his wines. At the first opportunity I reassured him that the shareholders "liked the wines." He gave me one of those looks. It was the best I could do: the conversation had already resumed, in French.

The St. Supéry board was led and dominated by Robert Skalli. After all, this was his dream project. Like his father before him, he was the wine guy in the family. It was he who had convinced other family members to co-invest with him in Napa Valley. He once told his cousins that St. Supéry was his *danseuse*. (Similarly, another winery proprietor likened his own winery to "his yacht.") Jokes aside, everyone understood that these were not dalliances, but serious businesses.

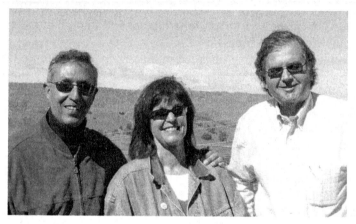

Claude Skalli, the author, and Robert Skalli at Dollarhide in 2008

Robert's cousins and uncle deferred to his wine industry knowledge and judgment, and in spite of occasional disagreements and even slightly bruised feelings, there was never any residual resentment or ill will. The Skallis are a tight knit family.

I made a point of personally documenting the board meetings in order to capture the decisions made, and the reasons why they were made. In this way, over my 21 years as CEO, I wrote a detailed business history of St. Supéry. My reports were written in English for the benefit of the management team, as they would be responsible for execution of decisions taken. Time allowing, I added a brief summary in French for Uncle Albert. He was the other major shareholder, with Robert, and the only one who spoke no English. I know he dutifully, laboriously pored over the English language meeting materials and reports.

Albert was the patriarch, the *éminence grise* of the interlocking family enterprises. He said little, but what he said was worth attending. I was honored to make a quick trip to Marseille solely for the purpose of attending the ceremony where the French government awarded him the *Légion d'Honneur* for his contributions to Marseille's economy.

By contrast, serving on the board of directors of Silicon Valley Bank from 2001-2011 provided a different board education. There I was exposed to the governance of publicly traded companies, tech entrepreneurs, how bankers make money, venture capital, equity compensation, risk management, and regulation of financial institutions. All of these were new to me, since St. Supéry was closely held and funded with equity from France.

Until I got a look at Sarbanes-Oxley, a 2002 law passed to rectify corporate accounting scandals, I had thought the wine industry was highly regulated. I will never complain again about winery regulation, silly as some of it is. Banks win that contest.

41 THE BOSS

When I was younger I was uncomfortable with the word "boss." I never wanted to work *for* someone, I wanted to work *with* others. Although I still feel the same way about work relationships, eventually I found it easier to adopt the common term rather than use circumlocutions to avoid it.

My thinly cloaked aversion to hierarchy predated joining Domaine Chandon as employee #2 in 1973. Founder John Wright didn't mind because he actively disliked hierarchies; long before business gurus acknowledged flat organizations as nimble and collaborative, he had built one. He didn't seem to notice that I avoided calling him "boss."

John Wright never made the mistake of telling me what to do, which I would have resisted; instead, he asked and I willingly complied. The idea of being "bossed around" was anathema to me, which John seemed instinctively to understand. Maybe he read stubbornness in my face. More likely, his Virginia-bred mother brought him up to be polite.

When it was my turn to be the boss, I found out what it was like to be on the receiving end of the B word. At first, I didn't realize other St. Supéry employees were addressing me, since I didn't identify with that title. It was like the rare occasions when I was called "Mrs. Rodeno." Was my dear mother-in-law in the room? Blessed with an unusually memorable first name, I prefer being called Michaela. Of course that informality did little to reduce the endemic boss-subordinate barrier.

The St. Supéry sales team was particularly good at calling me "boss" in an affectionately teasing manner, which made it easier for me to accept. As the reader can see from the language and stories in this book, I've gotten over bristling at working for or being called a boss.

42 THE GREAT DIVIDE

It came as a shock to realize that there was a wall between me, St. Supéry's newly arrived first-time CEO, and the other employees. It hadn't felt like that at Domaine Chandon. I didn't like this barrier, but I learned to accept that it comes with the territory.

My first clue was delivered at the employee holiday party in 1988. I'd been on the job almost six weeks and was still striving to match names with faces, and who did what. When Dave the bottling line supervisor walked in, all dressed up and sporting a pork pie hat, I greeted him with a smile and commented "Nice hat!" I thought I had successfully managed an admiring tone to conceal the wonderment I felt at seeing such hipster headgear in Napa Valley.

Two weeks later Dave was in my office, wanting to know what I had meant by that remark about his hat. Clearly, he'd been stewing about it since the party. I felt awful, as I certainly hadn't intended to torture him. Lesson learned: when the CEO speaks, people pay attention to every word, inflection, and expression. And they don't necessarily understand when you're kidding. This was going to be hard.

I found myself wondering whether my former boss John Wright realized how uncomfortable I was when he uncharacteristically invited me to lunch at Domaine Chandon one day. We were both constantly entertaining winery guests there, but in ten years of close collaboration somehow we'd never had a meal alone together in the winery's restaurant.

I couldn't help wondering what was on his mind, and got uncharacteristically nervous. Was he finally going to fire me? Well, no. He just wanted to relax and chat. I was anxious to the point of paranoia for no good reason other than he was my boss. It was a surprise to realize that the boss barrier did exist, at least in my mind, even in that freewheeling organization.

One thing that helps bridge the great divide is when the boss can laugh at him or herself.

As a believer in the bonding value of company parties, not to mention the fun, we found many occasions to celebrate at St. Supéry. For

Halloween, most of us came to work in costume. One cellar hand worked all day in a grass skirt and bra made from coconut halves, a tour guide showed up as a pregnant nun, and I dressed as a witch, in black from my pointy hat to my shoes, with a big spider carefully drawn on my nose with eyebrow pencil. It wasn't very imaginative, but everyone seemed to enjoy the allusion. I should have added a hooked nose, painted my face green, and donned red shoes.

Harvest always offered an opportunity to celebrate. After we'd all toasted the first load of grapes with a flute of sparkling wine, every week during harvest a different St. Supéry department would provide a potluck lunch for the crush crew. All the other employees were invited to join in after they'd eaten. I once stayed up until 2:00 a.m. cooking a gigantic pot of *carbonnade de boeuf* for a crush lunch, using Foster's lager instead of the traditional Belgian beer to honor our Aussie winemaker. It was a hit, but I never again cooked anything that time-consuming.

Winemaker Michael Beaulac, with the author and all employees welcoming the start of crush 1999 with magnums of Chandon

At another such potluck, the cellar supervisor seated next to me slyly offered a pepper from the supply he kept in his pocket. It was ominously small, no more than ¾"-long, and dark green. The entire crew stopped chewing to watch me expectantly. I knew I was in trouble, but had to accept. One cautious nibble on that lethal fruit and my lips started burning, my eyes turned bright red, and tears rolled down my cheeks. My mouth and throat were aflame. I couldn't even croak "Water!" My tormenter casually popped an entire pepper in his mouth, looking pleased with himself. Everyone else refrained from laughing; perhaps they admired my courage. I am thankful no one tested me like that again.

When the regional managers gathered at the winery for their annual national sales meeting, the winery-based employees invariably challenged them to a softball game. Everyone and anyone could play; the only prerequisite was to be employed by St. Supéry. Some had actually played softball in their youth—there was at least one ringer in the sales group—but most, like me, hadn't touched a bat or ball since middle school.

I was assigned to center field because it was unlikely the ball would get that far. It was, in fact, peaceful out there, quiet enough to allow sips of beer throughout the game. All players kept their beer cans near their feet whether in the field or in the dugout, even the catcher.

When it was my turn at bat, those underhand fast pitches slowed noticeably, and no one tried very hard to throw me out at first base. "Safe!" The next batter also got a hit, so I took off for second. Realizing that I was about to be tagged out, and flashing on the recent movie "A League of Their Own," I was inspired to charge the second baseman.

That brave soul, a retired naval architect who worked part-time in the visitor center, stood his ground. As I thundered toward him at full speed, my left brain started yelling at my right brain to stop before somebody got hurt. Too late: we crashed in a tangled heap. He didn't drop the ball, but I was called safe because, in the absence of a bag, no one knew precisely where second base was. My gentlemanly victim pulled a freshly laundered cotton handkerchief from his pocket and dusted me off.

Another occasion for levity occurred when I had an opportunity to drive an 18-wheeler. This one was loaded with ten, two-ton bins of Dollarhide Cabernet grapes waiting to be tipped, one by one, into the stainless steel hopper whose auger fed clusters into the stemmer-crusher. The driver's task was to inch the big truck four to five feet forward to position the next bin under a hoist for dumping.

Jim Eakles, the truck's owner, invited me to give it a try. I climbed into the cab, where he showed me how to operate its multiple unfamiliar gears, and the brakes. Whatever I did instead made his truck jerk and bounce like a demented low-rider until it arrived at the desired spot. The entire crush crew was laughing at me. I was laughing at me.

43 COMPANY CULTURE

"You're a real piece of work," a nervously smiling Pat Tracy said to me. I was his new boss, and we were chatting at one of our first employee gatherings at St. Supéry in late 1988. He and the handful of others I had inherited were uncertain why they were standing around holding a flute of Chandon Brut late on a Friday afternoon.

For me, this was a normal way to wind down a long work week and, better yet, to give people from different parts of the company an opportunity to catch up, to bond, and to ease into the transition to the weekend.

We'd been doing this for years at Domaine Chandon, where invariably someone would set aside the work in progress and pop a cork, attracting others as they finished their work. Enologists, riddlers, and cellar rats mingled with management, admins, and marketing staff; tour guides, kitchen staff, and servers dropped in as their duties permitted. This Friday get-together seldom lasted more than half an hour, but everyone appreciated the relaxed time together.

My new team at the as-yet unopened St. Supéry didn't get it. They stood in a shallow arc, silent and confused, waiting for something to happen. Maybe they were expecting me to make a speech. I think I did offer a toast, but my first attempt to bond with my new crew was not an instant success.

This was just one example of how unusual the Domaine Chandon way of doing things must have seemed to the rest of the world in general, and my new staff in particular.

Too green back then to realize just how enlightened a "manager" John was, I now realized how lucky I had been to fall into the opportunity to work in such an unconventional business environment. Moët-Hennessy made a leap of faith when they handed him the reins of their groundbreaking, multi-million dollar investment in the U.S., but they clearly liked his intelligence, creativity, and belief in the viability of fine California wine in the American market—which was not obvious in 1972.

In spite of academic exposure to a variety of management styles while working on my MBA at UC Berkeley's Haas School of Business, I proceeded to instill the Domaine Chandon "way" at St. Supéry because it had worked well for me and others. My former boss John Wright was a most unusual manager, perhaps because he wasn't one. He was a leader, and we all loved working for and with him.

He reveled in the affectionate nickname, Juan Correcto, bestowed on him by the kitchen crew. John brought an element of knowing—if dark—humor from his previous career as a management consultant for Arthur D. Little, captured in a chart showing the stages of a project (his version was in Portuguese, as he'd spent time in Brazil for ADL clients).

The Six Phases Of A Project:

1) Enthusiasm

2) Disillusionment

3) Panic

4) A Search For The Guilty

5) The Punishment Of The Innocent

6) Praise And Honor For The Non-Participants

In addition to the above, I started pinning choice cartoons about leadership, many from *The New Yorker*, on my office's bulletin board. One of my favorites was a Booth cartoon entitled "Take This Job and Love It," depicting a top-hatted, mustachio'd ringmaster cracking his whip over a manic menagerie of goofy looking dogs doing gymnastic tricks. Another was a fish branded "CEO" leading a school of similar fish. Perhaps anticipating what was to come, I loved the William Hamilton cartoon of a boardroom full of captains of industry bemoaning that "in a few years, we'll all be women." And, of course, the round white lapel button with a red border and a diagonal red slash through "No Whining" had pride of place.

When Robert Skalli noticed "Six Phases of a Project" on my bulletin board, he immediately asked where St. Supéry was in that progression. I facetiously replied "#3," meaning panic. His stricken look revealed that was not the answer he expected, as it was still quite early in my tenure as

CEO. He wanted to hear "#1. Enthusiasm." Telling jokes in a second language is a high-risk proposition.

I had often witnessed John Wright thumbing through his copy of Peter Drucker's classic tome *Management* when a new situation would arise, in much the same way a first-time teacher will read one chapter ahead of his students. Drucker understood that people, not processes or policies, are the root of the innovation and entrepreneurialism vital for success in business.

With hindsight it is clear that John Wright deserves credit for giving talented people the freedom to do their best with or without *à priori* credentials, and then getting out of their way. I loved that freedom. When it was my turn to lead, I gave others the same opportunity to contribute more, and more creatively, than I could ever conceive of asking of them. It would take me a while to understand that not everyone appreciates that much latitude.

I still find it hard to accept that some prefer the shelter of a well-defined box to the freedom to explore, black and white over shades of gray, certainty over ambiguity. Those people didn't last long in our new enterprise that, like Domaine Chandon, deliberately lacked an organization chart and job descriptions. Why impose limits on what people can contribute? Why hire people who need marching orders and four safe walls around them in a startup situation? Those who worked best in that environment invariably departed St. Supéry of their own accord, shaking their heads in disbelief.

People come and people go, but there were magical times when every individual on St. Supéry's management team was of such high caliber that I felt like a charioteer trying to steer five fast charging thoroughbreds in a high stakes race around the Coliseum. A roomful of brainy, hardworking, innovative, dedicated executives is surely every CEO's dream. I loved not having to hand out orders. There was no need: everybody understood the mission, and his or her part in making it happen.

Teamwork was essential at St. Supéry. Each executive was accountable for his or her area of responsibility (vineyards, winemaking/production, marketing, sales, finance), and each was expected to offer and accept help from the others in service of our common purpose. Territoriality, silos, and office politics were not in our vocabulary.

These extraordinary people were also confident, competent, and at ease working independently. Rather than ask me what to do, they understood that I wanted them to bring their ideas and plans to me for discussion, testing, affirmation, or even just information.

Their independence and reliability freed me to be a leader. Although I made it clear I was available if needed, I rarely got a call when I was on the road or on vacation. I trusted their judgment, and they rose to the occasion. I was confident this approach would work, with the right people, because it had worked at Domaine Chandon.

I once tried to create an organization chart for a meeting of St. Supéry's board of directors. There were so many dotted lines and shared boxes that it looked more like a plate of spaghetti than a graphic representation of an enterprise's structure. We never used it.

I also brought with me from Domaine Chandon an aversion to private offices, that is, offices with doors. Since the newly constructed winery had only five offices, each too large for one person and inadequate for two, we had outgrown the space before moving in. Believing that open work spaces encourage transparency and communication, I made sure that the remodeled offices had doors only on the bathrooms and the conference room.

This open door policy worked reasonably well, although people who wanted to speak with me rarely just barged in; they usually knocked on my office wall to announce their desire to speak with me. There were unintended consequences, too.

On the rare occasions I went into the conference room with someone and closed the door, everyone else was instantly alert that something must be afoot. Why so secretive? Why are we not invited to the meeting? Is that person being reprimanded or even fired? I never found anyone with a glass held against the wall, eavesdropping, but some probably would have liked to do so.

The accounting department eventually persuaded me to let them have office doors on the premise that the adjacent cellar noise was distracting them from their work; then HR requested privacy for personnel matters. Fair enough. But I did find a former CFO running a personal business behind his closed door on St. Supéry's time, an abuse of trust that lead to his departure.

Some things I learned at Domaine Chandon I chose not to bring to St. Supéry. John Wright abhorred formal meetings, preferring to drop by someone's desk for a chat about whatever was on his mind. This made our rare group meetings a major event.

Everyone from the lab through the management team would show up for the occasional sales meeting in John Wright's office (the commandeered former conference room), unwilling to be left out of anything that might be important. This helped me understand that employees had the right—and the need—to know how and what the company was doing. Or thinking about doing.

At St. Supéry I instituted quarterly company-wide meetings where everyone helped build the agenda, the management team reported on their department's progress toward goals, and the financials were presented for discussion. The questions were thoughtful and pertinent, and the answers were frank.

At these meetings we also recognized the Super Citizen of the Quarter, selected by the management team based on nominations from any employee. The Super Citizen's name and photo were added to the informal hall of fame in the lobby, and the winner was showered with work-related perks. Several star employees earned this honor more than once for their extraordinary contributions, well beyond their non-existent job descriptions.

Departments took turns providing breakfast for the company-wide meetings, which always started early to minimize disruption of the workday. When it was their turn, the production crew invariably served up hefty breakfast burritos from La Luna market in Rutherford. The visitors center team tended to healthier fare, like quiche and fruit. As in most workplaces, leftovers were gone by the end of the day.

The May meeting always took place at Dollarhide, a spectacularly beautiful vineyard that we all loved to visit. It helped us appreciate the origin of our wines, especially those whose work seldom brought them into the vineyards.

Everyone departed the meeting with a sample bottle of each wine, no matter how rare or expensive, released since the prior company-wide meeting. For those who had the day off, it was more than an incentive to attend the meeting; it helped prepare employees for the questions that every one of us, regardless of job description, regularly fielded about our workplace and products from friends, visitors, and colleagues.

Perhaps because our children were two and four years old when I joined St. Supéry, family-friendly policies were important. Instead of traditional sick leave, we offered paid personal time to be used for anything from caring for a sick child or filling in for an absent babysitter, to scheduling health care appointments, or staying home with the flu instead of sharing it at work. We were also early adopters of paternity leave, over and above maternity leave.

We had an annual kids' Christmas party with a piñata and gifts for all the employees' children. I once took a turn playing Santa Claus, and can attest that the rented red suit is hot and the fluffy white beard maddeningly itchy. I don't think I fooled any of the kids, but even the shyest among them played along and whispered their wishes to weird Santa.

When the Ms. Foundation launched "Take Your Daughter to Work Day" in 1992, St. Supéry jumped on board. Four young girls, including my 8-year daughter Kate, came to the winery to learn what their parents and others do all day. After watching me work on my computer, talk on the phone, and meet with employees for a couple of hours, Kate finally got exasperated and said "So when do I get to do your job?" Then she informed Piper Murray, who had just joined our public relations department, that "she'd fit in nicely here." Our in-house chef, Jamie Purviance, saved me and the other working parents by whisking the girls off to learn about wine production, marketing, and sales, and to help make themselves a wonderful lunch. No one was eager to do it again, even when the program was expanded to include boys almost ten years later.

In retrospect, we had a lot of company parties. You already know about Halloween at St. Supéry.

The grownups had a party of their own for the year-end holidays. It was the occasion for all of us to get dressed up. The cellar rats shucked their rubber boots and put on dancing shoes. Live music, a fine dinner (once on the Wine Train), and goodwill made this a treasured annual event. One time I had my hair done in an up-do for this party, resulting in several employees failing to recognize me. I enjoyed being the mysterious stranger.

A busload of Japanese visitors went into a photography frenzy when they spied the giant Easter bunny in the garden, handing out candy and helping our employees' children find eggs.

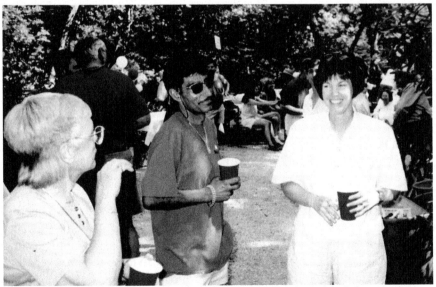

A typical St. Supéry crush party in a grove of oaks behind the winery near the Napa river. Pit-roasted cabral, cerveza, wine, colleagues.

Harvest parties are *de rigueur*, though after a few years they got a bit out of hand and we tried to limit them to production employees. That didn't work, as everyone felt connected to harvest and wanted to be there.

The summer picnic for families took place in different parks in Napa and Sonoma for years, under Christine Carey's creative guidance.

Pickup soccer games on the front lawn at St. Supéry
required neiher uniforms nor skill.

For a time we celebrated individual birthdays with cake and bubbly, but when the gifts got out of hand we switched to one collective party per month with birthday cards signed by everyone instead of gifts.

We also held creative events for our wine club. Marketer Lili Hsi Thomas created a lantern festival to celebrate Chinese New Year. She festooned the heritage oak in front of Atkinson House with red lanterns, while taiko drummers pounded fast and furious rhythms and wine flowed.

The most ambitious wine club event we ever did was a blending tasting for 300. The logistics of setting up on the lawn, dividing the members into teams, providing each team samples of Cabernet, Merlot, Cabernet Franc, Petit Verdot, and Malbec along with graduated cylinders, wine glasses, tasting sheets, and instructions, were formidable. Then we judges (winemaker, vineyard manager, CEO) had to taste the blends and pick winners while 75 proudly competitive teams crowded around, watching us closely as we sniffed and gargled and spit. This event was so successful we repeated it several times; returning club members started creating funny labels to enhance their blends, and one even humorously wrapped a twenty-dollar bill around its offering to bribe the judges.

Some of the informal good fun had to be curtailed. When one of the cellar workers broke his elbow during a lunchtime pickup basketball game on the crush pad, OSHA pronounced it a work-related injury and our insurance rates went up. No more basketball in the workplace. Soccer on the lawn was the next to go, when Robert decided we were ruining the landscaping.

The leadership naturally has a major influence on company culture. As a believer in education, especially higher education, I made a strong pitch for tuition reimbursement, but the shareholders would agree only to $250/year for courses whose content applied directly to an employee's job. (Education at all levels is government-subsidized in France, so the Skallis may have been puzzled by the cost of American education.) With university courses beyond our limit, this meant that only community college courses qualified.

Napa College was expanding its wine industry related offerings, but I was disappointed that only a handful of our employees took advantage of this opportunity to add value to themselves as well as the company.

Community relations were also important in a place where there was a distinct "town and gown" problem, with the small percentage of the population who are vintners often perceived as wealthy and arrogant by other county residents.

In the late 1980s there was a ruckus in Napa Valley about the growing number of wineries, and wineries expanding into activities—weddings, concerts, food service—not welcome in zones where protecting agriculture is the first priority.

The growing local antipathy to too many wineries perceived as doing whatever they wanted resulted in a new county regulation, the 1990 Winery Definition Ordinance (WDO). It was meant to clarify exactly what wineries are and are not allowed to do, especially in terms of marketing activities. The signs declaring "By Appointment Only" required of wineries built since 1990 still confuse visitors who infer that those wineries must be elitist and unwelcoming. Pre-WDO wineries retained the privilege of being open to the public.

In this faintly hostile atmosphere, I was determined that St. Supéry would earn a reputation as a good citizen of the Napa Valley. The winery's spacious galleries were loaned to local nonprofits for their fundraisers and provided space for local artists to exhibit their work; our managers chaired committees and otherwise served proactively in the Napa Valley Vintners

(NVV) association; our employees volunteered in community activities; and, like most vintners, we supported numerous charities with donated wine.

Within the decade, new leadership at NVV would take these bridge-building efforts to a higher level, improving the relations between the community and the vintners. Nonetheless, today there is another – the third in my wine career -- resurgence of anti-winery feeling that Napa County's leadership and the vintners are working together to address. The economic engine that keeps Napa Valley green is not well understood by all.

44 A TRAGIC ACCIDENT

My mother liked to say "there is no rest for the wicked," but I think the same may be true for CEOs.

St. Supéry's foreman at the Dollarhide ranch, Rutilio H., lived there in a small house with his wife and two young daughters. He stored all the vital information about Dollarhide in his head: the location of the pumps and valves in the extensive water system connecting seven lakes; how the block-by-block irrigation system was organized and controlled; which parcels produced the best grapes, which required special attention; and how to manage a group of vineyard workers varying in size from a dozen in winter to 150 during harvest.

During a major recruiting drive in Napa Valley in 1985, the United Farm Workers union had beguiled a handful of these workers to lead the others into voting to join the union. They started giving Rutilio a hard time, viewing him as management and therefore not to be trusted, but he refused to rise to the bait and stayed focused on getting the work done.

In 1991 his wife gave birth to their third child, a son, an event that made the family exceedingly happy. One month later on a Friday night, the proud father was celebrating with the vineyard's crew chief, talking, drinking beer, and taking turns shooting a pistol at empty soda cans in his backyard. In rural areas of Napa County, this was typical Friday night entertainment.

Inside the house, the phone rang. It was Rutilio's brother calling from Mexico to congratulate him on the birth of his son. Rutilio was crouched, pistol raised and ready to be leveled into firing position, when his daughter tapped on the window to call him to the phone. He looked over his shoulder at the sound, lost his balance, and fell backward. The pistol fired, hitting him in the head.

The crew chief cradled Rutilio, still alive, in his arms as they waited for the ambulance. The sheriff arrived first, concerned that a crime had been committed. As his employer, I got the call shortly after Rutilio arrived at St. Helena Hospital and raced to Angwin to join his family and co-workers, assembled silently in the waiting room. No one knew his status.

Two hours later, the emergency room doctors decided to transfer Rutilio by helicopter to the Queen of the Valley hospital in Napa. That was the only glimpse we caught of him: he was wheeled past on a gurney, unconscious, with what looked like a shower cap on his head. At that moment it became clear there would be no good news.

The family, vineyard manager, and I all raced the 26 miles from Angwin to the Queen. After another interminable wait, the hospital chaplain arrived to console the family on the death of their father/uncle/cousin. There was nothing to do but go home, exhausted in every way.

Later I learned that Rutilio's crew chief, still covered in blood, had been detained at the ranch until 5:00 a.m. the next morning, when the sheriff finally concluded that the gunshot wound had been accidental. He remains traumatized by the events around the sad loss of his friend all these years later.

The next piece of bad news came from St. Supéry's insurance company. Although premiums were up to date on the company-paid term life policies for all employees, the carrier was refusing to pay the claim on the basis that Rutilio's death was a suicide. Finally, there was something I could do to help.

Using my CEO title for all it was worth, I sent a strongly-worded letter to our insurance carrier detailing all the reasons why this happy new father was not a suicide candidate. His death clearly had been a tragic accident. I was ready to continue, but they gave in. The policy paid, I'm grimly pleased to report, double for accidental death—although no amount of money can ever replace a *père de famille.*

The entire Hispanic community turned out for Rutilio's funeral at the Catholic Church in St. Helena. It seemed to me that everyone held their breath when our vineyard manager, respected but not well liked, walked alone to the front of the church to pay his respects at the open casket. I thought he did the right thing. I remained at the back of the church, a saddened outsider.

Years later and with considerable effort, we mapped the complex water storage and irrigation systems at Dollarhide. The cause of a perennially soggy area below the Big Lake dam, bad news for vine health, was discovered to be a long-forgotten drainage pipe overgrown by tree roots. Once cleaned out, the spot dried and the Merlot planted there started to thrive. Rutilio would have known how to prevent that problem.

45 ASSIGNING BLAME

Few of us have experience with major construction projects, which is a shame because they are often rich with useful learning experiences.

When I arrived at St. Supéry shortly after the harvest of 1988 as its first CEO, the winery building had just been completed except for the public areas and landscaping. Planned renovations to Atkinson House, the Queen Anne Victorian on the property, had yet to be undertaken.

My first office was in one of its freezing former bedrooms because Napa County would not allow us to occupy the non-production parts of the winery building until the landscaping was completed. This policy was intended to prevent owners from promising to install landscaping and failing to deliver once their new facilities were operational and occupied.

Prompted by the prospect of several bleak winter months in unheated Atkinson House, with stiff fingers I typed a letter to county officials begging them to let us move into the brand new but empty winery offices. Fortunately, they accepted my assurance that it was in our interest to complete the landscaping as planned because the winery was due to open to the public in mid-1989.

Unfortunately, our small staff had outgrown the winery offices before we could move in, so we had to camp out in the unfinished tasting room for a month during office reconfiguration. I don't know of any new winery that plans adequately for office space; square footage devoted to overheads must seem an unnecessary luxury compared to revenue-producing production facilities.

While all of us were packed into the unfinished tasting room space—the ultimate open office—I invited Domaine Chandon's Mac consultant Bryan Bell to help us address the new winery's growing computer needs. Naturally, I wanted all Macs.

Our first stop was a visit to Apple headquarters in Cupertino to explore its shop for computers, peripherals, software, and some irresistible logo wear, all purchased on Bryan's developer license.

After scouting the layout of the winery, Bryan crawled around the as-yet unoccupied admin and production office spaces, punching holes in just-painted walls to install Ethernet cable so we could network the computers. Ours may well have been the first Mac-based intranet in a winery, cobbled together and kept updated and operational for years by Bryan from his home in Seattle.

His next task was to set up St. Supéry's first email system and devise ways to improve the quality of communications between Macs (us) and PCs (the rest of the world), systems that were then largely incompatible. Soon St. Supéry's new retail shop was sporting an Apple point-of-sale system. Even the accounting department worked on Macs at a time when PCs dominated the business market.

As St. Supéry expanded, stretching our jury-rigged Mac system to the limit, successive CFOs insisted on replacing aging Macs with the PCs they were used to. Less expensive than Apple products, over time PCs spread inexorably from the accounting department throughout the winery.

Within 12 years, the only Macs left were my own and those in the marketing department. My justification was that rank has its privileges. The marketing department had a better reason: they needed the powerful graphics capabilities of Macs.

When iPhones were introduced in 2008, even the PC users wanted one.

Back in the unfinished tasting room bull pen, the scramble was on to prepare for the main event—opening to the public in late July 1989. We were on track to complete construction in time until, one month prior to ribbon cutting, the State Fire Marshall announced that no one had ever requested a final inspection and—horrors!—the public side of the building had failed. The half-inch sheetrock in the ground floor ceiling was too thin to provide a sufficient fire block to protect the upper floor; further, the lobby atrium would be an invitation for a fire to rise quickly to the upper floor.

The architect blamed the contractor for not requesting a Fire Marshall inspection early in the process. The county, which had approved the plans, said it was not their responsibility to assure that state fire codes were met. The contractor, unsure who was to blame, was sweating bullets. And I, on behalf of the owner, was trying to find a way to solve this problem in time for opening day.

Even the Skalli family friend who had been the owner's on-site construction project liaison before returning to France, had no idea how the required three-quarter-inch sheetrock had shrunk to half-inch sheetrock during construction.

The only solution was to rip out the entire ceiling in the public areas of the winery and replace the sheetrock, then redesign the accesses to the upper floor to prevent fires from escaping upward. Our temporary office was festooned with wires dangling from the ceiling, but we were soon to be relocated—serious demolition was about to start.

To satisfy the Fire Marshall, we had to seal off the atrium and install panic doors at the top and bottom of each stairwell, not exactly an aesthetically pleasing welcome to visitors. All this cost more than $100,000 and plenty of frayed nerves, but the work was finished, barely, in time for opening day.

Who would pay was the next issue. The same routine ensued: the architect blamed the contractor, the contractor blamed the architect, and the owner ultimately was stuck with the bill. Adding insult to injury, the architect sent the winery a supplemental invoice for revising his own plans *ex post facto* to meet fire codes. The contractor's revenge was to edit a photo of the construction sign, abbreviating the name of the architect's firm from XXY and Associates to XYZ and A...you can guess the rest.

46 EVERY STARTUP IS DIFFERENT

My first startup, Domaine Chandon, was born with an identity and a mission. We would make Napa Valley sparkling wine in the traditional *méthode champenoise*. The enterprise would be blessed by the imprimatur and support of the largest of the *grandes marques* champagne houses, Moët & Chandon. It would have the advantage of being the first major investment in the U.S. by a respected, established French wine producer at a time—the early 1970s—when California wines were just starting to gain recognition for quality.

St. Supéry was a different matter. Fifteen years later, the U.S. wine market for still wines had become crowded. Apart from the financial support and business acumen of its French owners, the Skalli family, the mission lacked competitive advantages. Unlike Domaine Chandon, whose parent and its products were well known in the U.S., the Skalli name was not linked to its revolutionary varietal wine project in the south of France, Fortant de France. Further, Fortant was targeted at a lower tier of the U.S. market than the Napa Valley wines would be. To avoid confusing consumers and trade, the new winery's identity would have to be created from scratch.

When I joined the entity known as Skalli Corporation late in 1988, the first harvest in the new building was winding down. The 1986 and 1987 vintages from very young Dollarhide vines had been custom crushed elsewhere and were awaiting bottling. Robert Skalli had contracted with marketing guru Terrence Clancy to write a brand plan. His goal had been to go to market in 1989 with the 1986 Cabernet, 1987 Chardonnay, and 1987 Sauvignon Blanc.

I read the business plan, which was predicated on the notion that low prices were the only way to sell 500 producing acres worth of fruit as bottled wine under an unknown brand. That may have been correct, but it was a short-term answer to a long-term problem. Even if successful in moving a lot of product initially, this plan would make it difficult or impossible later to raise prices, thus limiting the return on the Skalli family's considerable investment in vineyards and winery.

The Australians are still trying to overcome their strategy of entering new markets like the U.K. and U.S. at low prices to gain market share quickly, only to find their wines stuck for years at suboptimal prices. I suggested to my new boss that this plan should be rethought.

The brand was to be Skalli-Atkinson, perhaps inspired by other successful hyphenated winery names of the time like Kendall-Jackson and Ferrari-Carano. The designer had to compress this long name into illegibility to fit the limited space available on a front label. I advised Mr. Skalli that a name change should be considered.

When we tasted the young wines, still in tanks and barrels, it was clear to me that, given the durability of first impressions, it would be wise to wait for better quality wines to launch the new brand. I recommended that we keep the 1986 Cabernet for sale only at the winery under a simplified brand label, bottle the 1987 Cabernet, and wait for the more-promising 1988 whites before launching the new brand yet to be created.

Not everyone survives telling a proud owner that his name on the label will not be an asset. Or that six years of intensive vineyard development work had not yet produced a market-worthy white wine.

Perhaps surprised by my American directness, instead of firing me on the spot Robert Skalli agreed to give me a year to get it right. That year was the only time in my long tenure at St. Supéry that I didn't have to get on an airplane, and I loved the opportunity to hunker down and lay a foundation for the future.

I used to marvel at how John Wright, my boss at Domaine Chandon, continually found good questions to raise. Now I was the one asking questions. In a startup situation, there is everything to do: build a team, create products and business plans, develop systems, point everyone in the same direction, and get to work! I who had unspoken reservations about my ability to lead a company realized that I had answers as well as questions. What I'd learned at Domaine Chandon during its startup phase proved useful in this new venture.

47 NAMING THE BABY

The first order of business was to find a name for the new company that would be authentic, memorable, and maybe even easy to pronounce (although I was not convinced about the importance of that, given the enormous popularity of tongue-twisting Pouilly Fuissé some years earlier).

I gathered a dozen right-brained friends and colleagues for a creative session upstairs in Atkinson House. Over two long days we papered the walls with references to local history, flora, fauna, landmarks, pioneers, literature, astronomy (stargazing is spectacular in Napa Valley), and so on, until we ran out of airspeed, altitude, and ideas.

Empty-handed, I was on the point of starting over when one brainstormer said she kept thinking back to a 1903 Napa Register article we'd found. It mentioned a 38-year-old French winemaker named Edward St. Supéry who had married into the Chaix family of Oakville, and briefly owned the nearby Rutherford property. As soon as she said "St. Supéry" I realized that the name had been tugging at the back of my own mind, demanding attention. It was obviously memorable, at least to us two, and its ties to the winery property made it authentic. It even sounded French, in honor of the owners. We had our name!

I sent a fax to Robert Skalli enumerating the reasons why this would be an excellent name for his family's winery, noting its authentic linkage to the site's history and, as reason #9 or #10, that it "sounded French." This was a positive thing because many Americans still equated French wine with fine wine, and of course the owners were French. The name didn't sound at all French to them! They even checked the Paris telephone directory and reported finding only two St. Supérys listed.

When we started selling wine, people would often ask whether St. Supéry had been named for the famous French author, Antoine de St. Exupéry, whose children's book *The Little Prince* is well known to American families. Some also mentioned possible links to a third growth Margaux, Château Malescot-St. Exupéry. These are both credible assumptions, and we were pleased at the positive associations, but that's not how we named St. Supéry.

I purposely kept the accent on the "e" in Supéry as a subtle nod to the winery's French ownership, but that mostly backfired. The name is often mispronounced Saint Supree by people valiantly trying to remember their high school French, in spite of ongoing efforts to assure everyone that the anglicized pronunciation (Saint Soup'-er-ie) is preferred. It's also often misspelled St. Suprey.

Now that we had a name, it was time to start building the brand. I would spend most of the next six months focused on getting the winery ready to open and preparing to launch the first vintages.

48 CREATING AN IDENTITY

One of the best parts about starting a new business is the opportunity to be creative. Inventing a brand identity is step one.

Once we'd settled on a name for Skalli Corporation's new winery in Rutherford, it was time to start translating that into a brand. I launched a search for a designer who understood the mission.

There were many excellent designers serving the wine business in 1989. After interviewing eight of them, all reputable and experienced, I began to fear I wouldn't find one capable of producing what I wanted: not just a label, though that was certainly important, but an identity.

Belatedly I thought of calling my architect friend from Domaine Chandon's winery construction project, Jerry Gabriel of ROMA, to see if he had any suggestions. He did. I didn't learn this until much later, but Melanie Doherty—newly returned to San Francisco after four years in Rome—nearly declined to meet with me after several disappointing presentations to vintners. It's a good thing she gave it one more try, because she was the one. Melanie understood that we needed an entire system, not just a label, to build the St. Supéry identity.

Other than the facts about the business, its ownership, and goals, the only guidance I provided Melanie was that I thought St. Supéry's brand image should reflect both modernity and tradition, and be visually memorable. I wanted people to be able to recognize our bottles from across a dimly lit restaurant. I had no idea what that would look like.

Melanie returned with nine directional concepts for us to consider. One was a spectacular label with a die-cut spiked crown we all loved, but which would have been impossible to apply by machine. We did enjoy watching our bottling line foreman's face blanch when we presented it to him as our new label design.

After that, we winnowed the concepts down to two, and would have selected one if Melanie hadn't suggested we let both finalists ferment in our brains for a while.

Within a week, we had tired of our first choice and grown an appreciation for the design she had undoubtedly wanted us to choose all along. The design called for varietally coded color blocks and logo type bars, combined with classic Garamond and Copperplate fonts. This created an elegant look that was also easily identifiable at distance.

A small gold-embossed medallion featuring a robed monk wearing a halo and dancing with two women was an intentional wink that embellished the label and the top of the capsule. The dancers were surrounded by the motto *Salta Pota Bonus Es,* which is how a UC Berkeley Latin professor had translated "drink, dance, and be good" for us.

We would have preferred to substitute "merry" for "good," but decided to avoid unnecessary label approval pushback from the Bureau of Alcohol, Tobacco & Firearms (BATF), whose aversion to anything sounding or looking like fun is legendary. Business cards, stationery and collateral materials all integrated the same look. St. Supéry had a brand image that would serve for twenty years.

Melanie was mercifully subtle at guiding us toward good design decisions. I managed to prevail on her to increase the font size on St. Supéry's label as my eyesight (and presumably that of my Boomer cohorts) weakened with age.

She proposed a wonderful concept for our new Meritage wines in the mid-90s, signaling their individuality and specialness with a commissioned illustration for each new blend. Selecting the artists with Melanie every year for Élu and Virtù was one of my great pleasures; nearly all of the illustrators, many of whom had *New Yorker* covers in their portfolios, produced imaginative variations on the "saint" theme.

After ten years, we updated the bi-color packaging of the main St. Supéry labels by reducing the label height and placing the new, smaller labels higher on the bottles; these slight changes refreshed the packaging while maintaining the integrity of the brand identity.

Eventually the time came to enliven the subtle color palette of St. Supéry's main labels, a simple matter of eliminating the gray tones in the original color blocks. We were all in favor of this move, but to my great surprise Robert Skalli—a strong marketer and usually receptive to change, especially if modernization was involved—reacted negatively.

He worried that any change to our labels, no matter how slight, could

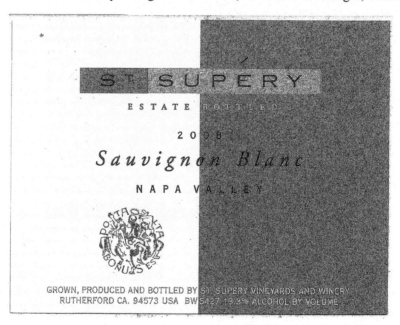

undermine the success the wines were enjoying. Making a mental note not to invite the French contingent into future packaging discussions, I proceeded with the necessary update. A year later, it was his turn to be

surprised when I happened to mention how well the market had received the slightly brighter colors. Robert hadn't noticed the change, and was not pleased that I hadn't respected his opinion.

After the departure of a vice president of marketing in 2002, I decided to resume responsibility for marketing, mostly the packaging and advertising. Neither required much more time than export, airlines, and cruise lines, for which I was also responsible. I did mention we ran a lean ship, did I not?

I reasoned that it would save me time and the company money, as my experience with newly arrived marketing managers had been that the first thing they wanted to do was change the packaging. I then would have to defend our carefully nurtured brand identity from discontinuous changes. It seemed easier, faster, and cheaper to manage this myself. Besides, I enjoyed working with Melanie.

Needless to say, shortly after I retired my successor changed St. Supéry's packaging.

49 A FOCUSED PRODUCT LINE

With a name—St. Supéry—and a visual identity established, the job of building a coherent brand remained. I was mindful that we would be lucky to get a nanosecond of attention from overwhelmed trade and consumers. Only a tightly focused message would stick.

Given our vineyard resources, it was clear from the beginning that St. Supéry would produce high quality Sauvignon Blanc and Cabernet Sauvignon. With the Sémillon, Merlot, and Cabernet Franc that had also been planted in lesser amounts by the Skallis in the early 1980s for blending, we had a Bordeaux-style lineup.

Chardonnay, the most popular white wine in the marketplace, had also been planted at Dollarhide. We had our first outlier in the Bordeaux-style product lineup. We also needed a guaranteed crowd pleaser for the tasting room; emulating Robert Mondavi Winery's success, we added a low alcohol, aromatic Moscato to complete the offer. In ascending order of importance and volume, St. Supéry would offer Moscato, Chardonnay, Cabernet Sauvignon, and Sauvignon Blanc.

Then in 1990, the Merlot craze exploded. We had 50 acres at Dollarhide intended for blending purposes that we decided, opportunistically, to bottle as a varietal Merlot, adding one more Bordeaux-style varietal to our product line. The portfolio had grown to five wines.

A never-ending challenge for brand builders is maintaining focus. It wasn't long before the winemaker and vineyard manager started hinting that a little Syrah would be an interesting addition. I resisted on the grounds that Syrah didn't fit into our (mostly) Bordeaux-style brand profile. They kept hinting. I did not encourage them. This went on for several years until I relented, mostly to keep them happy, and agreed to plant three acres of Syrah on the far edge of Dollarhide. Partly because of rabbit and deer damage, that little vineyard block failed to thrive. It produced barely enough wine for the wine club, not sufficient to create any confusion about St. Supéry's identity.

Given the success of my own family's Sangiovese planting, only about four miles distant from Dollarhide in a similar microclimate, I briefly considered Sangiovese as an addition to the St. Supéry portfolio. I slapped my own wrist.

And then there was the Chardonnay. My palate had been attuned to high acid, unoaked wine during fifteen years in the sparkling wine world. I was not a fan of the buttery, creamy, oaky, soft, sometimes frankly sweet style that had made Chardonnay the biggest volume wine in the U.S.

Chardonnay was never a stellar contributor to St. Supéry's bottom line. The expense of barrel fermentation and aging, and the need to compete aggressively against the huge volumes of similarly styled Chardonnay on the market made it barely as profitable as St. Supéry's distinctive and successful Sauvignon Blanc. Selling Chardonnay also required disproportionate time and effort from the sales team. I wanted to allocate our resources elsewhere.

In 2003 I convinced our noticeably reluctant winemaker that an unoaked Chardonnay would be worth trying. It would show the variety's delicious fruit character, long obscured by oak and malolactic fermentation, and it would be different from that generally offered, overblown style. Perhaps it would even be easier to sell because of that differentiation.

I was pleased with the dry fruitiness of the wine, labeled "Oak Free" because our winemaker thought "unoaked" sounded as if a barrel-fermented wine had somehow had its oak removed.

This radical change of direction for Chardonnay worked—in a small way. St. Supéry's tasting room, a wonderful market research laboratory, revealed an even split between those who loved the new style and those who didn't even recognize it as Chardonnay. Soon a few brave wineries followed suit with their own "naked" or "unoaked" or "no oak" Chardonnay, but in the marketplace, oaky Chardonnay remains dominant.

I wasn't ready to give up. As St. Supéry's success with Sauvignon Blanc grew, we were facing limitations on its growth. There was little of Dollarhide's arable land remaining unplanted, and we didn't want to buy grapes from other vineyards that might not offer the same characteristics as our estate fruit. So I made the case for replacing our Chardonnay acreage with Sauvignon Blanc, and the Skallis agreed.

We had finished top grafting all but twenty acres to Sauvignon Blanc when the Skallis returned for a regular board meeting with second thoughts about the decision to get out of the Chardonnay business. If the meeting had been a week later, we would have finished top grafting and back pedaling on the Chardonnay decision could not have happened.

Eventually I got the shareholders' support for top grafting most of the remaining Chardonnay to Moscato. As expected, it had proved a tasting room star from the time the winery opened to the public. It was also a favorite of the Skallis, perhaps because the variety's irresistible aromatics evoked happy childhood memories. With very little Moscato planted in the north coast, it made sense to grow it in our estate vineyards rather than continue to search for good grapes to buy.

That left just enough estate grown Chardonnay for the wine club, whose members could choose oaked or unoaked versions.

50 ROOKIE CEO THINKING

After dubbing the new winery St. Supéry and redeveloping its go-to-market strategy, I was ready to attack the financial translation of our plan. Motto Kryla & Fisher (MKF), our accounting firm, reformulated for my Mac a complex, 10-year interactive forecasting model that started with vineyard development and ended with after-tax profits.

I set out to test the validity of our strategy. The assumptions fed into the model are a cautionary tale. While some of the givens could not easily be changed—notably the nearly 500 acres of vineyard already planted—there were many estimates and assumptions that would affect the model's output.

We had to guess at the optimal yield levels where economics intersect with quality. Four tons per acre for Cabernet? More for Sauvignon Blanc? Lower yields on the hillside parcels and more on richer alluvial soils? How long would it take to reach full production? How much should we expect to spend on farming and wine production? We didn't consider the possibility of the ultimate black swan, phylloxera, or any other bumps in the road.

The assumptions we fed into the model seemed reasonable, at the time. How could we know what we could not know? I take some comfort in my belief that predicting the future is either a rare gift or dumb luck. Here are some of our remarkably naïve assumptions:

All vintages are good in the Golden State. Our extensive vineyards in Pope Valley and Rutherford would produce reliably every year, with quality and tonnage increasing over a reasonable period of time to a theoretically optimum level.

The grapes would be of high quality, suitable for, and indeed all bottled as St. Supéry Napa Valley wine. We would need to buy neither grower fruit nor bulk wine to achieve our production goals. Nor would we produce excess grapes or wine.

We would sell every bottle produced through our supportive trade partners and directly to our many thousands of visitors, at reasonable prices (by Napa Valley standards).

I kept this tattered, poster-size version of a graph
depicting the model's rosy forecast on the wall facing my desk
for 21 years, a reminder that nature abhors straight lines.

Innovative marketing would be effective in building our brand. We would develop a huge cadre of loyal consumers, allowing us to reduce sales and marketing expenses in the long term.

We would raise our reasonable prices at regular intervals to compensate for reasonably rising costs.

Left out of consideration were recessions, vine pests, droughts, competitors, earthquakes, price pressures, inventory shortages or overloads, Mother Nature's vagaries, or any other negative inputs that might derail this idyllic plan.

Nonetheless, we made our first profit in 1996, only one year later than the 1989 model predicted and three years ahead of the 10-year benchmark, by doing things that weren't in the 10-year plan.

I have since observed that doing unplanned things is how most annual budgets are achieved, and not just in the wine business. This is not to say one shouldn't plan, but rather to stay alert and be flexible.

51 BUILD IT AND THEY WILL COME

Although the launch of St. Supéry in mid-1989 didn't get the media attention that Domaine Chandon had enjoyed as the first major French wine investment in the U.S., the new Rutherford winery had a prime location on Highway 29 between Mondavi and Beaulieu. Naturally, we expected a Calgary Stampede of visitors from the moment the doors opened.

I should have known better. After four years of working behind the scenes, when we opened Domaine Chandon in 1977 anticipating thousands of eager visitors, only the media took notice. Visitors were disappointingly slow to discover the winery, perhaps because of our "green" initiative to keep the building's profile inconspicuous by nestling it into the rocky, oak-studded hills west of Yountville. They quickly sniffed out the restaurant, however.

The same thing happened or, rather, didn't happen, when we opened St. Supéry in mid-1989. It hadn't happened at Mondavi, either, when that iconic winery opened in 1966 as the first major new winery in Napa Valley since Prohibition. Michael Mondavi loves to tell stories about trolling for visitors on Highway 29, driving slowly to back up traffic behind him and then turning into the winery in the hope that one or two cars might follow him.

Nonetheless, we thought it would be different in 1989 and were primed for the onslaught that didn't come. Potential visitors would cruise by on Highway 29, glance at the new winery with the unfamiliar name, and keep going. That is, if they even saw the winery sign. Napa County's sign ordinance is so restrictive that it is very difficult to effectively identify one's business. That's why we eventually planted two stately King palms at the highway entrance to St. Supéry, to supplement the low-profile signage passersby would miss as often as not. At one point I considered painting a line of bright yellow footprints along the highway shoulder and into the winery's driveway to lure visitors, but my team convinced me that was going too far.

Then the Loma Prieta earthquake, which occurred three months after St. Supéry opened to the public, put a temporary halt to all Bay Area tourism.

It wasn't until consumers had become familiar with the brand, having seen the St. Supéry label on shelves in their home markets, that visitors began to stop in.

We welcomed them warmly, did our best to make friends, and stayed in touch. Our visitors center staff was highly aware of the value of building relationships, not just selling some wine today.

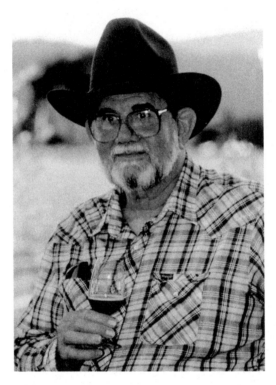

Don Hollingsworth, emeritus St. Supéry tour guide

They are a personable group, and always have a good story to share. Don Hollingsworth liked to pull out his wallet and show visitors a creased snapshot taken of him as a bikini-clad, well-oiled body builder in the 1950s. That was a conversation opener. Now retired, Don proudly recalls that "we were where other wineries sent guests to learn how wine was made." He delighted in showing visitors the two cork oaks near the demonstration vineyard, which inevitably lead to a dissertation on the evolution of wine corks.

157

Visitors are, of course, the Holy Grail of brand building in the fine wine business. From the first day we started building a database from our direct contact with visitors that would become the foundation of a highly successful wine club that still today contributes mightily to St. Supéry's bottom line.

52 WINEMAKING CONSULTANT

Six years after joining St. Supéry, I had become concerned that we were not getting the best results possible from the estate vineyards. The winemaker and I spent long hours talking about how to make our wines more interesting, but little changed. Tired of hearing that there was nothing more to be extracted from the vineyards, in 1995 I decided to hire a consultant to help.

My friend Bill Wren told me about Michel Rolland, who had first been hired in California by Zelma Long when she was president of Simi Winery. Since St. Supéry was focused on Bordeaux varietals and Michel is a *bordelais*, I thought the idea had possibilities even if he was best known for his work with red wines. At that time, I was more interested in developing the full potential of St. Supéry's Sauvignon Blanc.

Michel accepted my offer and St. Supéry became his second California client. Although he was well known in Bordeaux, this was before his consulting practice had grown to 100+ clients all over the world.

By the time I had a first exploratory meeting in Napa Valley with Michel, our winemaker had voluntarily departed St. Supéry. So Michel alone blended the wines being readied for bottling early in 1996 while we launched a search for a new winemaker.

Although neither technically trained nor a gifted palate, I'd been in the wine business since 1973 and had tasted with many professionals. I was impressed by Michel's ability to taste and especially to blend wines to their best potential. It was a real gift.

Within months of engaging the services of Michel Rolland, we were able to hire a first-class winemaker, Michael Scholz. He and I agreed that it would be useful to continue the consulting arrangement in spite of the expense. He understood and appreciated the opportunity to learn from Michel.

Eight years later, I was beginning to think we had gleaned all we would from Michel, or at least all we could reasonably apply. Some of his recommendations seemed best suited to wines costing $100 per bottle or more.

Consultant Michel Rolland (l) and winemaker Michael Scholz
at a St. Supéry blending tasting in the late 1990s.

Michel wanted to be involved in vineyard decisions, but his full schedule kept him away from Napa at the times when farming decisions had to be made. Pruning was finished before his May visit, and when he returned to Napa in late August it was too late for leafing or crop-thinning recommendations.

This is why I proposed, I thought reasonably enough, to reduce Michel's annual visits from three to one. We highly valued his expertise for the all-important blending sessions early in the year, which did fit nicely into his increasingly full travel schedule. Naturally, to me this meant his fees and expenses would be reduced to reflect a single annual visit.

Michel refused, saying that I didn't understand the work of consultants. It was to be all or nothing. Adept at managing client relationships, he had made sure that Robert Skalli believed his advice was crucial to our success, so I chose not to fight that battle. The consulting relationship continued until … *Mondovino*.

Mondovino is a 2004 documentary film apposing artisanal winemakers and "international" winemakers. Many in the wine industry thought it was a hatchet job: large producers like Mondavi are bad, tiny *vignerons* in the Lubéron are good. It was clear that most of the vintners interviewed had no idea the filmmaker would edit the footage to suit his doubtful premise.

Michel Rolland figured large in this documentary, portrayed as an international consultant indifferent to *terroir* who makes the same style of wine everywhere he goes, while making jokes at his clients' expense.

In my experience Michel is an excellent wine consultant, has a wonderfully dry sense of humor, and is quite likeable. For efficiency, as depicted in the film, he does hire a chauffeur in order to meet every week during harvest with each of his sixty clients in Bordeaux. He explained to me that it took him longer to shake hands and say "Hello, how are you? And the kids?" than to taste the client's six fermenters, make recommendations, and move on to his next stop.

It's probably not a coincidence that not long after *Mondovino* was released, Michel reduced his client load. I, already on record as wanting to cut back on his time commitment and fees, must have been at or near the top of his list. He dropped St. Supéry as a client. We had benefited from his advice for ten years, and paid him well for it—a fair exchange.

Four years after I retired, Michel is once again consulting for St. Supéry.

53 HIRING STARS, FIXING MISTAKES

Anyone who has to hire and fire people will tell you it's extraordinarily difficult, especially the latter. If there was ever an admission of failure, that's it.

Hiring isn't much easier. Trying to pick a winner based on a résumé, an hour or two of interviews, and reference checks that seldom reveal anything useful is like an arranged marriage: sometimes you get lucky. Here are four success stories, and two of my regrettable failures.

As part of my ongoing education on how to delegate effectively, in the early 1980s I decided Domaine Chandon needed an in-house public relations director. I didn't have to look farther than the visitors center to find an outstanding candidate. Sally McFadden (later to marry artist Steve Gordon) is one of those rare, genuinely caring people who exudes warmth and empathy and who is, as a result, universally loved. She listens and communicates well, has excellent taste, and knows how to entertain with style.

Keeping in mind the Domaine Chandon mantra that potential and talent trump experience—a cultural keystone that had worked for me—I offered Sally the job. She was a natural. She quickly developed relationships with journalists and strategic partners that served the winery well for many years. In an annual review I fear I hurt her feelings by suggesting she work on her writing skills, but she rose to the challenge and put an end to my blue pencil itch. Working with talented people is such a pleasure.

I nearly missed one of the best hires of my career.

In 1996 St. Supéry was looking for a new winemaker. This was either perceived as a plum job, or there weren't enough winemaker slots available for all the assistant winemakers wanting to move up; dozens of eager candidates applied for the position. Reviewing that mountain of résumés may be the genesis of my aversion to the word "passion" when linked to career ambitions in the wine industry. It became an inside joke on St. Supéry's management team that interviewees who used the P-word had just flunked the CEO's primary sorting device.

After eliminating the winemakers who claimed they wanted to be left alone to make great wine and damn the expense, I interviewed those I thought had potential to fit in at St. Supéry. This narrowed the field to three candidates to invite back for a second, group interview with the management team—my standard process for selecting a new executive. Since we'd all have to work together, I believed that a diversity of opinions would lead us to the best candidate and assure a good fit with the team. On this occasion, unusually, a previous commitment to an event in New York would preclude my participation in the group interviews.

On the eve of my departure for New York, something was bothering me. One of the candidates I had liked but not added to the short list was lingering in my mind like an uncompleted task, a sure sign that I had missed something. (Good decisions invariably left me in peace.) I thought his background and winemaking philosophy were perfect for St. Supéry, but was concerned that he couldn't explain why his current employer had not given him the title of winemaker, even though he had been making all their wines for three years. (I later learned that titles were reserved for the proprietor's family.)

Something wasn't right, and the gremlin in the back of my head kept nagging, demanding I give this more thought.

That night I called St. Supéry's public relations director, Sandy Flanders, and asked her to try to get this candidate onto the next day's management team interview schedule. She succeeded in spite of the short notice, and Michael Scholz was the team's unanimous, enthusiastic choice. His first vintage changed St. Supéry's Sauvignon Blanc into a "Wow!" wine that instantly became the winery's signature. I have paid attention to my gremlin ever since.

About the same time, the management team suggested I hire an assistant. That seemed extravagant, as I felt quite self-sufficient with my Mac and we had only just achieved our first profit. Although I didn't want to increase expenses unnecessarily, I took the recommendation in the helpful spirit in which it was offered and started thinking about how to justify the expense.

Rather than give myself the luxury of a full time assistant, I created a hybrid position of assistant/export coordinator/local restaurant sales. It's hard work to sell wine in Napa Valley, as there are many more wineries than wine lists.

A tall, attractive young woman presented herself, announcing that she wanted to work for *me*. She had useful experience, having worked in the U.K. and for our Sacramento wholesaler, so it was easy to say yes. Lesley Keffer promptly appointed me her mentor. I was fine with that, too, but on my own terms; I would not spoon-feed her a development program, but would be available for anything she wanted to ask or discuss.

After Lesley had put in a few years of very little "assistant" work, a lot of local and international sales, and then direct-to-consumer marketing, she decided to get an MBA. I encouraged her to focus on a serious academic program, rather than a quick and easy "get your MBA in one year" offering. I did not know until later that Berkeley/Haas had marked its MBA tuition and fees to market, on a par with the Ivy League schools, long after my graduation back in the days when California better supported higher education.

Expecting to lose Lesley once she earned her Berkeley/Haas MBA, I was delighted to have an unanticipated and highly strategic growth opportunity available in 2003. I expected the Commerce Clause protecting free trade among the states to prevail over the restrictions created by the 21st Amendment repealing Prohibition, once the issue reached the Supreme Court. I charged Lesley with preparing St. Supéry for the direct-to-consumer market explosion that was sure to follow a favorable ruling on direct shipping. That unpredictable moment arrived sooner than expected, in May of 2005. Even though the decision wasn't all I'd hoped for, St. Supéry was ready with a strategy, systems in place, and trained staff. Our direct-to-consumer business boomed, the wine clubs grew, and profits climbed.

On my recommendation, Lesley Keffer Russell was promoted to Vice President of Marketing and Direct Sales for St. Supéry. She was often invited to speak about direct marketing strategy and operations at industry symposia. In 2013 she accepted an offer to lead St. Helena Winery.

Hiring a vineyard manager was not as easy as hiring Lesley had been. The job involves optimizing the fruit from nearly 500 diverse, challenging acres of wine grapes while supervising a workforce that could rise to 150 people at harvest. In 1999 I was in despair, having interviewed a series of experienced but burned-out candidates with the help of my good friend Mike Black, the retired Vice President/Vineyards for Simi Winery. He was very familiar with the microclimate of Dollarhide ranch because his grandfather is buried at nearby Juliana vineyards. He also grows and bottles an outstanding Merlot on his own vineyard in Napa.

Mike, too, was disappointed with the candidates who'd presented themselves for St. Supéry's vitally important job. Then he had a wonderful idea: we could hire a recent viticulture graduate and Mike would devote three years to training him or her. Bingo!

My boss in France was not thrilled at the prospect of handing over $20 million of Napa Valley vineyards to an inexperienced manager and resisted. I resisted back, patiently explaining the unacceptable quality of the candidates we'd found, and having no other prospects. Mike's willingness to train the new manager minimized the risk to near zero, but still Robert Skalli hesitated. I was on the verge of telling him I'd rather quit myself than hire an inferior vineyard manager when he capitulated. I'm pretty sure Robert could read my mind; he nearly always seemed to sense when I'd reached my limit.

Within a week we had a winner. Josh Anstey came with a Master's degree in Agronomy and one lonely viticulture class from UC Davis on his résumé. But he clearly had the will and energy to take on the job. He didn't tell us, but his coach did when I called for a reference, that Josh had been a two time All-American on the UC Davis football team. That told me a lot about his character.

After only two years of working closely with Mike, Josh was ready to go it alone. He took responsibility for St. Supéry's 510 acres of vineyard, and a lot more (he loves building things and ranching), until after 15 successful years he succumbed to his entrepreneurial urge to create a business of his own.

In 2002 St. Supéry needed a marketing coordinator. Everyone knows that advertising a marketing job in the wine business is an open invitation to be deluged with hundreds of applications, most from people who think anyone can do marketing. Word of mouth can be an effective, efficient way to find candidates, but I wasn't interested in an industry veteran for this job. I wanted fresh thinking.

I was also tired of seeing résumés full of typos and grammar errors, and was eager to divest my self-assigned chore as St. Supéry's copy desk and proofreader. What I wanted more than anything for this position was a bright, creative person who could read and write. Then inspiration struck: I would put a blind ad on Craigslist, then still a fairly new enterprise, and require a résumé and a half-page writing sample.

I received six, not six hundred, applications. Three did not include a writing sample. Of the remaining three, two presented third-grade texts. The last one submitted a cogent, engaging movie review without any errors, so I gratefully invited its author in for an interview. Tina Cao bounced into my office at the appointed time, announcing "This is my dream job!" And St. Supéry benefited.

For six years Tina was a tremendous asset, using her intelligence, energy, and charm to coax the resources she needed from every department in the company while developing effective internal and external communication channels. She is now a fast-rising brand manager responsible for business development in European markets for Blue Diamond, a large almond growers' cooperative based in Sacramento. I've been serving their roasted salted almonds with bubbly for years.

From left, Lesley Russell, Tina Cao, the author,
Josh Anstey, and Emma Swain in 2009.

I love success stories. And I am proud of my protégées, although they have seldom needed more from me than the opportunity to shine.

Not all of my personnel decisions were so fortunate. I was obliged to fire a highly recommended CFO after I discovered he was running a private business from his winery office that competed with St. Supéry, on St. Supéry's time. Wait, that's not quite right. I had discussed my intent to let him go with the rest of the management team. One of them either tipped him off, or the CFO had read the tea leaves, because he walked into my office for our scheduled meeting and quit before I had a chance to fire him. He then proceeded openly to vie with St. Supéry for customers.

The only other management team member I had to let go in my 21-year tenure as CEO was just as difficult, but for different reasons. I had hired a talented executive with an Ivy League MBA who did outstanding work but who proved expert at "managing up." This is biz-speak for treating peers and superiors deferentially. (There are other terms for this, but the euphemism is more popular in self-help management books.) The unfortunate corollary, until then unknown to me, is that, unlike peers and superiors, subordinates find themselves on the dark side of these managers: stifled, browbeaten, and disrespected.

While I was away on business, this management team member summarily fired a young assistant and had her escorted out of the building within 30 minutes as if she had been stealing state secrets. Since I made sure that St. Supéry was an open book to the employees, there were no secrets; and it was certainly not part of our culture to make exiting employees do a perp walk on the way out.

On my return the fired assistant requested an exit interview, where I heard enough to launch an investigation. It soon became clear that this executive had also driven away a valuable manager who had been unwilling to say why he was leaving, and had been abusive to other employees. It was painful to discover how toxic this person's behavior was. *Finis.* Interestingly, some on the management team were unhappily surprised by my quick, unilateral decision, having themselves been successfully managed up.

It took me too long to recognize a manager-upper. My wont is to give people the benefit of the doubt, a chance to do the right thing. But after that episode it was harder to fool me.

My purpose was always to hire smart, energetic people, share the mission and strategy, and then give them room to run. The more technical assignments require appropriate education and experience, but many of my management hires offered at first little more than talent and enthusiasm. I was delighted with new ways of thinking and doing things, and encouraged those behaviors.

I was available if needed, but woe to the manager who wanted to be told what he/she should do about a problem; the job was to bring a proposed solution to me, if in the manager's judgment such a discussion was needed. I would ask questions to make sure the manager had considered all the pertinent issues, which would usually take us quickly to agreement. I also strongly encouraged people to work together for the good of all; anyone who showed signs of playing political games for personal aggrandizement was a misfit.

There are those who believed I favored hiring women. That's not true. It is, however, fair to say that I didn't assume women couldn't compete. It's also likely that a female CEO attracts a disproportionate share of women candidates. My purpose was simply to hire the best talent our business could afford. In my 21 years as CEO, the gender balance on St. Supéry's management team ranged from 5:1 to 1:5 and everything in between as people came and went.

On the rare occasions when we were obliged to let an employee go for a bad fit or even unsatisfactory performance, I tried to make it as painless as possible. I am convinced that people perform well when doing work they enjoy, and that there is a right place somewhere for nearly all who want to work. If St. Supéry wasn't that place, and I'm the first to admit my management style could be described as eccentric, I wanted to acknowledge the hiring error by helping him/her find a better fit.

This is why I'd send an exiting person off in search of a new job, personal pride and confidence intact, while keeping him or her on the payroll for a few more weeks and providing a letter of recommendation focused on the positives. Since I consider litigation a sign of failure, I am a bit proud of never having been sued by a former employee. I am more proud that many who voluntarily or involuntarily moved along almost always landed in a job where they were happier, and retained good memories of our time together. It seems that having St. Supéry on one's résumé is a plus for job seekers.

Occasionally current and former St. Supéry employees remind me that I once said something that resonated with them, advice they never forgot that had guided them forward. No CEO could ever be better compensated.

54 BACK TO BORDEAUX

I never expected to return to Bordeaux after the year I spent there as a participant in the University of California's "junior year abroad" program. UC students from all nine campuses who wanted to study in France were sent to Bordeaux; the Stanford contingent went to Tours; other universities sent their students to Aix-en-Provence or even—the lucky ones—to the Sorbonne in Paris.

In 1966 Bordeaux was a dingy, gray, cold, damp city that hadn't yet recovered from WWII. Its inhabitants were famous for being *renfermés*. Pedestrians never made eye contact and few of the French students were interested in getting acquainted with the Americans spending *une année scolaire* in their midst. Nonetheless, it was a great learning experience.

In my junior year abroad, I learned to play bridge, smoke unfiltered *Gauloises*, appreciate Armagnac, and drink *vin ordinaire*. As impoverished students, we were barely aware that great wines were grown nearby; we couldn't afford them even if we had had an invitation and transportation to the *grands châteaux* of Bordeaux.

I also learned to swear in French, order *café crème* and *une demi* like a pro, appreciate cathedrals from an historic and architectural point of view, enjoy plain yoghurt and omelettes, and admire the note-taking of our French classmates.

Armed with five colors of ink, often ingeniously housed in one ballpoint pen, they took copious notes in perfect outline form as the professor lectured sonorously for three hours without a break. They memorized these notes, to be regurgitated at examination time. The eighteenth-century century lecture halls were overheated and smelled of wet wool, rough cigarettes, and unwashed bodies.

At every opportunity, we'd hitchhike to Paris.

Halfway through our academic year, classes were moved from the historic *facultés* in the center of Bordeaux to a new, American-style campus in the suburbs. Talence was a half-hour bus ride from the city center where we Californians lived in rented rooms within walking distance of the *facultés*. It was still a construction zone, a veritable sea of mud. Worse, there were no cafés where we could drink and smoke and play bridge. Most of us stayed in *centre ville.*

When the year-end examinations came around in May—French students get one chance to succeed (or fail) every year—most of us did well thanks to our long-suffering tutors. The *Université de Bordeaux* was in agreement with the University of California that we young Americans could not possibly comprehend lengthy academic lectures delivered *en français,* so a French graduate student was assigned to the Americans to meet with us weekly to make sure we were grasping the material in our classes.

Our tutors, who became good friends, spoon-fed us all we needed to know. One of them, Marie-Hélène Huët from Armagnac, later became a professor at UC Berkeley. With the exception of one girl who'd hurt herself falling off a curtain wall in the medieval city of Carcassonne on a field trip, we all returned to California with good grades and full credit for the year-long courses we'd taken, prepared to graduate on time. For me, graduate school was in the cards before I joined the workforce.

During the fifteen years I spent at Domaine Chandon, my business travel in France favored Champagne and Paris. Then in 1988 I joined St. Supéry, where part of my job was to develop business in international markets.

Export was new to me, since Domaine Chandon's mandate had been to supply high quality sparkling wine only to the U.S. market. For different reasons and in spite of its paltry per capita wine consumption, I believed that the best opportunity for relatively costly Napa Valley wines like St. Supéry would be the large, wealthy U.S. population.

It was hard for me to understand how competing with established, lower-priced European producers on their turf could be successful for St. Supéry. It would take significant effort to achieve even small sales volumes, perhaps at most 10 percent of our production, which would yield lower margins because of higher selling expenses.

I was not enthusiastic about our export prospects—but my new boss Robert Skalli was, so I found myself returning to Bordeaux on a regular basis more than twenty years after my student days there.

VinExpo, the biannual wine trade fair started in 1985 as a showcase for the wines of Bordeaux, quickly became equally important for producers from all over France and other winegrowing regions. The main attraction was the presence at VinExpo of serious buyers: importers, distributors, airlines and cruise lines, liquor control boards and monopolies, and on and off-premise chain buyers from around the world.

My first VinExpo, in 1989, is best remembered for a tremendous heat wave, when the kilometer-long metal exhibition building at Bordeaux Lac (a huge dedicated exhibition space far from the city center) posted temperatures over 100 degrees Fahrenheit throughout the week, with humidity to match. The building was not air-conditioned.

Proudly displayed bottles pushed their corks, red wine running down their sides and staining the labels. Sweaty and miserable in business attire, no one felt like tasting wines, negotiating deals, or even chewing the dessicated sandwiches on offer—the only food available in that isolated location. Two people are said to have expired from heat prostration. The Australian contingent, housed in an overflow tent, made it clear they would not come back unless air conditioning was installed and they were given space inside the main building.

In spite of VinExpo's early success in attracting buyers and sellers, Bordeaux was not prepared to accommodate 2,000 producers and 50,000 buyers during the last week in June every other year. Along with the Skalli team from the south of France, that first year I was housed in a small, stuffy motel closer to the airport than to Bordeaux Lac. Its amenities included road noise late into the night, cardboard walls, dim lighting and, of course, no air conditioning.

For the next VinExpo, in 1991, management had installed a swamp cooler system in the massive building. Ironically, the weather was unseasonably cold and wet that June. Accommodations were scarce, with every available hotel room booked a year to the day in advance for the upcoming trade fair.

That may have been the first year my boss took pity and found me a room in one of the plastic, expensive chain hotels near the exposition halls. I could walk there in 10 minutes, avoiding the huge, daily traffic jams in and out of Bordeaux Lac. It took another ten minutes to navigate through the building to the California pavilion near its center.

Sandy Flanders and I had hatched a plan to decorate the Napa Valley stand (within the California pavilion) with live California poppies. This required persuading an accomplice on the Skalli team to plant the seeds we mailed to France at just the right time to bring the blooming poppy plants to the exhibition hall for opening day. It worked perfectly, although the symbolism of our state flower was almost certainly lost on all but the Californians in attendance.

Then Sandy came down with a wretched case of the flu. Every night, her French roommate would bounce in after partying until 4:00 a.m. with the Skalli team and rouse her from an exhausted, fitful sleep. Our French colleagues loved to eat, drink, and dance, but it didn't stop them from showing up punctually at work the next morning. I found it hard enough to be starting dinner at midnight, after nine hour days of standing on aching feet. I love to dance, too, but not under those conditions.

171

The California vintners decided early on that VinExpo, being full of interesting wines, badly needed some good food to match. Guided by Axel Fabre of Robert Mondavi Winery, they launched a temporary restaurant in a tent and named it the California Café. Axel imported chefs, sommeliers, kitchen equipment, non-French foodstuffs like tomatillos and cilantro, tableware, decorations, and servers to recreate an authentic California dining experience complete with California wines for VinExpo week. (This may have been the genesis of today's pop-up restaurants.)

Deprived producers and buyers from around the world, including California, immediately lined up for lunch in the California Café. The following VinExpo boasted a few more temporary regional restaurants. Soon, the entire length of the exhibit hall had sprouted tented restaurants sponsored by generic German, Spanish, Italian and specific AOC winegrowing regions and featuring their wines, so everyone was better nourished.

Margrit and Robert Mondavi with the author, enjoying a
Michelin three-star lunch in the Skalli stand at VinExpo in 1993.

The biggest buyers and most sought-after journalists were always spirited away from VinExpo by helicopter for a fabulous lunch in one of the nearby *grand cru* châteaux. Home court advantage to the *bordelais*.

Although it was supposed to be against VinExpo rules, Robert Skalli was able to create a private restaurant inside the building, within the Skalli stand. With one of the Pourcel twins—chef/owners of *Le Jardin des Sens*, a Michelin three-star restaurant in Montpellier—manning the stove, buyers and journalists were eager to be invited to lunch. This caused the large, perpetually busy Skalli stand to become a madhouse at midday.

Bob and Margrit Mondavi joined me for lunch several times over the years in the Skalli stand; in 1993 the three of us were squeezed into a closet-size private room, with gawkers and paparazzi outside the open door hoping to get a photo of them.

Thereafter the Skalli team abandoned this format of multi-course luncheon menus and private rooms, designed to allow the confidential business negotiations that are VinExpo's *raison d'être*, in favor of three-star small plates and flexible seating. This proved easier to manage and accommodated more guests.

In 1995 the Napa Valley Vintners Association organized its first pre-VinExpo trade tasting in Paris, graciously hosted by U.S. Ambassador Pamela Harriman in the official residence on the rue du Faubourg Saint-Honoré.

This palatial venue, plus wonderful Neal's Yard cheeses and Napa vintners pouring their best wines, was a huge success. In a diplomatic coup, Ambassador Harriman flew to Bordeaux the next day, where she created a bigger commotion touring VinExpo than had the French prime minister and his entourage. The media loved her.

After several VinExpos, Robert decreed that St. Supéry move out of the Napa Valley group stand and into the adjacent Skalli stand to join its sibling wineries from Corsica, Languedoc, and Châteauneuf du Pape. It made sense to have all the Skalli-owned wineries in one location, particularly since the French sales team would soon be responsible for selling St. Supéry wines in international markets. But it also created a problem for St. Supéry. Buyers seeking Napa Valley wines were unlikely to look for them inside a French producer's stand.

The Skalli stand was purposely located directly across the aisle from the Napa Valley stand. This proximity had made it easy for me to dart over to entertain American VIPs at lunch in the Skalli stand. Now this proximity would make it easy for me to cross the aisle in the other direction, into California territory, to take an occasional shift pouring all the Napa vintners' wines, including St. Supéry.

This was also a good way to learn more about our Napa neighbors' current vintages and, oddly enough, them. We vintners got to know one another best when traveling together for a common purpose, without the distractions of working at home in Napa Valley.

I enjoyed pouring Napa wines for an international audience; there was a great deal of curiosity, since many of the buyers and producers had never been to California, much less Napa Valley (that's near Los Angeles, *non?*). The restored classic car that Far Niente Winery customarily shipped to

Bordeaux as part of their booth's décor also attracted admiring attention. Or it could have been the delicious little bites provided by their jovial in-house chef, Michel Cornu.

This cooperative arrangement worked well. Since most of the time I was in the adjacent Skalli stand, my Napa colleagues would generously refer potential buyers or even bring them across the aisle to meet me. It has long been standard practice for Napa vintners to support one another.

After a few VinExpos of trial and error, we found the solution to St. Supéry being hard to find. A separate exterior entrance was created for the St. Supéry section of the Skalli stand.

It was well branded with a panoramic mural of our scenic Dollarhide vineyard and a prominent display of St. Supéry bottles. Dollarhide's rolling green vineyards contrasting with golden hillsides and specimen oaks sent a strong message that this was California territory. Oddly, in a country where *appellations d'origine contrôlées* are revered, it took more than one VinExpo to get the signage right; replacing "California" with our strongly preferred "Napa Valley" seemed an unimportant detail to my colleagues in France.

Lesley Keffer Russell, then in charge of export for St. Supéry, and I were the greeters. Like spiders lurking in a web, we waited behind a small podium in the St. Supéry booth entrance, alert for interested passersby. Catching someone's eye, we would offer a tasting of the always well received Sauvignon Blanc and Cabernet Sauvignon. Building relationships over a taste of wine is a very Napa Valley way of creating customers.

At VinExpo, the serious business is all done by prior appointment with specific buyers. It's more about price and volume negotiations than discovery. Producers who naively arrive at Bordeaux Lac without a book of appointments are seldom satisfied with the return on their substantial investment to participate.

As the producers' stands grew ever more elaborate over the years, the competition for buyers' attention grew fiercer. Winegrowing associations started offering free, large-scale regional or varietal tastings that I found educational. I'm sure they were helpful for journalists, too, but I doubt they resulted in the desired immediate commitments. Bordeaux châteaux continued to poach journalists and buyers for their private events, building business relationships on extraordinary VIP treatment.

In 2001 the Skalli team came up with a creative idea that attracted a crowd of 80 top-flight journalists to the stand. It was a sit down tasting of wines from thirty of consultant Michel Rolland's clients, with a three-star Pourcel small bite matched to each wine. Michel was the sole commentator, and only wines from outside Bordeaux were presented.

Commenting publicly on his Bordeaux clients' wines on their home turf would have been beyond even his considerable diplomatic skills.

Michel did a fine job of finding something positive to say about each of thirty wines from places as diverse as India, Napa, Argentina, Sonoma, South Africa, Washington, and Italy. The Pourcel food pairing developed to accompany St. Supéry's 1997 Élu, a red meritage blend, was amazing: a wonton skin stuffed with a bit of *foie gras,* then folded into a butterfly shape, deep fried and sprinkled with sea salt. It was ethereal, and showed the wine to perfection.

Haute cuisine small plates are not always to American taste. One afternoon Lesley was munching an unidentifiable three-star tidbit and enjoying it, until I casually noted that she was eating snails. She paled, as horrified as if I'd told her she was eating worms. Another time she had a laugh on me when I couldn't manage to swallow a bony mouthful of eel, a Bordeaux specialty that felt like disjointed vertebrae in slime. Just call us squeamish. I likewise couldn't bring myself to order anything too adventurous when dining with the Napa vintners at La Tupina, famous for innards, in downtown Bordeaux.

One of the highlights of VinExpo for Robert Skalli is the closing party called *La Fête de la Fleur.* The châteaux take turns hosting this grand event for 1,500 people with a champagne reception, the robed induction of members into the *Commanderie de Bordeaux*, a black tie dinner, and entertainment. It can get competitive.

When it was their turn, Château Lynch-Bages erected an enormous round white tent spacious enough to allow costumed jugglers on 10-foot stilts to mingle among the guests. But there was more. Acrobats were slingshot in a high arc from opposite sides of the tent, crossing in midair. The *pièce de résistance* was a beautiful woman suspended just below the apex of the tent—easily 50 feet above our heads. Her dark green silk skirt unfurled to create a 25-foot tall Bordeaux bottle. Only then did it become apparent that she was the cork. It was all very Cirque du Soleil, and quite wonderful.

A couple of years later *La Fête de la Fleur* took place at Château Smith Haute Lafitte, site of a fourteenth-century defensive tower. Not surprisingly, the entertainment had a medieval theme. Acrobats dressed as jesters were performing leaping somersaults in the vine rows, which must have obscured the trampolines that allowed them to sail into the air with such ease; it looked a bit like a game of whack-a-mole without the whacking. Owner Daniel Cathiard's daughters were swanning about in couture gowns, lovely as Vogue models as they mingled with their guests. Leather-clad falconers launched various birds of prey, some with six-foot wingspans, which soared at low altitude over the guests' heads. Dinner was in the cellar, cleared of barrels for the evening. The party went on into the wee hours.

With some effort I eventually convinced Robert that I was less enamored of *La Fête de la Fleur* than he, and excused from further duty. I don't think he understood that I was exhausted. If I were in charge of VinExpo, *La Fête de la Fleur* would be the opening event, while everyone is still fresh and full of energy.

The Californians had the counter-cultural idea to host a casual party far from Bordeaux Lac in the middle of VinExpo week. Only a couple of the Skalli team accepted my invitation to join us—Yvelise Kinsey and Xavier Logette, both honorary Napans at heart—and we enjoyed everything from line dancing outdoors (imagine a French band playing Texas two-step music) to rock 'n' roll in a castle. It was at one of these parties that I first met Jean-Charles Boisset. Like most of the French people I know who seek opportunities in California, Jean-Charles has the entrepreneurial gene that makes him at home in the U.S.

I was just getting the hang of surviving and succeeding at VinExpo when I retired from St. Supéry in mid-2009, which didn't save me from making one last appearance at Bordeaux Lac. Wouldn't you know: too late for me, a five-star hotel was under construction across from the *Grand Théâtre* in downtown Bordeaux.

In 2008, Hong Kong anointed itself the wine capital of Asia by eliminating the duty on imported wines, putting neighboring countries at a severe disadvantage. China, whose wine tariffs remain high, did not follow suit; this quickly led to a thriving wine smuggling trade from Hong Kong into China.

It's no surprise that VinExpo Hong Kong quickly became where the action is for the *bordelais* and wine exporters from all over the world eager to grow sales in promising Asian markets. Since the same group manages both VinExpo Bordeaux and VinExpo Hong Kong, these wine trade fairs alternate—meaning that east or west, there's now a VinExpo every year.

55 LEARNING ABOUT WINE

While at Domaine Chandon I was occasionally invited as a guest to the Napa Valley Women in Wine tastings, held at 9:30 a.m. on alternate Mondays in a member's home or winery. The tastings were businesslike, usually taking no more than an hour.

The original group included Napa Valley pioneers like Belle Rhodes, Lila Jaeger, Marge Stafford, Virginia Van Asperen, Jamie Davies, Veronica di Rosa, Kathy Collins, Katy Spann, Renate Wright, Linda McGrew, Janet Trefethen and Barbara Eisele, all women I knew and admired. I would have loved to become a member but could not justify the time away from work.

When I made the transition from sparkling wine to still wine at St. Supéry, I finally could rationalize playing hooky: I had much to learn about non-sparkling wines.

For our tasting sheets, artist Veronica di Rosa designed a whimsical logo for the group featuring a tasting cup similar to the famous coupe,

complete with nipple, purportedly modeled on Marie Antoinette's breast. A photo of the original graces the cover of Patrick Forbes' seminal work on champagne.

As the years passed, the tasting group lost members to demanding jobs, family changes, illness, or death, and new members were invited to join.

Carol Anderson and her daughter-in-law Tracy, Daphne Araujo, Cathy Corison, Margaret Duckhorn, Marie Oliver, Diane Livingston, Janet

Pagano, Willinda McCrea, Dawnine Dyer, Karen Cakebread, Joan Crowley, Julie Johnson…the group renewed itself on a rolling basis.

With the arrival of new members, some of whom (like me) had inadvertently broken the unspoken rules, it seemed helpful to share the rules as I understood them. This aroused discussion and eventually provoked some changes.

- ✧ All tastings are blind.

- ✧ Tastings should be educational.

- ✧ Everyone is assigned a date to organize and host a tasting; if you aren't available, it's your responsibility to switch dates with someone who is.

- ✧ No media allowed.

- ✧ Guests may be invited with the host's consent.

- ✧ No men allowed, except at the annual Christmas bubbles and potluck dinner.

- ✧ Never put your own wines into a blind tasting.

- ✧ Everyone is expected to inform the host if they are unable to attend.

- ✧ The treasurer reimburses the host for the tasting wines.

- ✧ Pay up when the treasurer says it's time to replenish the bank account.

Twice a month was too much for some busy schedules, so after many years we switched to monthly tastings. Some would like to invite an occasional wine writer, but that remains controversial. Everyone knows—after Jamie Davies organized a spectacular *tête de cuvée* champagne tasting some years ago that depleted the treasury by $1,000—to keep costs in mind.

The annual coed holiday dinner went by the wayside after several spouses departed this earthly coil; it's now a holiday potluck lunch, always with bubbly, but only for the tasting group. This is the one gathering that nearly everyone finds time to attend.

One host started offering interesting cheeses to try with the wines after we'd blind tasted, ranked, revealed, and discussed them, which was brilliant. Cheeses are now a standard tasting amenity; the wines change dramatically and usually for the better both with aeration and with carefully chosen cheeses.

Occasionally the Monday morning tasting is transformed into a field trip to a new or interesting winery, so far including Dana, Jarvis, Hagafen, and Palmaz. We're always graciously received, and find these local excursions educational.

Many of us try to follow the example set by Belle Rhodes, a formidable researcher, by providing printouts on the tasting wines once they've been unveiled. Always noted: brand, appellation, price, alcohol, vintage, varietal, descriptors, and often a bit of history.

Some of the wines generate *ad hoc* foreign language lessons or extemporaneous travelogues, others provoke lively discussions about alcohol levels, or packaging: aesthetics, ethics, carbon footprints. There is often hilarity over back label content.

This is an efficient group, nearly all (you know who you are) arriving promptly at 9:30 a.m. and departing after a satisfying learning experience between 10:30 and 11:00 a.m. It takes discipline not to lapse into friendly chatter, but we manage, mostly. The holiday lunch is the exception; bubbles and efficiency are not a natural pairing.

I feel only slightly guilty for revealing the secrets of Napa Valley Women in Wine, because I hope others will be inspired to follow this congenial model for shared learning about wine.

56 WOMEN FOR WINESENSE

This is a long story because establishing the context is important.

In the mid to late 1980s there was a rising crescendo of anti-alcohol sentiment in America, stoked by experts at manipulating the media like the Center for Science in the Public Interest. By providing sensational headlines and selective studies about the damage attributed to alcohol, they were able, for a time, to control the public debate.

The Bureau of Alcohol, Tobacco, and Firearms reacted by imposing a requirement that wine labels carry the warning "contains sulfites" starting in 1987. Since sulfites are a natural result of fermentation, and winemakers nearly universally add a bit more to protect their wines from oxidation, their presence in small amounts was indisputable.

However, the rare severe allergic reaction to sulfites was not caused by wine; the culprit was salad bars where oxidation-prone items like lettuce and guacamole were loaded with 5,000 ppm of sulfites to keep them appetizingly green for hours on buffet tables. No matter, the warning label for wine was required, probably to Do Something or, worse, to scare us away from alcohol.

Not long after, a second warning label was mandated by the feds. Forty-two words long and highly objectionable to the wine industry, it took up valuable space on back labels to warn women that any consumption of alcohol before or during pregnancy was dangerous to a fetus, and that operating heavy equipment (!) while drinking was inadvisable. There was no science to support the first, and the second was plain common sense (and limited to the small part of the population qualified to operate bulldozers and cranes). Once again, the government seems to have felt the need to Do Something.

Mothers Against Drunk Driving, whose laudable mission was to prevent drinking and driving, was also having success influencing elementary school curricula. Suddenly, children were being taught that alcohol *per se* is a drug like cocaine or heroin ("alcohol and other drugs" was the standard phrase), which caused considerable confusion in households where wine on the dinner table was customary.

Here in the Napa Valley, children who were well aware that Daddy or Mommy was neither a pusher nor an addict would slyly ask winegrowing parents "Why are you making drugs?" They were curious. In our household, we simply replied "We're not making drugs," and the kids were satisfied.

There were many similar stories. A school in Sonoma sent third graders home to change from winery logo T-shirts to more politically correct clothing. When ZD Winery offered to donate a used computer to a Napa elementary school, the principal, teachers, and students were eager to accept this gift. A lone parent objected so vehemently to the word "winery" on the planned donor plaque that the donated computer ultimately had to be refused. In Seattle, a waiter took it upon himself to refuse to deliver a cocktail ordered by a pregnant woman; she protested and the server was fired.

It was in this context that many in the California wine business felt these anti-alcohol attacks were targeting women and women's issues. The public debate was one of extremes: *laissez-faire* libertarians battled with media-savvy anti-alcohol forces, with no one speaking up on behalf of the moderate middle.

Common sense told us that wine, far from being an evil influence, has been part of enduring cultures and religions for millennia. Evidence from large, longitudinal studies in Europe showed that alcohol in moderation was good for health, contrary to nearly daily alerts in the American media about the dangers of fetal alcohol syndrome, addiction, cirrhosis, and various forms of cancer.

Most vintners were aware that our California wine trade association had an extensive library of wine and health research that could illuminate the public debate on alcohol, but its strategy seemed to be "this too shall pass." Laying low seemed safer than joining the fray in a litigious society, so the response was limited to labeling the anti-alcohol crowd "neo-prohibitionists."

In February 1990, I was among several women attending a wine industry conference in Santa Rosa who had gathered in the lobby during a break to share our frustration that no one was speaking up on behalf of wine.

Five minutes into this venting session, Julie Williams of Frog's Leap Winery looked straight at me and said "*We* could do something about it." I knew instantly she was right. As a mother of young children, I was not happy that strangers were trying to control our family's lifestyle. As a vintner, I also felt my livelihood potentially threatened. So in spite of a full work-family schedule, and contrary to my not-a-joiner nature, I said "Yes, we could!"

We were stunned by the power of this idea. There were gigawatts of pent-up energy among women in the wine business that found an outlet in this nascent effort. Margrit Mondavi, patron saint of most worthy causes, hosted the first meeting. Dozens of women showed up, eager to be involved.

The first task was, as usual, to find a name. We wanted to be understood not as experts but as proactive women on a mission to save wine from its attackers by espousing a thoughtful, moderate, and sensible lifestyle that includes responsible wine consumption.

Since most of the kerfuffle focused on alcohol in general, Julie's husband John contributed the useful comment that we were "women for *wine* sense, not women for alcohol sense." Should we include men? Sure! Just not in the name of the organization. We settled on the proactive name Women *for* WineSense and went to work.

My former boss Robert Skalli may be dismayed to learn that 25 years ago we burned out St. Supéry's new copy machine producing hundreds of packets of the published studies and articles that supported our mantra of moderation. There was plenty of sound research to refute the assertion that wine, being a beverage that contains alcohol, is intrinsically bad for people; on the contrary, wine has proven health benefits.

Most of this research came from carefully designed longitudinal studies done in Europe. (Many of the studies cited by the anti-alcohol forces in the U.S. were unreliable, being based on as few as 6 people and/or of short duration.)

I recall one study from the Netherlands that for years tracked the drinking habits, and health results, of 26,000 nurses. The researchers came to a startling conclusion: of the very small subgroup identified as binge drinkers—defined as consuming an eye-popping liter of vodka daily—only 10% produced babies showing fetal alcohol syndrome damage.

And we moderate wine drinkers in America were being warned that even a single glass of wine could cause fetal alcohol syndrome! I found it insulting to our intelligence that American women were being led to believe that even the most moderate wine consumption during pregnancy was dangerous; it also seemed cruel to add needlessly to the natural anxiety all mothers feel for their unborn children.

Physicians soon joined the abstinence bandwagon, whether out of belief, fear of malpractice suits, or political correctness, we'll probably never know. Only a few well-informed American researchers like Dr. Curtis Ellison of Boston University had the expertise and the courage to speak publicly in defense of moderate wine consumption before, during, and after pregnancy, and for the health benefits of moderate wine consumption in general.

Thanks in part to certain Surgeons General, today this urban myth has nearly all American women convinced that the only way to avoid any risk to an unborn child is to abstain. Zero defects is a peculiarly American goal, and an odd standard to apply since the medical community has long acknowledged that 75 percent of birth defects are of unknown origin.

It is worth recalling that in France, Spain, and Italy, women do not give up wine with meals while pregnant. As late as the 1980s, American obstetricians and pediatricians were recommending a glass of beer or wine to stressed mothers-to-be, women who were likely to go into premature labor, and nursing mothers, but they don't anymore—at least publicly.

After educating ourselves, we mailed the hefty Women for WineSense research packets to policy makers and the media. Their reaction took us by surprise. Lobbyists promoting an agenda are normally so far out on the extreme ends of a given topic that a group like ours, coming from the moderate middle perspective, was welcomed by those we approached. Maybe it was just the power of a group of women on a mission.

Legislators in Sacramento and Washington were eager to meet with us. The media wanted to hear more. I have never felt or seen such energy in my life, before or after the early days of Women for WineSense. It was heady. We began to appreciate the powerful undertow of a (non-religious) crusade.

Margaret Duckhorn, Rosemary Cakebread, Kit Wall, Lynne Carmichael, Dawnine Dyer, Zelma Long, Lili Thomas, Annette Shafer, Susan Sokol Blosser, Gabrielle Saylor, Cathy Clifton and many others worked tirelessly with Julie and me to get the Women for WineSense message of moderation in front of the public.

Margrit Mondavi helped us continue the educational mailings with a grant for postage money. *Vineyard & Winery Management* magazine put a Women for WineSense group on its cover in 1991, which helped attract even more support.

Marvin Shanken asked for a side meeting at the Napa Valley Wine Auction Napa Valley. It was a wonderful surprise when he handed me an unsolicited $10,000 grant from his Wine Spectator Foundation to Women for WineSense.

In November 2001, Morley Safer finished the job we'd started. On the widely viewed *60 Minutes* television news show, he interviewed French researcher Dr. Serge Renaud—over a calorie-laden, multi-course lunch washed down with good burgundy in a famous Dijon restaurant—about the health benefits of moderate wine consumption.

THE BOTTOM LINE RESOURCE FOR GROWER & VINTNER

VINEYARD&WINERY
MANAGEMENT

MAY/JUNE 1991

THIS ISSUE!
Women For WineSense Ready To Meet.
Virginia Tech Hosts Chardonnay Conference.
Material Handling Management: Conveyors.
A Look At Wine Marketing Demographics.
Valves for Wine Processing.
Fertigation Management.

Dr. Renaud explained the French Paradox: the French blithely enjoy foie gras, butter, cheese, and other potentially dangerous rich foods, yet their mortality rate is better than ours in America. Why? Because they also drink red wine with their reasonably sized, nutritious, balanced meals.

This absolution set millions of American television viewers free to do what they liked and wanted to do anyway. Overnight, red wine with meals became part of the lifestyle for the nine percent who drink 91 percent of the wine consumed in the U.S. at that time. Others joined them.

A probably apocryphal story had little old ladies marching into restaurants and ordering their statutory two glasses of red wine with dinner—even though they hadn't been wine drinkers before that *60 Minutes* broadcast.

And what of Women for WineSense? Our mission accomplished, we debated whether to declare victory and disband, or keep on. None of us really believed we'd won the war—the battle, yes—so in a strategic planning meeting in 1994 facilitated by Karen Jess-Lindsley and Linda Cyrog we decided to keep the organization intact in case we needed to defend wine again. (As of 2015, such attempts have been minor or laughably self-interested, as with a short-lived arsenic scare.)

In the meantime Women for WineSense would provide a forum for networking and education for women in the wine industry, and for women and men interested in wine.

An added benefit was to continue building on the wonderful friendships we'd discovered by working together. Women for WineSense is still going strong, and celebrated its 25th anniversary at the biannual national conference in Napa Valley in spring 2015.

We haven't heard much from the Center for Science in the Public Interest recently. After the anti-alcohol campaign fizzled, they took a run at Girl Scout cookies (proclaiming them the "least healthy cookies in the U.S." to loud guffaws from the press). The subsequent "heart attack on a plate" campaign against *fettuccine Alfredo* was similarly received. In the meantime, wine has become so clearly identified with a moderate, healthy lifestyle that I doubt they'll try again.

In 2011, the U.S. became the largest wine market in the world in spite of its still-low per capita consumption.

57 FORTUNE CALLING

"What's it like to be a woman in the wine industry?"

What I wanted to say: "Very nice, thank you. I imagine it's much like being a man in the wine industry."

The media loved this question, which I got often as one of the rare female CEOs who was a professional manager rather than an owner or winemaker. I came to think of it as the story that would not die—yet I was grateful for the publicity opportunities this question offered for St. Supéry. So I usually tried to answer helpfully.

Even so, I nearly blew it when a reporter for *Fortune* magazine called, and I thoughtlessly responded "Oh, that again?"

Mentally kicking myself, I quickly added there were many angles that had not yet been explored and offered encouraging suggestions and additional sources to the reporter. The result was a seven-page article in the April 2000 issue of *Fortune* with one-third of its title spread devoted to

a color photo of St. Supéry's CEO. This visual honor was certainly due to me being the only one to show up for the photo session wearing the black blazer normally reserved for my frequent business trips to New York. This was *Fortune*, after all, not our local favorite *Wine Business Monthly*.

186

The six other women pictured in the article wore typical wine country work clothing that apparently resonated less with Manhattan photo editors.

It will be a fine day in America when women's contributions are more newsworthy than their scarcity in leadership roles.

58 BONVERRE

In the early days of St. Supéry we had more grapes from our two estate vineyards in Napa Valley than brand equity, which is even slower to develop than vineyards. Such an imbalance requires creative solutions unless one is prepared to undermine long-term brand positioning to address a short-term oversupply problem.

I believed that brand building was key to the long-term financial health of St. Supéry, so we chose not to flood the market with all the St. Supéry-labeled wine we were then capable of producing. That would have sent prices tumbling and forever condemned the brand to suboptimal margins.

There are other ways to deal with excess inventory, whether grapes or wine. Obviously, one can sell grapes—if there are interested buyers. Even in the vaunted Napa Valley, demand for grapes goes up and down, usually with a significant lag to what's going on in the bottled wine market. Another is to sell excess wine on the bulk market, but supply and demand, and therefore prices, fluctuate there even more than in the grape market. It is rarely the most remunerative solution. The other options of private label or buyers' own brand wines were common in the UK market but had not yet appeared in California.

With every price point today teeming with competitors, it is difficult to believe that in the early 1990s there was a gaping hole for an $8 brand. Gallo and the fighting varietals producers dominated the low end of the market, and Napa/Sonoma the high end. Remarkably, the middle was wide open.

Bonverre was thus born of necessity and opportunity. It differed from a typical winery second label in being based on a surplus of estate fruit, rather than on grapes or wine deemed unsuitable for a winery's main brand. It offered a more controllable, more profitable way to deal with excess fruit than the grape or bulk wine markets. And we could have a little fun with it, since it wasn't the primary brand. Bonverre's tongue-in-cheek packaging would bring a bit of rare humor to the sober-sided wine business.

The name Bonverre was pure invention, resulting from a few hours of playing with words on my computer. It can be loosely understood as "good glass."

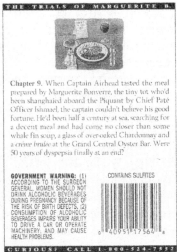

BONVERRE

CALIFORNIA
CHARDONNAY

LOT NUMBER 7

PRODUCED AND BOTTLED BY BONVERRE VINEYARDS
RUTHERFORD, CALIFORNIA, USA ALCOHOL 12.5% BY VOLUME

THE TRIALS OF MARGUERITE B.

Chapter 9. When Captain Airhead tasted the meal prepared by Marguerite Bonverre, the tiny tot who'd been shanghaied aboard the Piquant by Chief Pâté Officer Ishmael, the captain couldn't believe his good fortune. He'd been half a century at sea, searching for a decent meal and had come no closer than some whale fin soup, a glass of over-oaked Chardonnay and a *crème brulée* at the Grand Central Oyster Bar. Were 50 years of dyspepsia finally at an end?

GOVERNMENT WARNING: (1) ACCORDING TO THE SURGEON GENERAL, WOMEN SHOULD NOT DRINK ALCOHOLIC BEVERAGES DURING PREGNANCY BECAUSE OF THE RISK OF BIRTH DEFECTS. (2) CONSUMPTION OF ALCOHOLIC BEVERAGES IMPAIRS YOUR ABILITY TO DRIVE A CAR OR OPERATE MACHINERY, AND MAY CAUSE HEALTH PROBLEMS.

CONTAINS SULFITES

CURIOUS? CALL 1-800-524-7552

I enjoyed developing the packaging with designer Marianne Agnew. We had already decided to create a story for Bonverre, which quickly became the adventures of tiny Marguerite Marie Madeleine Bonverre. Marianne created a Bonverre family crest bearing daisies in her honor (in French, daisies are *marguerites*), and added the sailing ship—anachronistically looking like the Santa Maria—that transported our young heroine and her family across the Atlantic to Ellis Island. The final flourishes were a glass of wine and a *fleur de lis*, all topped by a banner exhorting us to *"Buvez un bon verre de vin."*

To capture the imagination of consumers, we developed an illustrated back label saga recounting chapters in the exciting life of an intrepid 10-year-old French immigrant on her own in America, back in the day. With each vintage and varietal we published four consecutive chapters so fans wouldn't have to wait a year for the next installment. Marianne, longtime Domaine Chandon and St. Supéry newsletter writer Herb McGrew, and I had a fine time creating some forty illustrated mini-chapters of *The Trials of Marguerite B.* over the brief lifespan of Bonverre.

For McGrew those precious 100 words on a back label were a wonderful challenge, as difficult as writing poetry. Early on he condensed our heroine's full name to tiny Marguerite to save space. Puns and alliteration abounded. I loved the story line, the Beth Leeds watercolor illustrations art directed by Marianne, and the whole creative process.

Shanghai'd on arrival in America, brave young Marguerite extricated herself from a series of misadventures by using the culinary gifts she learned at her *maman's* knee. She tamed Brix Baxter the beastly pirate captain with her heavenly *choucroûte*. She barely survived the long wait for spring to free her popular Hudson Valley river restaurant, *l'Ile Flottante*, from its icy prison on the Erie Canal by inventing and selling Buffalo Chicken Wings. Her Thanksgiving brownies brought peace to the Iroquois Nation. She headed west, escorted by a pudgy pastry-loving former pirate, into territory where the locals favored guns, not buns.

The excellent quality Napa Valley appellation Cabernet, Chardonnay, and Merlot we offered at attractive prices under the new Bonverre label resulted in near-instant success. Distributors liked it because it was easy to sell. Consumers liked it because it offered excellent value. I enjoyed the marketing. We bottled more.

Within three years Bonverre sales had rocketed to 42,000 cases, a big number for a young winery. This had not passed unnoticed: the big boys were quick to understand they, too, could create wine brands for this and every other price point. And they had serious marketing budgets.

As more and more of our estate grapes were needed for the growing St. Supéry brand, we gradually migrated the Bonverre appellation from Napa Valley to California, supplementing our remaining excess Napa Valley fruit with purchased bulk wines. This novel idea came from St. Supéry's owner Robert Skalli, who had created a leading négociant business in the south of France for varietal wines. (While the norm in California, varietal wines were an innovation in a country where wine labels traditionally bear place names, like Bordeaux or Chablis.)

Négociant wines were then essentially unknown in Napa Valley. Today, several changes in the federal regulations later, "virtual wineries" are a widely accepted business model and négociant brands abound.

The Merlot craze exploding in the U.S. market in the early 1990s led us to another innovation. We realized that the fifty acres of Merlot originally planted at Dollarhide for blending with Cabernet was enough to bottle an estate St. Supéry Merlot.

We returned our formerly excess estate Merlot grapes from the Bonverre program to the St. Supéry portfolio. With buyers everywhere clamoring for value Merlot, we looked to the bulk market to resupply Bonverre, but the big producers had already cornered every gallon.

Discussing the supply dilemma in a meeting with Robert Skalli, he offered "But we have Merlot in France. How much would you like?" And that's how St. Supéry began importing bulk Merlot from the Languedoc for its Bonverre program.

When the first sausage-shaped container of French Merlot arrived in Rutherford, looking like a fat bomb suspended in a metal frame, we St. Supérians gathered around to marvel at this unique way of shipping bulk wine.

The next wonderment was discovering that American consumers seemed not to notice that Bonverre Merlot now bore a Vin de Pays d'Oc appellation on its front label.

We added a French-sourced Viognier to the Bonverre lineup, and reluctantly ceded to a new national sales manager's request for more serious looking packaging.

As the competition from well-funded large wineries increased, selling Bonverre became more challenging. After consulting with my friend Steve Boone, founder of the retail chain Beverages, and more! (now BevMo) about our limited ability to compete, we decided to shelve the program. Bonverre had served its purpose of profitably using the surplus grapes from our estate vineyards as we built up the St. Supéry brand. And it had been fun.

Today, importing and exporting bulk wine is done as a matter of course, shifting with changes in supply and foreign exchange rates. Big producers import inexpensive wines from afar as needed to fuel their mass-market labels. They also export bulk wine for bottling in the market where the wine will be sold, to save the expense of shipping heavy glass. While many of these value wines have critter labels or cute brand names, few offer an entertaining read on the back label.

59 ANOTHER VINOUS ADVENTURE

I don't remember which was our first vintage of Mt. Madrona, but it was in the early 1990s. This was the original name for St. Supéry's kosher wine, which we changed to Mt. Maroma when a winery in the Sierra Foothills named Madroña objected to our label.

Making kosher wine was one of several tactics we employed to put more of our 500 acres of grapes to beneficial use; the nascent St. Supéry brand couldn't yet absorb that much. The idea came from owner Robert Skalli, who knew that a number of Bordeaux châteaux set aside a small part of annual production for top quality kosher wine.

There was only one problem with this plan: no one at St. Supéry knew anything about kosher wine production. Several of us had heard of Mogen David and Manischewitz, but those wines were from a distant world. And so began another phase of our winemaking education.

We learned that the Orthodox Union (OU) divides the U.S. into two regions for certifying kosher wines and, on a much larger scale, food products. The first step to kosher certification was to pay $2,500 for an annual license, a large expense to spread over our planned small production. This entitled us to add the OU emblem to our labels, certifying that the wine is kosher—provided we follow the processing rules.

Wine certified at the lower, less expensive level remained kosher only if opened and served by a rabbi. Since there aren't enough rabbis for all those who might wish to invite one to dinner, we elected the higher level of kosher certification, known as mevushal. Civilians can open and serve mevushal wine without causing it to lose its kosher status, which is particularly useful for wines sold in restaurants.

Our UC Davis-trained winemaker was appalled to learn that traditionally, mevushal status was achieved by boiling the wine. Today, technology provides a better solution: flash pasteurization. We acquired a used flash pasteurizer from a Sonoma dairy that could raise the temperature of liquid very quickly to 140 degrees, and immediately cool it. The process had the unexpected benefit of "fixing" or preserving the fruit characters in the wine, so it had a surprisingly positive impact on wine quality.

The other requirement for making kosher wine is that a rabbi must be the only person to touch the wine during processing. The head man at OU headquarters in Los Angeles would assign one of his rabbinical students to be the "hands on" person whenever cellar operations required the wine to be touched, e.g., during fermentation, transferring from one tank to another, filtering, topping up barrels, etc. (Interestingly, rabbis weren't required to pick the grapes for kosher wines.)

St. Supéry was paying the rabbi's salary and travel expenses, so we did our best to organize kosher cellar operations to minimize his wine country visits. Before returning to Los Angeles, the rabbi would place a seal on each fermentation tank and barrel to assure the wine's kosher status was maintained in his absence.

That first kosher crush was challenging. Our production crew was working long shifts to process hundreds of tons of grapes for St. Supéry and its custom crush clients, and by the time we started on the kosher Chardonnay and Cabernet project they were exhausted and irritable. The additional layer of complication—teaching the visiting rabbi how to handle pumps, hoses, fittings, barrels and filters properly, and especially coping with the lack of operational flexibility—eventually caused so much disruption that we nearly had a mutiny among the increasingly cranky cellar rats.

Just before blowing a figurative gasket, our winemaker either remembered or discovered that a large custom crush facility in Sonoma named Vinwood had an employee on its production team who happened to be a rabbi. In mid-crush, we outsourced all kosher winemaking to Vinwood.

The following year we knew better what to expect and how to plan for it, so we took the kosher winemaking back in-house to eliminate the incremental expense of outsourcing.

Once we were set up for kosher winemaking, Ernie Weir, a former colleague from Domaine Chandon, brought his first Hagafen wines to St. Supéry for kosher vinification.

This time, Los Angeles assigned us two rabbinical students. One was large and jolly and friendly; the other old before his time, and aloof. His superiors quickly recalled the jolly one.

Rabbi Ben stayed on, and we all grew to like him even if he wouldn't shake hands with any of the women. He was our kosher guy until we terminated the program after a few years. The St. Supéry brand was growing fast, offering a higher return on those estate grapes.

60 PHYLLOXERA

Just as the Skallis were nearly finished planting 475 acres of new vines at Dollarhide Ranch, my alma mater, UC Davis, announced that AxR-1, the rootstock it had been recommending for years, was susceptible to phylloxera.

Phylloxera is the microscopic root louse that had devastated the vineyards of Europe and California a century earlier; the solution had been to replant desirable European wine grape varieties onto phylloxera-resistant American rootstocks.

This was very bad news in 1989, since by then 75 percent of Napa Valley vineyard acreage was planted on the otherwise high-performing AxR-1 rootstock. Phylloxera blazed through the valley floor in the early 1990s, killing vines in two to three years by devouring their root systems. This scourge, which created a huge demand for capital to replant, was among the reasons for Robert Mondavi Winery's decision to go public in 1993.

It took until 1996 for phylloxera to manifest at Dollarhide; its mountain location provided a temporary buffer from the carnage on the valley floor. Another bit of not-quite-accidental good fortune was that only half of Dollarhide's vines had been planted on AxR-1.

In the early 1980s, Robert Skalli had hired Professeur Denis Boubals of the *Université de Montpellier* to consult on developing Dollarhide Ranch. As one of the most respected viticulturists in France, his credentials were impeccable.

Professor Boubals had explained that AxR-1 has a small amount of vinifera genetic material that makes it susceptible to phylloxera and that although this rootstock had performed well originally when tried in French vineyards in the 1920s, it had collapsed before the expected productive lifetime of a commercial vineyard. So it had been removed from the list of recommended rootstocks in France.

Dollarhide's vineyard manager discounted the professor's counsel to avoid using AxR-1 rootstock, noting that "things are different here in

California." The compromise had been to plant only half the Dollarhide vineyard on AxR-1, with the rest on reliable old St. George rootstock.

I doubt Professor Boubals ever said "I told you so," but he might have been tempted.

It was a hard time. Afflicted vineyard owners shook their heads in disbelief (denial), then furiously demanded why Davis had recommended this rootstock for so many years (anger), then set about trying to figure out a solution that wouldn't break the bank (bargaining), grew saddened by the sight of their vineyards dying off (depression) and finally started planning for the future (acceptance).

Then followed an additional stage not to be found among the five "grief" classic ones: the forceful conviction, at least here in Napa Valley, that this disaster would have a silver lining.

The untimely replanting of most of Napa's vineyards, some only a few years old when phylloxera took them down, created the opportunity to apply recent viticultural learning that would otherwise have had to wait out a normal commercial vineyard life cycle of 25-30 years.

As a result, vineyards in the Napa Valley and other areas where phylloxera had struck were replanted on a broad selection of new rootstocks (except AxR-1). No one would ever again risk a rootstock monoculture.

The new rootstocks, and some old tried and true ones, were carefully matched to certified clonal selections, and to specific microclimates and soils. Updated thinking on which varieties to plant where (and why), trellising, row orientation, vine spacing, and irrigation practices all made these new plantings far superior.

Some growers and wineries went into organic and a few even further, into biodynamic farming. Grape quality made a great leap forward, pushing Napa Valley wines to new heights and resulting in sales that helped pay off those big loans.

61 CALL IN THE EXPERTS

The wine industry has long been notorious for its lack of useful data, partly because so few wine companies are publicly traded, but also because there are so many different business models. This contributes to the difficulty of making decisions, especially given the lengthy cycles for vineyards, winemaking, and brand building. This also makes comparing one's performance to competitors a challenge.

Vic Motto, whose accounting firm Motto Kryla Fisher (MKF) reviewed St. Supéry's financial statements every year, also offered consulting advice to client wineries. Eventually consulting became MKF's primary business.

I occasionally called on Vic as a wine industry expert when I needed an independent third party opinion to back me up in board meetings. Until St. Supéry made its first profit in 1996, I was subject to an insistent drumbeat from St. Supéry's shareholders to get there faster. My response was always the same: we were doing the right things, and building for long-term success. That patiently repeated explanation did little to halt the nudging.

So I invited Vic to a board meeting in 1995 to lay out for the shareholders the typical growth pattern of a vertically-integrated Napa Valley winery. This was nothing new. I had often presented this information, but it was time for them to hear it from someone else. Enter Vic.

He laid out the rule of thumb for a vertically-integrated premium wine business starting from bare land, through bricks and mortar and inventory buildup, to breakeven: it takes ten years *from the time you have something to sell* to make a profit. This time, the shareholders heard the message and dropped their wishful contention that the ten years began with investing in bare land.

None of us will ever forget Vic's communicative illustration, quickly sketched with a green marker on the conference room whiteboard: St. Supéry was still a sapling that would one day grow into a giant sequoia. Since that meeting, any mention of a sequoia would start the entire board of directors chuckling.

Today, owning a bricks and mortar winery is no longer part of the federal permit requirement to make and sell wine. Not investing in vineyards and a winery greatly reduces capital needs, and a new (to Napa, anyway) business model developed. A clever négociant can buy bulk wines, blend, and bottle them in someone else's winemaking facility and— if a good salesman—sell the labeled wine before the bills come due. The rule of thumb still applies to the "bare ground to saleable inventory" model, but there are faster paths to profitability.

MKF developed one of the best sales tools I ever used. It was a benchmarking study based on their access to nearly 300 Napa and Sonoma winery clients' financial reporting and related company information like sales volumes, pricing, product lines, and distribution.

If the anonymous, aggregated data showed that a winery like St. Supéry should expect to sell eight percent of its total Sauvignon Blanc volume in Texas but sales there were only five percent, distributor performance discussions could be data-driven and more productive. Distributors were just as starved for market information as wineries, and were interested in and accepting of the benchmarking information. I was disappointed when MKF stopped producing this useful analytic tool after a couple of years.

Another smart data accumulator, Silicon Valley Bank's fine wine division, uses access to its numerous winery clients' financial information to build peer groups with similarly anonymous, aggregated data. The peer groups are customized for volume, price point, years in operation, financing, and profitability. These comparisons, though imperfect due to the multiplicity of business models in the wine industry, help bank clients evaluate their relative performance.

The largest wineries can afford internal market research departments, but it wasn't until formation of Wine Market Council (WMC) in 1994 that market research became affordable for smaller producers.

Since its inception, WMC has conducted an extensive annual tracking study that follows wine trends in the U.S. It was this study that first alerted vintners to the early adoption of wine by Millennials, or Echo Boomers, important because this young cohort of 70 million will eventually replace the 77 million Boomers who have been driving wine consumption in the U.S. since the 1960s. With the Millennials all of legal age in 2015, we're waiting to see how the iGeneration will behave.

In recent years WMC has added topical research projects, including "Wine and the Economy" throughout and following the 2007-2009 recession, "The Boomers," and a focus group on Millennials. In progress: an in-depth look at wine clubs and another on direct-to-consumer sales.

American Generations
(Age ranges in 2015)

WW II (83 and over) 12 Million

Swing (70 - 82) 30 Million

Boomer (51 - 69) 77 Million

Generation X (39 - 50) 44 Million

Millennial (21 - 38) 70 Million

iGeneration (6 – 20) 61 Million

Wine **Market**
COUNCIL

Source: American Demographics, Census Bureau

The democratization of market research has been greatly aided by the Internet. Surveys that used to cost many thousands of dollars can now be cheaply and effectively implemented online. Even small producers can use Survey Monkey to find out what their customers are thinking. Transforming the resulting data into information, however, remains an art.

62 RESPECT FOR THE LAW

I am in the minority of Americans who like attorneys. I married one. It is partly his influence that led me to prefer lawyers who act as strategic business advisors, and avoid those with a preference for sparring and litigation. As the chapter on my dealings with the UFW will demonstrate, there are sound reasons for these preferences.

In the wine business, it's easy to run afoul of the law. Nearly anything creative, especially in marketing and sales, is likely to be illegal. There are federal and state laws to respect, and they aren't always synchronous. Compliance is a major task, made less labor-intensive in recent years by technology but still burdensome.

The former Bureau of Alcohol, Tobacco & Firearms, or BATF (which now bears "Explosives" at the end of its original name), an unholy trio lodged in the Department of the Treasury, is charged with approving the layout and information on every wine label, ostensibly to protect consumers from false or misleading statements about the product.

With the BATF already spending eighty percent of its time on guns and explosives, and with more than 130,000 wine labels submitted annually for approval, this administrative task took up most of the BATF's limited staff time for wine. They had few resources to devote to other forms of compliance.

The label approval process can be arbitrary, with previously approved label designs coming back rejected, or noncompliant labels easily winning approval. Many vintners would resubmit a rejected label in the hope that a different reviewer would approve it, which worked surprisingly often.

Vintners found it amusing, and annoying, that statements implying that a wine might have some therapeutic value, including words as innocent (and true) as "refreshing" or "healthy," would earn immediate rejection for their labels. BATF also rejected labels depicting naked ladies, although their attitude seems to have softened in recent years.

With the stage set, I will share a tale that demonstrates the need for attorneys who specialize in wine law, like my good friend Jim Seff of Pillsbury Winthrop Shaw Pittman LLP.

One of St. Supéry's custom bottling clients was a small Napa winery that had been sold by the Skoda family, when its patriarch died, to Fred Franzia, owner of the major Central Valley wine company named Bronco.

The former Skoda Works (as we called it) was named Rutherford Vintners and was, in fact, located in Rutherford. At first, Franzia continued to bottle Napa Valley wines under its Rutherford *Vineyards* (this minor name change later proved important) label, though the brand soon switched to a broader California appellation as it sourced grapes farther afield.

In accordance with BATF regulations, all of our custom services clients' wines were made and/or bottled under St. Supéry's federal permit, making St. Supéry responsible for obtaining their label approvals and reporting on production.

The first problem arose when Rutherford Vineyards asked us to obtain approval for a new label indicating that the Chardonnay to be bottled had been barrel fermented. Having vinified this wine, we knew that was not true and refused to submit for approval until the label was corrected. It was, and we did, and the corrected label was approved.

A bigger problem developed when Franzia began running full page, four-color ads for Rutherford Vineyards in the *Wine Spectator* showing a beautiful Napa Valley scene that prominently featured a row of rural mailboxes labeled with Cakebread, Beaulieu, and other familiar Rutherford winery names.

The ad's tagline was "Rutherford. It's the Neighborhood." The inference was that Rutherford Vineyards Cabernet came from the prized Rutherford appellation, even though the bottle shot clearly showed its correct California appellation on the front label.

Napa Valley vintners and growers are justifiably protective of their appellation(s), and this potentially misleading advertisement made some of them angry.

Larry Bettinelli, a grower, complained to BATF about the Rutherford Vineyards ad. The BATF, which had had contentious dealings with Franzia in the past, was eager to open an investigation. The ads were withdrawn.

Given Franzia's well-documented history of thumbing his nose at regulators, the BATF was not about to stop there. Their investigation turned to St. Supéry's production and bottling records for the Franzia-owned wines.

They discovered that Rutherford Vineyards had never been registered as a dba by Rutherford Vintners. This was a technicality, but it would do. Gotcha! The problem was, of course, that it wasn't Franzia the feds got, it was permit-holder St. Supéry.

This is where Jim Seff comes in. When the BATF announces, grimly, that you're in trouble even if they're really after Fred Franzia, you phone your attorney. It is a measure of how much the BATF wanted to nab Franzia that they sent a high-level bureaucrat from Washington, D.C., a tiny, gray-haired bulldog named Harriet Bobo to our dispute negotiation meeting in San Francisco. (Jim later told me that she had changed the spelling of her name from Beaubeau because no one could pronounce it properly.)

Harriet was out for blood. If she couldn't have Franzia's, she'd take some of ours. Fortunately, St. Supéry had good documentation on the "barrel fermented" label incident, proving our *bona fides* and respect for the rules.

After hours of careful (and carefully recorded) verbal fencing between Harriet and Jim, she backed off her original demand for a $30,000 fine and agreed to reduce the penalty to $20,000. It was a ridiculously unfair situation, but Jim was wise to the ways of BATF and kept me from making it worse by pointing that out to Ms. Bobo.

We invited Rutherford Vineyards to take its business elsewhere.

If only I hadn't made the mistake of assuming that Rutherford Vintners had done what wineries typically do: add dbas covering every possible permutation and combination of their brand name (e.g., Rutherford Vineyards, Rutherford Cellars, Rutherford Wines) to their basic permit. It would have saved St. Supéry a $20,000 fine, plus attorneys' fees. And a black eye with the BATF.

Earlier in our custom services relationship, Fred Franzia had wanted to meet Robert Skalli to discuss whether there might be additional ways they could work together, perhaps with the French wines from Skalli. Leery of Franzia's reputation for operating as close as possible to the edges of the law, I made a point of joining them for dinner. I'll never know what kind of hard luck and trouble I saved Robert and probably myself by advising against expanding dealings with Franzia beyond custom services, but I'm grateful he took my counsel.

63 THE WINE AUCTION

Domaine Chandon had been a member of the Napa Valley Vintners Association (NVVA) and I had served on numerous committees over the years. When I joined St. Supéry in 1988, NVVA asked if I would serve on its board of directors. I saw this invitation as both a community obligation and an opportunity to learn from my peers, and quickly accepted. I served from 1989 through 2003, an experience that helped me, and young St. Supéry immeasurably.

NVVA board of directors in 1989. Author is front row left.

Then NVV started asking when I could chair the June wine auction. This major annual fundraiser, originally modeled on the Hospices de Beaune, had been organized and run by vintners and volunteers since its inception in 1981. Sooner or later, as a winery principal it would be my turn to serve.

I was willing but wary, knowing that this honor would not be without risk. Several previous auction chairs' businesses had suffered because of the intense, 18-month commitment.

By 1997, I was beginning to feel comfortable that St. Supéry could spare some of my time. Hoping my involvement would give our wines broader exposure to fine wine enthusiasts and collectors, I accepted the responsibility of chairing the 1998 Napa Valley Wine Auction.

This became an even greater challenge when the sole auction employee, Shirley Knudsen, unexpectedly resigned. This left me and her successor Stacey Dolan with neither a road map nor the benefit of her 17 years of auction experience. Fortunately, there were returnees among the 30 volunteer steering committee chairs to provide continuity.

The Napa Valley Wine Auction board of directors was always concerned that the auction be properly understood as a charitable enterprise rather than as self-promotion for Napa Valley wines. Nevertheless, it was clear that bidders were attracted for reasons in addition to philanthropy, so I set out to make the 1998 auction entertaining for the attendees as well as financially successful for the beneficiaries.

With a small operating budget, a large steering committee, an attentive board of directors, and one thousand volunteers, running this business-for-a-year could be a formidable task. I felt fortunate to have learned the value of delegating, and thoroughly enjoyed being the temporary custodian of this worthy project. Three incidents, only one of them planned, will give you the flavor of "my" auction.

A perennial problem was enticing the guests away from the outdoor sparkling wine reception and into the big tent so the live auction could begin. My solution was to add to the vintners' Big Bottle Parade a lively troupe of Brazilian dancers and musicians to lead everyone inside. The dancers would be brightly costumed in Mardi Gras bling, festooned with sequins and plumes, and sporting (gasp) thongs. How could that fail to attract willing followers?

To my disappointment, this was considered too risqué. Instead of thongs the dancers covered their toned bottoms with diaphanous skirts decorated with feathers and sequins. Their colorful costumes, lively music, and contagious energy did successfully lure the guests into the tent, but it could have been even more fun.

The weather in early June is generally fair, and occasionally hot. In 1998, Napa Valley was unseasonably cold and gray. This boosted sales of auction logo sweatshirts, but rain threatened to derail the plans for the post-auction supper outside on the Meadowood fairway.

Stacey and I and Linda Rieff, executive director of NVVA, were outside the tent huddled over weather updates as the live auction bidding began early in the afternoon. Linda and Stacey wanted to move the supper under the shelter of the tent, but I was in favor of maintaining the original *al fresco* plan. A decision had to be made within the next half hour to allow time for the crew to implement changes, as seating 2,000 people for a meal is a major logistical feat.

Chris Ligouri, a thoughtful former FBI agent who had volunteered to chair the security committee, had been observing this discussion from a few feet away. Sensing an impasse, she pointed toward the tent and suggested "Why not ask them?" Brilliant!

We then did something that had never happened before: we halted the live auction. I climbed onto the stage to explain the threatening weather issue and the need for an immediate decision. I then asked for a show of hands from those risk-takers present who were willing to bet it wouldn't rain. Fortified by great wines and excited by auction action, a large majority cheered and raised their hands.

I then asked the risk-averse who feared it would rain to vote. A scattering of hands went up, but there was a clear mandate for sticking with the original plan. The live auction resumed, ultimately yielding $3.8 million for the beneficiaries.

The post-auction outdoor supper, featuring a delicious Mexican menu prepared by Meadowood's chef de cuisine Pilar Sanchez, turned out to be memorable for another reason. Someone launched a tortilla into the air. (A surprising number of vintners have confided to me they were the first to let fly.) Someone else retaliated. Within seconds the Napa Valley version of a food fight ensued, with hundreds of tortillas sailing around like frisbees. It didn't last long, but it was fun.

The instant the dance band finished playing at the scheduled hour of 10:00 p.m., the skies opened and down came the rain.

One privilege of chairing the auction is hosting the "big bidder" dinner the night before. We decided to do a Tuscan dinner among the vines at my home. Remembering the chickens loose in the courtyard at Badia a Coltibuono (highly recommended wines, olive oil, and restaurant, not to mention Lorenza di Medici's cooking school), I asked our vineyard office manager to raise a dozen chicks. She jury-rigged a cardboard carton that had once contained a refrigerator with a light bulb for warmth, and installed the chicks. They soon graduated to an outdoor pen.

On party day, the 6-month old birds were released into my garden to add to the décor. I thought they might wander off, or run away in fright. No, they mingled with the 100 guests, seated at long tables in the vine rows, and happily scratched and pecked for bugs. One young bird showed a macabre interest in the grill where chickens were browning nicely. After the party, I kept six of them and sent the rest back to the ranch. It was a pleasure to find that, once they started laying, "the girls" produced green, brown, tan, and white eggs for us to enjoy.

A perennial dilemma is the June auction's dress code, "Napa Valley casual." Here are interpretations from (left to right) previous chairs Karen Cakebread, Beth Novak Milliken, Janet Pagano, Paula Kornell, the author, Mary Novak, and Nancy Duckhorn. Anything goes, from strapless dresses to cowboy boots. My choice was linen.

Several years later it was decided that all 24 preceding auction chairs should team up to co-chair the 25th auction, now renamed Auction Napa Valley by the renamed Napa Valley Vintners.

These two dozen movers and shakers, all strong leaders and supporters of Napa Valley Vintners activities, had been pondering better ways to deal with the challenges they had faced when individually chairing the auction. They had big ideas. The first planning meeting auction ran for hours, as all 24 co-chairs shared their accumulated wisdom to improve the 25th auction.

It was a marathon meeting. We eventually realized that if we couldn't restrain ourselves, or at least manage to be brief, our next meeting would end with the co-chairs falling asleep, hurting one another, or giving up. With that insight, we started operating as a team and the planning progressed smoothly.

The 25th auction incorporated a number of the past chairs' long-cherished innovations and was, as usual, a success. It raised more than $10 million for the beneficiaries.

For what is probably my final Auction Napa Valley role, Molly Chappellet invited me to serve on the steering committee for the 2012 auction chaired by her family. I was happy to accept, and volunteered to take on the public relations committee. It was fun to be working with the vintners again after my mid-2009 retirement from St. Supéry.

A trained artist, Molly's "look and feel" incorporated massive installations depicting the life cycle of grapevines from birth to ashes, accompanied by imaginative jazz and classical music piped throughout Meadowood's grounds. Unusually, almost all of the decoration was outdoors; inside, the auction tent itself was bare except for jumbo TV screens high behind the stage to ensure that all 800 guests could track the fast-moving action.

ANV 2012 brought in more than $8 million in spirited bidding. A clear signal that the effects of the Great Recession were fading away was the huge success of Auction Napa Valley 2013, which raised $16.9 million.

Over the past three and a half decades, Auction Napa Valley has distributed well more than $145 million to the local beneficiaries—primarily health care, youth, education, and housing programs—that fill needs in the community.

64 MEDIA TRAINING

The joke among consultants is that you fly in, provide your advice and an invoice, and depart, leaving the client to make it work.

Most of the consultants I have known have offered useful information and guidance. Some have provided excellent value for money. When there's an important problem to be solved and the expertise isn't available internally, the right consultant can be invaluable.

Media training is an excellent example.

Winery spokespersons, if they are to be effective, often need to be taught how to communicate desired messages clearly. Few face challenges from investigative reporters, since wine stories are seldom controversial—but it can happen. More often, the problem is a garbled message or a missed opportunity.

When our public relations agency suggested media training, I readily agreed. I had no idea this would involve revealing videotapes of me making error after error.

The first media training session I endured was a real eye-opener. I didn't know I had so many tics, avoided making eye contact, and said "uh..." so often. (I am more poised and articulate when speaking French, possibly because I was reading elegant, classical French literature in grad school.)

Tics aside, it was useful to learn not to rise to the bait instead of making a smart aleck remark when asked a provocative question, and how to bridge to the points I wanted to make rather than simply answer the question as posed. This training made me a greatly improved winery spokesperson—when I remembered to use it.

My preference is to speak extemporaneously, and usually I get away with it. On the rare occasions when I prepare extensive notes, or even write a real speech, the delivery falters. I once spent all fourteen hours of a flight from San Francisco to Sydney writing and rewriting a speech to be delivered at Australia's annual wine industry conference. My assigned topic, the future of wine in America, was vast. When the time came, I ignored my scribbled speech and delivered an extemporaneous talk that ran unpardonably long past the scheduled 30 minutes.

When I was invited to speak about foreign investment in the wine industry to a conference for certified public accountants—this was, I believe, Vic Motto's idea—I again wrote out a speech, this time because I thought accurate figures would be important to a group of professional number crunchers. I read the speech carefully, certain that my lack of eye contact and animation was putting the audience to sleep. The CPAs applauded when I finished. Either the content was interesting enough to overcome the presentation, or they were simply relieved I had finished reading aloud.

In his native French Robert Skalli is a polished spokesperson. In English, he felt on less certain ground. In a media training session intended to set him at ease with American media, I played the part of interviewer while the professional trainer observed and offered feedback.

She collapsed when I asked him to talk about the prophylactic methods used in vineyards in the south of France. Since we were using the word in its French sense, neither Robert nor I understood why she couldn't stop laughing. I believe that videotape is in her media training hall of fame.

Another time we decided that vineyard manager Josh, our bright and entrepreneurial former college football star, would make an excellent spokesperson for St. Supéry. Surrounded by dirt and dogs, he was in his element and could talk to anyone, including large groups, for hours. Waxing enthusiastic about viticulture, the market, wines, heirloom turkeys, he was downright eloquent.

I didn't know until our public relations agency put him in a conference room full of marketing people and turned on the video camera that he would freeze. He was in agony, too uncomfortable to speak. Fortunately, one of the trainers understood and called off the session before we further traumatized him.

65 FOR SALE

I flew to Paris in 2000 prepared for what I expected to be a typical all-day St. Supéry board meeting. After greeting me, Robert Skalli ushered me into an adjacent conference room full of investment bankers from Crédit Lyonnais and Crédit Agricole. He introduced me, asked me to brief them on St. Supéry, and returned to his office.

It's fair to say that I was nonplussed. Investment bankers help clients buy and sell businesses. I had had no indication that the Skallis were thinking of selling St. Supéry, which could be the only reason for me to brief these bankers. I spent several hours doing my best to explain the business and answer the bankers' questions, but I was in a state of shock.

Later, Robert explained that one of the minority family shareholders had, for personal reasons, expressed a desire to be bought out. That had necessarily launched a valuation of the family's extensive holdings. The rather large numbers thus revealed caused additional family members not actively involved in running the businesses to decide they, too, would like to cash out.

To accommodate their desires, some part of the family enterprises would have to be sold. As St. Supéry was the only Skalli owned entity located outside France and its sale should generate sufficient cash to buy the shares proffered, it was the natural choice. Enter the investment bankers. My job description had just expanded to include helping sell the business named St. Supéry.

Usually when a business is offered for sale, the investment bankers prepare a detailed memorandum outlining its assets, performance, and potential. They then share this document with a carefully selected list of likely buyers, who sign confidentiality agreements in exchange for a look. Confidentiality is intended to protect the interests of both buyers and sellers.

In this case, the offering memorandum was scattered to nearly all of the larger wine businesses in California, and some in Europe. This put me in a difficult position. My boss had sworn me to secrecy, but my management team was hearing from indiscreet industry colleagues that they'd seen a document offering St. Supéry for sale. Naturally my team reported this to me, and I reported it to Robert Skalli. I told him it was untenable to withhold information from my team, and got his agreement to work out a "stay" bonus program for them.

For nearly a year we met with New York-based executives of Crédit Lyonnais and Crédit Agricole, and various potential buyers. I was assigned to make the sales pitch and although my heart was not in it I did my best to carry out the family's wishes. Selling a business that you've helped build for the long term is hard, especially when the future giant sequoia is not yet an adolescent.

During this anxious period St. Supéry suffered some damage. In spite of my best efforts to persuade him to wait it out, our star quality winemaker accepted a job from a small winery that offered more security and, a rarity in the wine business, a promise of equity.

Thanks to the wine industry's efficient gossip mill, St. Supéry's distributors got wind of a possible sale. Fearing distributor changes under new ownership, they shifted attention to suppliers they expected to continue to represent in the future. Sales sagged.

I sensed that I wasn't the only one whose heart wasn't in it. For nearly two decades St. Supéry had been Robert Skalli's pride and joy; he had agreed to sell from his strong sense of family unity. Throughout that long year he seemed uncharacteristically deflated, and did not participate in meetings with potential buyers.

When serious negotiations developed with a certain buyer, I decided it was finally time to give up my good soldier role and speak my mind. I upset the investment bankers by saying in a meeting with the buyer that I believed Robert Skalli didn't really want to sell St. Supéry. "Oh yes he does!" asserted a banker who probably wanted to throttle me.

Soon after, I privately shared with Robert my true feeling about the offer on the table: it wasn't a good deal. Besides, I added, I didn't believe he really wanted to sell. I'll never know whether this burst of frankness had any impact on the family's ultimate decision to abandon the idea of selling St. Supéry, but it was important to me to tell him what I thought about it. To my surprise the Skalli family instead sold almost all of their pasta businesses in 2001.

Today, St. Supéry is the sole remaining wine business owned by the Skalli family. They sold their French wine assets in 2011 to the same family, the Boissets, from whom they had bought the St. Supéry winery site in Rutherford in 1986.

66 REMEMBERING 9/11

After an all-day meeting in Paris with St. Supéry's board of directors, I was en route back to San Francisco on a nonstop United flight. We were only three hours away from landing in SFO when the pilot tersely announced that we would be putting down in Calgary in 20 minutes. Anxiously, the passenger seated next to me turned and asked *"C'est normal?"*

Most of the passengers were probably worrying about whether there was something wrong with the aircraft, but not me. I was thinking about how any delay could derail two tightly scheduled events that had taken months to organize.

I had plans to fly to Seattle the next day to conduct a St. Supéry tasting for the Wine Society there, followed by another for the Wenatchee Wine Society in Leavenworth, WA, on September 13. Both events had been organized with the help of an enthusiastic St. Supéry wine club member from Wenatchee, Alex Saliby. There was little margin for error under the best of circumstances, and now I was faced with a delay of unknown proportions.

Our plane landed safely in Calgary, the first to be grounded there on the morning of September 11, 2001. It was not an emergency landing in the mechanical sense, and no one had any idea why our flight had been interrupted.

When the ground crew opened the hatch, from where I was sitting I could see the shocked faces of our flight attendants; they had clearly just received horrendous news. What could possibly have happened? Had there been a huge earthquake that closed SFO? Was San Francisco burning? Was my family safe in Napa Valley? No one was thinking in terms of terrorist attacks then.

We passengers were herded off the plane into the empty terminal, surrounded by armed airport security staff warning against cell phone use, grimly refusing to answer questions, and barking at those who protested.

It got more surreal. A security officer hollered that there would not be enough hotel rooms in Calgary for everyone, so those traveling alone should find themselves a roommate...now.

I caught the eye of another apparently solo traveler and we tacitly agreed to share. This is the only part of the story, told when he called from Paris to find out whether I was safe, which made my French boss giggle; he couldn't imagine me sharing a hotel room with a young man I'd never met.

My next thought was: did I have anything decent to sleep in? I pride myself on traveling light, and am chagrined if I return home without wearing everything I've packed. Then I remembered a pair of old boxers and a t-shirt in my carryon. Mundane details can be comforting in the face of big, bad news.

It wasn't until my new roomie, Dave, and I were in a taxi headed to our assigned Holiday Inn on the outskirts of Calgary that we heard the radio reports of terrorist attacks and the consequent devastation of the World Trade Center and Pentagon. The rest of the day Dave and I were glued to the television, numb and disbelieving. He was especially affected, being a United flight attendant himself deadheading home to Los Angeles from Paris, and he lost colleagues that day.

I was grateful to have a cell phone with international service. I loaned it to Dave to call his wife, who was understandably worried about him. I called home, and then the winery to let everyone know I was safe in Calgary. Our export manager put in a call to St. Supéry's Canadian importers to let them know I was on their turf, unexpectedly.

In circumstances this stunning, everyone wants to help. That afternoon our importer's Calgary agent and his wife came to the Holiday Inn with a basket of fruit and wine, doubly welcome for its normalcy and because the hotel amenities did not include so much as a vending machine. This gave me an idea: since we clearly would be stuck in Calgary that night, perhaps a good dinner would distract my bereaved roomie.

The agent made us a reservation at the only restaurant in Calgary that carried St. Supéry wine, a very good restaurant. Dave and I shared a fine meal and rather a lot of St. Supéry red Meritage. In my line of work one gets acclimated to eating and drinking well, but Dave wasn't in the wine business; I like to think this wine-rich dinner helped him sleep when he might otherwise have fretted throughout the night.

Certain that the world would have resumed its normal pace, the next morning I caught the 5:00 a.m. hotel shuttle back to the Calgary airport. It had become a parking lot of grounded aircraft. The other two shuttle passengers headed off to rent a car. Still expecting to catch a flight home, I entered the terminal.

The sole visible employee was sitting behind a ticket counter reading her novel, waiting for the next half-hourly update from the authorities on when flights might resume. Getting the message, I hustled over to the rental car office and offered to share gas expenses with the two Canadians driving to Vancouver. I was grateful to be on the move again.

The Canadian Rockies are beautiful, but under the circumstances none of us enjoyed the scenic drive. When it became apparent that we would not arrive in Seattle in time for my St. Supéry tasting, I called our Washington distributor to see if he could arrange a last-minute substitute.

We pulled into the silent Vancouver airport at 10:00 p.m., moments before the rental car office closed for lack of activity and well after the Seattle Wine Society tasting had ended.

I could have stayed overnight in Vancouver after that long day on the road but, anticipating massive delays at the U.S. border, I decided to drive on to Seattle that night. Like most people, I was not in the habit of carefully inspecting rental cars, except perhaps for obvious dents that someone else had caused.

Oddly, at 1:00 a.m. there were miles of cars and trucks backed up on the U.S. side waiting to enter Canada, but only six vehicles ahead of me trying to cross from Canada into the U.S.

Every vehicle was being thoroughly searched, including the undercarriage. Watching the close inspections going on ahead of me as I waited in line, a rapidly developing paranoia went into overdrive. I was imagining the contraband (or worse) that could have been secreted in or on my rental car.

The border guard carefully circled my vehicle, checking under and inside, and then reappeared at the driver's side window to announce he'd found something in the wheel well. My heart sank. He enjoyed the look on my face for a moment or two, then grinned and said "Yeah, a Coke can."

Safe and friendly as Canada is, crossing the border was a tremendous relief. I was home in the USA. I hadn't realized how anxious I had felt until that moment.

Before heading home I had to detour east into the mountains for the long-planned Wenatchee Wine Society tasting in Leavenworth. Between this commitment and the continued blockage of air transport, it took me three days to get home.

I was so happy to be back in northern California that I didn't mind the additional three hours it took to drop off the rental car and retrieve my own car, parked at SFO. Planes wouldn't be allowed to resume flying until days after my return.

Non, madame, ce n'est pas normal.

67 DISTRIBUTORS

I am not good at sales, at least in the transaction sense. I enjoy talking about concepts. This may explain my lack of success with distributors, a deficiency near the top of my long list.

Until direct shipping started taking hold in the past decade, most vintners would answer the classic marketing question "Who is your customer?" by saying "my distributors." I found this odd. Distributors are middlemen and gatekeepers, as are restaurant and retail wine buyers, but the real customer is the end user – the consumer who will choose, purchase, and drink your wine. Vintners may be forgiven for this, given the power wielded by distributors.

In the 1970s, there were enough distributors in the U.S. to represent the wines, beer, and spirits on offer. Many were family-owned businesses into their second generations, having been founded when Prohibition ended in 1933. The best of them were on a mission to develop a market for fine wine in the U.S.

One such was Tony LaBarba, founder of American Wine & Importing in Dallas. A longtime Moët distributor, he was eager to help launch Chandon sparkling wines in 1978, as he had done for other fine imported and California wines.

He did this by welcoming visiting vintners to Texas, personally introducing them to key accounts and the local media at events he organized and funded and, perhaps most importantly, by training his sales team to build brands instead of making deals. His wholesale margins were intentionally high to provide market development funding for the wines in his portfolio.

That model slowly died out as the distribution tier proceeded first through years of increasingly tight focus on cost cutting and profitability, and then on consolidation. Margins were squeezed, portfolios were cleansed of unprofitable brands, and distributor salespeople ceased developing brands and became order takers. If they had to make new placements to achieve a quota, they sold on price.

Marketing was left to the producers, rather pejoratively called "suppliers" by distributors as if we manufactured widgets instead of creating delicious wines. Eventually the distributors' *raison d'être*, the sales function, also devolved in large part to the vintner brand owners.

As a handful of large distributors grew more dominant by expanding into multiple states and absorbing smaller houses, they increasingly focused their attention on the easiest way to make money: the large, well-known wine brands that flow easily and profitably through the three-tier system.

With these well-funded mega-suppliers taking care of marketing and sales support for their own brands, the distributor role could be reduced to shipping, warehousing, and local delivery service.

Distributors did not reduce their margins (they typically pay suppliers half of a wine's recommended retail price) to reflect these reduced services; the money that had historically funded distributors' sales and marketing functions went to their bottom line.

Distributors began using the relative handful of small, fine wine brands with demand pull (i.e., with high scores from key wine critics) as leverage to place less desirable wines that had to be moved to satisfy a powerful supplier. Brands without strong pull, most of them small, languished in warehouses or were summarily dropped by their distributors.

Medium-size wineries had to fund costly incentives and discounts to obtain an occasional slot on their distributors' monthly sales quotas. Wines not promoted in this way fell to the bottom of a distributor's priority list. These increased selling expenses, along with the cost of fielding winery sales managers and representatives while still paying full distributor margins, eroded much of the profitability of sales through the distribution channel for mid-size vintners.

These changes at the distributor level encouraged the development of an alternative route to market for smaller vintners: sales directly to consumers, legal as of 2015 in all but half a dozen U.S. states.

The Internet has been a key factor in the rapid expansion of this still young direct channel, making communications with the public affordable and effective. However, like distributors taking the line of least resistance by selling solely on price, the Internet could, through its transparency and reach, ultimately become destructive by facilitating online price wars. If that happens, the last one standing turns out the lights; no one will make enough money to stay in business.

The two wineries I helped develop over forty years were mid-size wineries. They, too, struggled to succeed within an inadequate distribution system.

St. Supéry started selling, cautiously, to the trade when the winery opened in late 1989. Aware that many distributors were not interested in unproven brands, we chose to sell directly to wine merchants and restaurants in the competitive San Francisco Bay Area, with national sales manager Vivien Gay leading a team of three (all women, as it happened). Lovotti Brothers in Sacramento became our first distributor, soon joined by fine wine specialist Silenus in Boston and then Opici in New York.

National Sales Manager Vivien Gay observing the author using all ten fingers to enumerate selling points at the Opici kickoff meeting in 1991.

Before technology made information accessible, distributors generally didn't want to share account data with suppliers; they wanted to maintain control of those relationships. Similarly, winery sales managers didn't want to report where and how they were closing sales that might conflict with brand standards.

St. Supéry had been working with Lovotti for nearly a decade when I learned that our rapidly increasing Cabernet sales were due, for the most part, to Lovotti selling large volumes to Costco for its rapidly developing fine wine program.

This raised three red flags: Costco's purposefully low margins could undermine the winery's recommended retail price positioning; other desirable retail accounts might drop St. Supéry rather than try to compete with Costco; and replacement business could be hard to find if Costco dropped St. Supéry. We decided to slow a planned production increase, and work to expand our account base to minimize these risks.

It wasn't until nearly 2000 that St. Supéry had the technology to track distributor depletions by account. TradePulse reports that detailed where our wines were being sold enabled us to keep distributors and our own sales managers on brand strategy, instead of defaulting to whatever it took to achieve volume goals. Sales incentives can be very effective in achieving results, but developing a program that works *as intended* isn't easy.

Vintners have to plan for the long term, or at least the minimum three years it takes to get a red wine ready to go to market. We build inventories, of necessity. Lenders keep an eye on how well we achieve our revenue plans, because backlogged inventory is a major financial risk to us and therefore to them. When distributors don't hold up their end of the bargain by achieving the mutually agreed annual sales objectives, it causes us vintners huge headaches.

Wine producers meet regularly with distributor management to keep them informed of new products, progress against goals, and the support available to help them succeed. They listen politely, remind us how difficult the market is, describe expected or real economic vagaries, eventually agree on goals, promise they'll do their best, shake hands and usher us out the door—and usher in the next supplier for a repeat performance.

One of St. Supéry's regional sales managers colorfully told me, following a typical revolving door meeting with a distributor, that they "were blowing smoke up my skirt." He also explained that distributors privately deride what they call "supplier math," the straight line extrapolation of favorable trends often used by vintner-suppliers to develop sales goals that distributors find unreasonable.

As there are many highly successful female sales managers in the wine business, I have to accept that it was I, not gender, at least partly responsible for St. Supéry's spotty history with distributors. Perhaps this was an example of marketing (me) and sales (distributors) being like oil and water. In my defense, I don't know any vintners or brand owners who claim to be satisfied with their distributors' performance.

Nearly all distributors seem to be hoping for the Next Big Thing, like broke teenagers buying lottery tickets and hoping for a jackpot instead of looking for a job. From the moment St. Supéry entered the wholesale world in southern California (recall that we were already working with Lovotti Brothers in Sacramento and selling direct to the trade in the Bay Area), we were obliged to switch almost annually to a new distributor. Disillusioned by the lack of instant success, each soon gave up.

Distributor changes are disruptive, setting back progress by at least six months in a market-building process that takes years. In 1994, Jim Allen of Southern Wine & Spirits (SWS) broke his company's rules (statewide representation or nothing) and took on St. Supéry solely for southern California. By 1996, Vivien had been enticed away by Sonoma-Cutrer. Her successor persuaded me to give up our newly profitable, 2000-account, direct-to-trade sales operation in northern California, ceding that prime market also to SWS. If Jim did get in trouble in 1994 his gamble paid off.

St. Supéry gradually expanded into national distribution. We had long relationships with some wholesalers, like Quality in Minnesota and Opici in New York. In other markets we endured troublesome distributor changes because of poor performance, distributor consolidation, or the arrival of a St. Supéry national sales manager with a different network of sales relationships.

In spite of trying everything we could think of to make our distributor relationships work, I had the unpleasant duty of personally firing SWS at different times in three states: Florida, Nevada and, finally, even California. Southern was not happy to lose brands, even brands into which they put no effort; perhaps they didn't want suppliers going to competing wholesalers.

Having to fire employees or partners is never a pleasant situation, but powerful distributors are particularly resistant to suggestions that it's time to break up. They are not used to hearing "no." One such meeting was a courtesy call meant only to deliver the bad news, but my interlocutor thought it was a negotiating session.

After patiently explaining for the fifth time in fifteen minutes why it was time to part ways—for years St. Supéry had done everything feasible to make this work, there was no point in trying again, the partnership had not prospered, we're done—this top distributor executive started getting angry. I had begun to imagine, alone with him in a remote location, that he wasn't going to let me leave until he got the second chance he was demanding. But his company had had plenty of chances. My decision was final.

I wish there had been a better answer. St. Supéry had good wines to sell, and our prices were reasonable by Napa Valley standards. We believed in marketing, and put serious effort into building brand recognition and demand pull. We did our work, and most of theirs, but we just couldn't get our distributors consistently on board. If I sound frustrated, I was—for years. This is one part of the wine business I don't miss, although I remain fond of individuals working in the distribution tier.

Since the early days of Domaine Chandon I have listened to leading vintners and importers proclaim the need for "clout" with distributors. This translates as being economically important to your wholesalers. To achieve clout, suppliers have grown bigger through consolidating brands and wineries, growing volume, and funding discounts and promotions to push sales. Long ago I came to the conclusion that there is no such thing as enough clout—why else are suppliers still struggling to achieve it?

Distributors have been fighting direct sales for years, fearing their own obsolescence. Even as direct shipping expands from its small but growing base, few distributors understand there will always be work for them in the U.S. Lacking storage, restaurants need frequent, small deliveries from local warehouses. Large wineries need distributors to move high volumes efficiently to market. As the trend for Americans to increase their wine consumption continues its upward trajectory, high volume, low margin products will continue to pay the rent, handsomely, for distributors.

Smaller, fine wine brands have to find their own way to market.

68 RELATIONSHIP MARKETING

In the fine wine business, brands are built on memorable experiences. St. Supéry was designed to provide one, with extensive square footage devoted to a gallery of museum-quality educational exhibits, viewing windows into the barrel cellar and bottling line, and an open overhead walkway through the cellar that allowed visitors safely to see, hear, and smell winemaking in action.

Here I will digress for a moment to say that I would not have recommended investing in such an elaborate gallery, but it was ready to be built out when I arrived late in 1988. The exhibits, by museum designer Gordon Ashby, featured interesting and useful information in easily assimilated presentations that visitors could digest at their own pace. With St. Supéry's permission, the Napa Valley Vintners used a reproduction of our climate mural for years. The plan for the final exhibit, however, struck me as emblematic of everything wrong with the way wine was marketed in America.

So I changed it. Instead of a display of wine bottle shapes and the corresponding stemware—bordeaux, burgundy, champagne—that was sure to make Americans even more nervous about wine service *faux pas*, we invented a low-tech, interactive exhibit called Smellavision (see Appendix B for a detailed description) that provided a memorable "Aha!" moment for many visitors.

Unveiled in 1989, Smellavision was still being written up twenty-two years later as an "on the cheap and surprisingly effective lesson about wine and 'nose' … that linger[s] in the mind." (Discover magazine, September 2011.)

It also caught the attention of Sarah Kemp, publisher of Decanter magazine, when she visited St. Supéry shortly after the opening. She asked if we would bring it to the upcoming London Wine Trade Fair. This was a tempting offer, and would have been a fine way to focus attention on our new brand, but flying a half-ton exhibit (it was built of heavy oak) across the Atlantic was too hard to justify. So we built four portable Smellavisions and sent them instead. I still remember one nice British lady asking how we managed to get the aroma from the display bottles into the sniffer tubes.

Those portable Smellavisions were compact, dismountable, and easily shipped, and our sales managers used them for years to good effect for promotions and in U.S. markets where tastings are not allowed in stores.

The Chandon Club is probably the best example of relationship marketing I know (see Chapter 33). We were able to scale it successfully by using regular communications to encourage enthusiastic visitors to spread the word to their friends, no doubt over a flute of Chandon. Today's equivalent would be a video going viral.

These self-appointed brand ambassadors happily shared their fondness for Chandon sparkling wine because we treated them as special friends, not like paying customers. We didn't sell them wine except at the winery, because direct shipping was illegal then. Chandon Club members reciprocated by accounting for 25 percent of the winery's total sales.

Having experienced the power of relationship marketing in action at Domaine Chandon, I was determined to build a strong base of consumers for St. Supéry.

From the moment we opened St. Supéry, we worked hard to connect personally with visitors and make sure they felt welcome. Our personable staff did their best to make friends and capture contact information so we could maintain these relationships.

In the early years we offered lifetime tasting passes, which recipients perceived as prized secret decoder rings. Traveling around the country, I frequently met St. Supéry fans who eagerly pulled out their wallets to show me the tattered lifetime pass that proved membership in our tribe. In a business where brands number in the many thousands and loyalty is notoriously difficult to achieve, positive memories of a winery experience are pure gold.

Unlike most wineries, St. Supéry respected the restrictive but largely ignored state laws forbidding direct sales to consumers; we only shipped directly to the states that had enacted reciprocal shipping laws. We did so mostly as a courtesy to visitors who didn't want to carry wine home, rather than trying to develop those direct markets. As I watched other wineries ship on demand to consumers everywhere, I thought I must surely be the only great fool in the wine business.

Then Kendall-Jackson and Cakebread were caught in a sting instigated by distributors worried about losing sales to direct shippers. (If any of our distributors had seen the promotional video taped by an early direct shipping company wherein I publicly endorsed direct shipping, it could have caused St. Supéry some grief.) The resulting fines and negative publicity caught producers' attention. After that, most took the legal constraints on direct shipping seriously. Cakebread courageously took a leading role in "Free the Grapes," a consumer-driven effort to rationalize archaic state laws dating back to Repeal.

The very communicative logo of Free the Grapes.

St. Supéry's wine club grew slowly, organically, at first. With the advent of our first website in 1999, we stepped up direct sales outreach.

We also expanded our product range by bottling new, small volume wines from St. Supéry's estate vineyards, including Malbec, Petit Verdot, Sémillon, and Rutherford Merlot. This gave us a broad enough selection of wines to create a regular bimonthly offering without duplication. It was also important that a majority of the club wines be exclusive to its members.

In 2015, with 43 states allowing direct shipments to consumers and the Internet facilitating consumer communications for even the smallest producers, nearly every winery has a club. The big change is that winery clubs are now more focused on transactional marketing, i.e., sales, than on relationship building. It should come as no surprise that there is pressure to offer discounts, and significant club membership churn is the norm. Brand loyalty remains elusive.

69 THE UFW AND ME

I was barely settled in my new office at St. Supéry when the winery's labor lawyer thrust a one-year United Farm Workers (UFW) union contract under my nose and told me I had to sign it. I resisted for good reasons, the foremost being never sign something you haven't read.

While Cesar Chavez' selfless work to improve working conditions in the Central Valley's backbreaking strawberry and lettuce fields was well known, my career in Napa Valley had not prepared me to deal with unions. I'd also had nothing to do with the election won three years earlier by the UFW, or the subsequent negotiations that had produced this first, one-year contract.

Even after reading it, I was not comfortable signing this document whose import I did not fully understand. St. Supéry's lawyer advised that it would be an unfair labor practice if I didn't sign, so I did. I also replaced him with a new labor lawyer who would not say annoying things to me like "Correcto."

That first year went by quickly, and soon it was time to negotiate the contract renewal. (For those also blissfully ignorant of how union contracts affect operations, the terms of the original contract remain in effect until a new one is signed.)

In the interim, several of our vineyard workers had confided that they did not like being union members because the dues cost them two percent of their gross wages, for which they received no perceived benefit. They didn't like the union's health and vacation programs, which were less favorable than what they had enjoyed prior to the election.

These same people had voted in favor of the union under pressure from UFW field representatives and the small group of vineyard employees who were pro-union activists; now they were asking me to get them out of this mess. They and I did not yet understand that under the terms of the Agricultural Labor Relations Act, there is little an employer can do.

In my maiden negotiation session with the UFW, I earnestly suggested that the workers who wanted to belong to the union ought to be free to do so, but those who didn't want to should not be forced. This is a free country, I was thinking. I probably should have discussed this idea with my new lawyer first. I didn't know that optional membership was a red flag for union organizers known as an "open shop" provision, anathema because it would diminish their dues receipts. The bull saw red, and charged.

The UFW immediately slapped St. Supéry with an unfair labor practice charge, a serious legal matter requiring a serious legal response. Meanwhile, our pro-UFW workers stepped up their ongoing, illegal work slowdown in the vineyards, using peer pressure and harassment to coerce the others to work at a snail's pace. This was a common union tactic to pressure employers into signing a contract.

In a complex vineyard like Dollarhide where the timing of operations is extremely important, missing the narrow windows of opportunity to plant, train, irrigate, or leaf vines can seriously diminish fruit quality. A work slowdown is also costly, since productivity drops but hourly wages remain the same. Worse, I learned that I was legally barred from helping employees who complained about being harassed by the union and its supporters.

As management, we were not allowed to discuss labor matters directly with the workers—that constitutes an unfair labor practice. Firing workers who repeatedly failed to appear for scheduled work resulted in unfair labor practice charges. Firing workers who consistently failed to meet normal production goals drew a charge. Even laying workers off, a common occurrence in seasonal agriculture work, would trigger a charge because some lower seniority workers with year-round skill sets had to be kept on. Hiring workers who had not been referred by the union resulted in unfair labor practice charges, even though the union seldom presented any candidates.

This constant barrage of charges by the UFW ensnarled the company in a costly legal dance that eventually ended in arbitration. Based on time cards and historic production records, we were able to prove the illegal work slowdown, and in mid-1991 the arbitrator ruled in our favor. He did permit himself to marvel aloud at how someone obviously as intelligent (his words) as I could be so naive about unions.

The celebration—our happy anti-union vineyard workers dancing to a country band under the stars at Dollarhide alongside St. Supéry's Napa Valley Wine Auction guests—was short-lived. The Agricultural Labor Relations Board, political appointees all, overturned the arbitrator's decision on appeal. St. Supéry was ordered to reinstate the workers fired for poor performance and pay them back wages.

Having painfully confirmed my belief that litigation is seldom the best solution, I found a thoughtful strategist for St. Supéry's next labor lawyer. Jordan Bloom understood the needs and especially the fears of union leaders, primary among them the downward trend in membership.

We continued to try to come to terms with the UFW, but made little progress. Every contract proposal or counterproposal we offered up was *ipso facto* deemed a subterfuge, greeted with suspicion by the union negotiators. Whether it was a language problem, or fear of being taken advantage of, or both, was not clear. The UFW negotiating team agreed to nothing we proposed, and we could accept only some of what they proposed and still manage the vineyards to achieve the desired wine quality.

The winery negotiating team always agreed to meet whenever the union asked, and not just because failing to do so would be—you guessed it—an unfair labor practice. The understaffed UFW tired of these lengthy, unproductive meetings that ran late into the night, and abandoned negotiations for many months at a time. Intimidation and harassment of workers who were pro-employer continued, but thankfully the strife never escalated beyond the occasional keying of someone's car.

From time to time the UFW would get fired up and picket the winery in preparation for requesting a meeting. They seemed to believe that public pressure would make us more amenable to agreeing on a new contract. I returned from a vacation in 1992 to find Cesar Chavez himself, and his diminutive Number 2 in command Dolores Huerta, leading a picket line on Highway 29 in front of St. Supéry.

I went out to speak with them, but Cesar didn't acknowledge my presence. That was Dolores' job. Looking up at me intently, she expressed disbelief at my lack of solidarity with the UFW's goals because, after all, "You're a woman."

This was a conversation going nowhere. Male or female, Napa Valley growers understand their dependence on reliable workers and treat them as the valued employees they are. Dolores had been fighting for so long in the Central Valley, she was unable to grasp that vineyard workers in the Napa Valley didn't need the UFW's help to receive fair wages and working conditions.

There were about three dozen people strung along the shoulder of Highway 29 that day, a few of them St. Supéry vineyard employees, waving red flags bearing black eagles and brandishing a carefully lettered placard declaiming "Our boos Michaela Rodeno is a bloodsucker."

While it was a singular honor to have a personal visit from Cesar Chavez, I couldn't help enjoying the misspelling of "boss," by far the simplest noun on their sign. My colleague Lesley Russell later gave me a cherished denim work shirt embroidered with St. Supéry's logo and "The Boos," front and back, and "Inhuman" on the sleeve placket.

Two years later the UFW decided to picket the Napa Valley Wine Auction, hoping that would somehow advance the intermittent negotiations with St. Supéry. It seemed unfair to drag the vintners, their guests, and especially the auction beneficiaries into this dispute, so I asked Hope Lugo, a leader in the Hispanic community in Napa, to intervene.

She did, for the sake of those who benefit from the auction's support for vital local nonprofits like Clinic Olé and Healthy Moms and Babies, many of them vineyard workers and their families. The picketers departed and the auction went on uninterrupted.

Seven long years after that first contract had expired, I was still struggling to find a way to resolve the near impasse with the UFW. (Because both parties were still trying to negotiate, however sporadically, we were not technically at an impasse.) Then an article in the *San Francisco Chronicle* reported the resolution of a dispute between the UFW and a Salinas lettuce growing family that had lasted two generations, through the intervention of Arturo Rodriguez. Arturo, who had succeeded his father-in-law as president of the UFW after Cesar's death, was described in the article as an attorney.

Perhaps, I thought, it would be possible to have a rational discussion with a negotiator whose legal education had trained him to see both sides of an issue. I asked Jordan to request a meeting with Arturo. He was doubtful, since we had never met with anyone in the UFW's top ranks, but placed the call.

Arturo quickly accepted. We reached an agreement in two hours, a sharp contrast with the lengthy, frustrating, and ultimately unproductive meetings with lower level union negotiators.

Arturo believed the membership would want our negotiations to appear more arduous than they had been, so we continued to meet for another two months before making the announcement and signing a three-year contract. End of work slowdowns, end of harassment, end of unfair labor practice charges, end of picketing. We had a contract that allowed us to manage the vineyards, and the UFW had what it wanted: a fair, signed contract.

Since then St. Supéry has had a productive working relationship with the UFW, but we never took them up on their offer to help us sell wine to union supporters.

70 MARKETING AND SALES

Because most wineries are small businesses, it is not uncommon to find the roles of marketing and sales commingled. These complementary functions ideally work separately but in tandem, as they require different skills that are seldom found in one person. In my view, a winery with a vice president of sales and marketing really has a vice president of sales and no marketing.

What's the distinction? Marketing is consumer focused, while sales is trade and transaction focused. Marketing creates products for and finds end users, and works to keep them for the long term; sales assures fulfillment of the demand "pull" thus created.

Without marketing, sales must "push" products through the distribution system. Without marketing, products can devolve into commodities, resulting in declining profits and risking that the biggest or most efficient producer will erode competitors' margins to the point where they go out of business.

At St. Supéry, there was never any question that we would have different people responsible for marketing and sales. When necessary, I acted as the marketer-in-chief, and enjoyed the opportunity to be creative. For me, marketing has always been the most enjoyable part of the wine business.

I was less likely to volunteer for sales duty, but a CEO has the pleasure of being involved in everything. My business trips were typically organized around a public appearance such as an event, a speech, or an important interview, and fleshed out with distributor meetings and sales calls.

I've met with and presented St. Supéry to retailers, restaurateurs, importers, and regional-national chain accounts all over the country. I occasionally knew the thrill of a successful sale. Armed with the MKF comparative market data, I could enjoy negotiating fact-based goals with distributors who were eager to learn how their performance stacked up against others.

I worked the market with distributor sales representatives. Theirs is a tough job. In New York and other densely populated cities, trudging from one account to another with 25 pounds of wine samples is affectionately known as "dragging the bag." In less urban markets, sales reps often use their cars as rolling offices. With a trunk full of point-of-sale materials, an ice chest of samples, and dog hair on the upholstery, they conduct business on the fly.

A good "work-with," as these visits are often called, can produce results for the winery, the distributor and, above all, the sales rep. After listening to winery stories and brand lore all day, he or she can more easily sell those wines in future.

More often a work-with or ride-along is a lesson in humility. While I am good at telling colorful winery stories and explaining concepts, I'm not much of a closer. I often forget to ask for the sale.

One of my most successful account calls took place in New York. The distributor on-premise sales manager who had organized our day together decided it would be a fine thing to take me, the female CEO, to call on a "gentlemen's club" on the lower West Side. I had no idea what a gentlemen's club was; perhaps something like the private clubs in London where elder statesmen nod off over *The Times* in their leather armchairs?

We arrived in mid-afternoon to find an oddly blank building, with no windows, a blacked-out front wall, no signage, and a security guard. He let us in the locked entrance, and we lugged our samples up a narrow flight of stairs to a large, empty room with several seating areas and bars. We appeared to be in a nightclub that would not open for several hours.

Off to the side, behind a desk decorated with photos of his wife and young children, sat the manager. After chatting for a while and tasting several St. Supéry wines, the manager began calling his colleagues over to taste. They liked the wines, too.

The manager explained their pricing policy, which was surprisingly high; when he added that they also sold plenty of $400 steaks, I began to wonder about the business model. Then a handsome, fit young man in charge of "the girls" came over to taste. He loved the Moscato, which would be a wonderful (and cheaper) substitute for the champagne that the ladies usually ordered while they were making friends with the gentlemen buying the drinks and steaks.

We sold a lot of Moscato and Cabernet that day.

71 MOTHER NATURE

When it comes to farming and the weather, I am one with Enlightenment philosopher Denis Diderot's fictitious protagonist *Jacques le Fataliste*. There's little we can do about it and, frankly, it's a relief not to be responsible for everything.

My boss Robert Skalli thought otherwise. Either he knew something I did not, or he had too much faith in my ability to influence outcomes. Every time I cited Mother Nature as the reason why something had gone wrong in the vineyards, he would give me that look and say, *"Eh, oui, Muzzair Nature encore."*

In December 1990 a hard frost hit the Napa Valley before the vines had hardened off in preparation for their winter dormancy. The still green, water-filled tissues expanded as they froze and burst the trunks, killing the vines down to the ground. We thought we'd lost all the prized Sauvignon Blanc in low-lying Parcel 5, but as we discovered the following spring, the roots had survived and sent up new shoots.

In June 1991 I was attending VinExpo in Bordeaux when St. Supéry's winemaker called at 3:00 a.m. California time to announce that we had just lost 400 tons of Dollarhide Chardonnay to a freak hailstorm. These happen frequently in Bordeaux, decimating the crop and inviting rot in the surviving grapes, so instantly the French vintners were all ears. Robert sought out Bordeaux vintner Patrick Léon, who advised an immediate anti-fungal spray not used in California.

There was nothing to do but try to reassure Robert that our naturally dry summer climate would prevent the type of rot for which the Bordeaux spray was designed. By the end of the growing season, the Dollarhide vines had rebalanced themselves by enlarging the undamaged berries and clusters. We harvested the tonnage originally estimated prior to the hailstorm.

Rain or high winds during bloom, usually in June, can reduce "set" by damaging a vine's tiny flowers before they can turn into berries. This is not uncommon and, again, there is nothing to be done but wait and hope the vines will rebalance themselves if the set is not good.

Vineyard managers in Napa Valley are on high alert during frost season. From bud break in March, when the tender new shoots start emerging, until danger of frost is safely past in early May, they don't get much sleep. Failure to start up the frost protection systems when the alarms go off can result in the loss of an entire crop.

In May 2008 freakish rivers of freezing wind randomly damaged even hillside vineyards in Napa Valley. Hillsides are seldom protected against frost with sprinklers or wind machines because cold air, like water, settles into the lowest parts of a vineyard. This pattern was different, and unpredictable, and caused significant crop damage. Robert wondered aloud if someone had been stealing our grapes.

One of my favorite sayings is "Sometimes you eat the bear, and sometimes the bear eats you." That's very difficult to translate into French.

72 THE ECONOMY

There have been six recessions during my forty-plus years in the wine business. As a marketer at Domaine Chandon, I paid little attention. As a CEO, my antennae were up. Economic downturns made a big difference, and not only because the three that occurred during my St. Supéry tenure were much bigger than the earlier ones. If I'd had a crystal ball enabling me to take corrective action in anticipation, the impacts might have been diminished.

The first occurred within a year of my taking on the leadership role at St. Supéry. For a new winery just entering the market, this economic downturn made a tough job more difficult as we struggled to attract the interest of overstocked distributors, retailers, and restaurants. Fortunately, this recession lasted only eight months, and the 1990s thereafter proved to be a period of strong economic growth.

The second recession started with the dot.com implosion in 2001. The immediate impact on St. Supéry was the rational but heartbreaking decision to divest a first-class, 250-acre Cabernet vineyard that we had just finished developing to meet growing demand for our wines—demand that had been stopped cold by the recession.

No farmer wants to sell a good vineyard. In Napa Valley it's practically guaranteed that you won't be able to replace it in the future, unless you're very lucky *and* able to pay much more. It's no surprise that, fourteen years later, Napa Valley would find itself suffering a Cabernet shortage.

Grape and wine broker Bill Turrentine captured these recurring cycles of mismatched supply and demand perfectly in his wise and funny "Wine Business Wheel of Fortune." (Appendix A)

The other lesson of the 2001 recession was the need to keep a close eye on inventories, especially those with a long horizon like Cabernet-based wines. Through the boom years of the 1990s, St. Supéry's Cabernet sales had risen steadily and we had continued to increase production, cautiously, to fuel that growth. When the bottom fell out of the market in 2001, we had an inventory buildup appropriate to meet demand that had been projected three years into the future.

When demand halted abruptly, we found ourselves with more Cabernet in the cellar than we needed. We were fortunate to find a good buyer for the new vineyard, but finding a home for the excess wines already in the cellar would prove challenging.

For two years we struggled to sell large amounts of now-excess wines into a flat market without damaging St. Supéry's brand positioning. This meant avoiding discounted retail pricing that would reveal stress, focusing instead on airlines, national accounts, and by-the-glass programs where any discounts necessary to move the wine would not be visible. We did fairly well, but not well enough, because many other wineries were also trying to solve the same problem the same way.

In 2003, St. Supéry's board took the decision to write down the value of our remaining excess inventory by several million dollars, which made 2003 our first unprofitable year since 1996. The good news is that over the following three years, we were able to sell the excess wines profitably enough to recover the entire loss and more—while carefully rebuilding St. Supéry's trajectory.

The 2001 recession also caused us to rethink St. Supéry's strategy. It had proven difficult, as the U.S. economy waxed and waned, to maintain the volume strategy familiar to the Skallis in their French operations.

With a view to optimizing use of our vineyard and winery resources, in 2003 we decided to adopt what Robert Skalli called a "château" strategy. This meant focusing more on margins and less on volume, a natural strategy for Napa Valley wineries.

We started raising prices and making our base of distribution more granular. Distributors who wouldn't or couldn't accept the changes had to be replaced. Consumers supported the new strategy, since the wines were excellent and remained fairly priced compared to many other Napa Valley wines.

The most recent and biggest recession, sometimes called the Great Recession, quietly started in December 2007 and ended, at least technically, when I retired from St. Supéry in mid-2009. Few understood how bad the situation was about to become until Lehman Brothers was allowed to fail on September 15, 2008, although the challenges of achieving our sales goals had already increased.

A distributor ride-with I had been trying to schedule for months to support our sales team finally took place on September 18, 2008. I met Alex Casella of Young's Market Company early that day in San Francisco and we set out to make account calls armed with appointments, samples, pricing, and promotional materials. We made a good sale at our first restaurant stop in the Financial District, but sold nothing to the seven or eight likely prospects we called on thereafter.

Wall Street's woes should not have been Main Street's woes, but clearly something was wrong. Alex is one of the best salespeople I've ever ridden with; we put in a full day calling on pre-qualified accounts; the wines showed well; and a visit from a winery CEO can usually get the attention of even the most jaded trade buyers. By the end of the day we were both scratching our heads. With hindsight, those accounts were anticipating or maybe already feeling the coming pain of the recession and were controlling their inventories carefully.

Were it not for the strong consumer base we'd cultivated over twenty years that had allowed St. Supéry to build a highly successful wine club, my last two years of reporting to the shareholders at board meetings would not have been pleasant.

73 THE PATRON SAINT OF LOST CAUSES

St. Jude must have been hovering over me throughout my wine career. I seemed always to be heading in a direction that everyone else at least initially perceived as a loser: sparkling wine instead of champagne, racy Sauvignon Blanc not soft Chardonnay, Meritage rather than fantasy names, Pope Valley instead of the watershed of the Napa River, unoaked Chardonnay vs the popular barrel-fermented version, dry rosé instead of sickly sweet pinkies, and Sangiovese—another "Next Big Thing" that failed to ignite (this last in my personal life, with our family's Villa Ragazzi winery).

When Domaine Chandon introduced its first sparkling wines in 1977, New Yorkers wrinkled their noses at this "fake champagne." West of the Hudson River there was a warmer welcome.

The neighboring vintners in Napa Valley kindly kept whatever reservations they might have had to themselves, and in fact embraced this first major French investment that confirmed to the world Napa Valley's status as a prime winegrowing region. Potential competitors remained wary. While closely tracking the progress of Moët's audacious California venture, other champagne houses seemed to fear it would fail. Piper-Heidsieck, Taittinger, Mumm, et al., gave Domaine Chandon a lengthy head start before deciding it was safe to follow.

Upon moving from sparkling to still wines in 1988, I found St. Supéry's most promising estate wine to be Sauvignon Blanc. The Dollarhide fruit had a certain verve that was unique and attractive. This was welcome news, as I had decided ten years earlier that Vichon winery's Chevrier Blanc, a blend of Sauvignon Blanc and Sémillon, was so delicious that we replanted our family's Oakville vineyard to those varieties. (The people who knew how to make money were planting Cabernet in Oakville, even before Silver Oak and Opus One blessed the area.)

The bad news is that Sauvignon Blanc grapes and wine are hard to sell even at low prices, as Robert Mondavi had discovered some years earlier. Renaming his wine Fumé Blanc didn't entirely solve the problem, but my predilection for Sauvignon Blanc remains, nonetheless, solid.

St. Supéry's solution to the market problem was to convoke a Sauvignon Blanc symposium for winemakers, the trade, and media in 1990 to discuss how to address the market's lack of appreciation for this varietal. We were well down the planning path when we discovered that Dave Stare at Dry Creek Vineyard was on the verge of founding what he had dubbed The Society of Blancs, aka S.O.B.

Rather than compete with one of the few U.S. champions of Sauvignon Blanc, we offered to join forces; the St. Supéry symposium would become the inaugural S.O.B. gathering. Dave brought along his friend Henri Bourgeois, an enthusiastic vintner from Sancerre who makes delicious wines. A real entrepreneur, Henri now also produces Pinot Noir in New Zealand.

At that first Sauvignon Blanc symposium, winemakers and marketers talked about how confusing consumers found the myriad of Sauvignon Blanc styles. These stretched along a spectrum from soft, Sémillon-laden blends to bright citrusy wines, then to wines dominated by ripe tropical fruit characters and finally to oaky, Chardonnay wannabe styles.

We talked about food and wine pairings. We discussed where to plant, best vineyard practices, and how to modify Sauvignon Blanc wine styles in the vineyard. We tasted dozens of Sauvignon Blancs. The day ended with everyone all fired up and ready to advocate for our favorite white wine.

In spite of the unfortunate acronym, S.O.B. members worked hard to promote good Sauvignon Blancs and enjoyed a measure of success. When Cloudy Bay started getting traction in the U.S. market in the late 1980's, it quickly became a sensation—rather like what happened with red wine after the *60 Minutes* report on The French Paradox.

Suddenly, everyone "got it," and zesty Sauvignon Blanc joined the ranks of accepted wines in America. Nonetheless, prices for high quality Sauvignon Blanc remain relatively low compared to Chardonnay and even Pinot Grigio, and volume remains small but steady at about four percent of the market.

As for St. Supéry, its success with Sauvignon Blanc resulted from a change in winemaking that released the full potential of Dollarhide grapes. Michael Scholz embraced the vibrancy of the varietal, eliminating the softening effects of Sémillon and oak aging to reveal a zingy, compelling grapefruit-lime-floral character that was an instant hit.

Blending was the next challenge we took on. It's hard to believe now, with winemakers marrying wildly diverse varietals in ever more creative ways, that in 1988 blending was still often suspiciously viewed in the U.S. as an attempt to stretch or dilute a wine.

Few then knew that the traditional way to create a wine better than the sum of its parts is by blending across varieties, traditional in Bordeaux and Champagne. Perhaps if the *bordelais* had been more transparent about their winemaking practices, Americans might have better understood the benefits and the art of blending.

Also working against blending as a way to make better wines is the typically American belief that if some is good, more is better, and 100 percent must be the best of all. In the 1980s, the federal government increased the 51 percent minimum requirement for varietal labeling to 75 percent to reinforce varietal character. Winemakers and consumers generally regarded wines without varietal labels as inferior, perhaps because the regulations offer only the pejorative-sounding alternatives of "red wine" or, worse, "table wine." In Europe, anything labeled table wine is considered plonk.

In 1974 Joseph Phelps was the first to make a bordeaux-style blend in the U.S., which he named Insignia to counterbalance the federally required "red table wine" designation in small type on his label. He was blending to make a superior product, and wanted that understood.

Soon after, more Napa vintners started making bordeaux-style blends carrying fantasy names. Opus One is probably the most famous among them. While these wines were nearly always superior in quality and high-priced to reinforce the point, this highly individualistic approach to branding did little to help American consumers understand the concept.

A group of vintners who were strong proponents of blending decided to take the matter in hand in 1988. Following months of effort to find a suitable name for this new category of fine wines blended in the Bordeaux tradition, they agreed on Meritage, a combination of merit and heritage.

Even though Meritage is an invented word and certainly not French, francophones and most Americans continue to mispronounce it as mair-eh-tahge. (Actually, it rhymes with heritage.) This word proved to have inherent, positive connotations of quality for many, and has been adopted by real estate developers and restaurateurs as well as wineries.

After a couple of years of energetic marketing to launch the concept, its founders lost steam and the Meritage Association dozed off. That was the situation when I stumbled onto the scene in 1997.

We had identified a choice lot of 1994 St. Supéry Cabernet Sauvignon and set those barrels aside for future consideration, perhaps for bottling as a reserve or a special blend. With the arrival in 1996 of winemaker Michael Scholz, a bordeaux-style blend became our first choice for this 1994 Cabernet.

A native of Barossa Valley in Australia, Michael was already well acquainted with Sémillon. It seemed appropriate to ask him to create a white bordeaux-style blend that could be released in late 1997 along with the special 1994 red wine he was to blend. There was only one problem with this excellent plan: what to name these new blended wines?

I was opposed to proprietary or fantasy names on the grounds that consumers were confused enough already, and a fanciful name would not be enlightening about the contents of the bottle. I did try to come up with one though, since my boss thought proprietary names were the key to success: witness Insignia, Soliloquy, Dominus, Ariadne, et al.

Our team brainstormed. We had company-wide naming contests. We researched. Nothing clicked. We were getting uncomfortably close to the planned release date when I came across a mention of the Meritage Association. It seemed the perfect solution, as Meritage is, by definition, a red or white blend of at least two bordeaux varietals. And of course everyone knew that, didn't they?

One month before the release of our inaugural 1994 Red Meritage and 1996 White Meritage, the *Wine Enthusiast* published a lengthy article pronouncing the demise of the Meritage concept, a silly idea (another failed "Next Big Thing") that had never taken hold. There wasn't time to soak off and replace our Meritage labels, and we didn't have an alternative name anyway.

My only recourse was to find someone involved in the Meritage Association and offer to become active in promoting or at least defending the concept. Orville Magoon, then owner of Guenoc Winery, was the association's president. I called him to offer help. After hello, his first words were "Would you like to be president?"

I spent the next five years as president of the Meritage Association, St. Jude hovering nearby. We rebuilt the membership, made progress convincing the trade to create Meritage sections on wine lists and in shops, and cleared up some consumer confusion.

Then adventurous winemakers started blending non-bordeaux varietals into their Meritage wines. Blending was finally catching on. Soon after came Syrah-Zinfandel blends, and Rhône-style blends. Even "Sem-Chard" blends. Blending had grown well beyond bordeaux varietals and was becoming a new creative outlet for winemakers and marketers.

Robert Skalli had never given up his notion that St. Supéry's blends should have a name we could own rather than a generic name like Meritage, so that debate was still going on. I ultimately conceded. Over a wine-heavy lunch, graphic designer Melanie Doherty and I came up with Élu for the red and Virtù for the white. Sorry, consumers: fanciful names rule.

In my defense, we did explain the Meritage concept and the precise varietal components of each vintage on St. Supéry's Élu and Virtù back labels.

In its first report on St. Supéry, in 1989, the *Wine Spectator* characterized Dollarhide as a high-risk proposition in "Napa's Outback." They were referring to its location in Pope Valley, which is one of several mountain valleys in the Napa Valley American Viticultural Area (AVA), or appellation.

There have been Pope Valley and other mountain grapes going into Napa wines since the nineteenth century. That is why Pope Valley and similar areas of Napa County outside the Napa River watershed were included in the Napa Valley AVA when it was delimited in 1981, with the support of Napa vintners.

Robert Mondavi himself made a fine speech to that effect at the public hearings held to determine what would constitute the "Napa Valley." Even now, three decades later, some still disagree about including the mountain valleys in the AVA. They should get over it.

When Robert Skalli purchased and started planting the Dollarhide Ranch in 1982, it was only the second vineyard of any size in bucolic Pope Valley. Today, many of its broad meadows of grasses and wildflowers have been converted to prime vineyards.

Nonetheless, 30 years ago there was a perception, particularly among Napa old timers, that the best grapes came from vineyards on the valley floor. They may not have known that many European appellations outright forbid planting wine grapes in deep, rich soils. Oregon's Willamette Valley AVAs, defined less than ten years ago, start at 200-feet elevation and go up. The mountain vs. flat vineyard debate rages on.

Over the years growers have become more sophisticated about Napa's many soil types, microclimates, exposure, moisture retention, and all natural things associated with differentiating *terroirs*. Pope Valley, like most of northern Napa Valley, is well suited to Bordeaux varietals (and Sangiovese), just as Carneros is a good home for Pinot Noir and Chardonnay. The proof is in the wines, not dated generalizations or *idées reçues*.

74 ON THE ROAD, STILL

I remember the exhilaration of arriving in Paris for the first time at age 19 after a ten-day Atlantic crossing on a spartan student ship, followed by three hours on the boat train from Le Havre. Several of us young Americans excitedly bounced into the first café we saw and asked the barman for a coffee. He was a kindly fellow, so instead of laughing he invited us to find a table and order from the waiter like everyone else.

Many trips to Paris later, the thrill remains. I love poking around its museums, reading the *International Herald Tribune* in public parks, and watching the daily fashion parade from a sidewalk seat in a café. But while our children were small, and they were only four and two years old when I joined St. Supéry, there was no time for such leisurely pursuits.

I organized my business travel to minimize the time away from home and family. I would take the non-stop red-eye flight from San Francisco to Paris, arriving early in the morning to go straight into an all-day board meeting, and take the first available flight home the following morning. This happened two or three times every year.

Similarly, during my last four years at Domaine Chandon when the children were even younger, I had honed my monthly business trips to New York to 24 hours total time elapsed. Leaving Napa Valley in the dark to catch a 6:00 a.m. flight out of San Francisco was standard procedure; arriving home at 3:00 a.m., I was often treated to a spectacularly clear, starry sky. Every time I returned from a business trip I was struck anew by the Napa Valley's beauty.

I wasn't able to control my schedule entirely. When traveling on Napa Valley Vintners (NVV) market visits, which for years were patterned after our 1979 Moët jet market-hopping adventure, NVV set the schedule. A typical five-day road trip covered one major market and three smaller markets close enough to reach within two hours. For example, Chicago was paired with Minneapolis, Detroit and Cleveland. Or New York with Baltimore, Washington and Raleigh-Durham.

As many as 100 vintners would fly into a target market in time for a media lunch, followed by an afternoon trade seminar and tasting. We'd get a one-hour break to rest our aching feet before the consumer tasting started at 6:00 p.m. Three hours later, we packed up after a long day that would be repeated three more times that week in different cities.

There wasn't time for dinner between the trade and consumer tastings, so the vintners would stampede to the bar (these events were often held in hotels because their ballrooms had the square footage required) for refreshments, usually beer.

It was on one such trip that Nancy Duckhorn talked me into my first martini, at the Ritz-Carlton in Atlanta. It came in a tall, elegant, easily tipped glass and I drank it like dry rosé on a warm summer day. The observant bartender saw an opportunity for a repeat sale and pounced. Sure, I'll have another. Two sips later the first one made its presence felt. My feet didn't hurt at all during the three-hour consumer tasting that followed. Since then, I treat myself to one martini, once in a great while.

The Napa Valley Vintners road shows gradually expanded to international markets. Europe was the first target, specifically the northern countries that produced little or no wine of their own, or those that produced mostly white wine like Switzerland and Germany. Canada proved to be a strong export market for Napa Valley wines in spite of its provincial liquor monopolies. The early successes in Japan sagged with its economy. And finally came China.

I was among a dozen vintners on the NVV tour to Beijing and Shanghai in the spring of 2008, surprised to learn later that it was the first group market visit to that intriguing country. I was instantly hooked by the energy and entrepreneurial spirit of Shanghai. I was eager to return.

Silicon Valley Bank, of which I was then a director, has commercial offices in Shanghai and Beijing. Together we planned a fall 2008 St. Supéry-Silicon Valley Bank networking event for the bank's clients and business prospects in a Shanghai restaurant, pairing five different wines with high-level Chinese cuisine (which is very high level indeed).

The next morning someone forwarded a tweet from one of the guests, a Chinese businessman who, with a few friends, had stayed late into the evening to finish all of the open wine bottles. He tweeted being "dazzled," a charmingly fractured way to describe overindulging in excellent Napa Valley wine.

I was often asked how much time I spent traveling on business. Compared to St. Supéry's sales managers, I was a piker. Perhaps 25 percent of my work time was spent on the road, spread very unevenly throughout the year. Of course such trips meant nights and weekends away from home, too.

Once our children arrived in 1984 and 1986, this would not have been possible without the support of my husband. His Napa law practice didn't require business travel out of the area, and he provided willing and able coverage for this often absent mom.

Although the physical displacement of travel grew increasingly tiresome as airlines cut costs and 9/11 added the pleasant overlay of TSA queues, I have always liked being in different places. The U.S. is a wonderfully diverse country, worth exploring in all its eccentricities. International travel is similarly stimulating.

Working in the wine business, unfortunately, seldom leaves time for more than airports, distributor warehouses—of which they are oddly proud—restaurants, wine shops, and hotels. When in Paris, however briefly, I liked to treat myself to a *hôtel de charme*, usually in the 6^e arrondissement. They offer a sense of place that is lacking in the international chain hotels, and are invariably less expensive.

Sometimes TSA staff, humorless as they are trained to be, can be inadvertently entertaining. I was departing St. Louis shortly after 9/11 with an opened, re-corked bottle of St. Supéry Cabernet in my carryon; it was going back to the winery lab for analysis because the wine had showed cork taint.

At that time TSA was confiscating open containers unless you took a swig in their presence to prove the liquid wasn't toxic. I made a futile attempt to explain why tasting that particular wine wasn't a great idea, but I couldn't comply anyway because another TSA crew had previously confiscated my Swiss Army knife. I had no corkscrew.

While the entire TSA team gathered around to discuss how to deal with this first encounter with an open but un-openable container, passing the bottle among themselves and finally calling over their supervisor to advise, the line behind me grew ever longer. Dozens of impatient travelers were craning to see what was blocking their progress, ensuring that my bottle of Cabernet got plenty of free brand attention. It was a fine opportunity for St. Supery's graphically memorable label to do its intended work.

In the end, TSA elected to confiscate the bottle. I've always wondered whether whoever surely succumbed to the temptation to take it home noticed anything odd about the wine.

In spite of all this time in the air I never had anything like a close call, not even an emergency landing. There were plenty of instances of flights delayed by a cockpit warning light, but nothing scary. Except the time that Domaine Chandon's winemaker Dawnine Dyer and I were going to Los

Angeles to do a tasting for the Committee of 200 at the invitation of John Wright's old friend and Harvard professor, Rosabeth Moss Kanter.

It was a stormy day in San Francisco, but the airport hadn't been closed. As we gained speed, the plane pitching and yawing to strong crosswinds as we skittered down the runway, Dawnine and I looked at one another wondering aloud, too late, "Do we really have to do this?" Once aloft the sun was shining and the air calm. The Committee of 200 proved a fascinating group of women leaders, but I remember that takeoff better.

I have the dubious honor of being a two million mile frequent flier with American Airlines as a result of years of business peregrination, making me platinum forever or until the next rules modification. At least I don't have to pay to check luggage, a recent airline innovation. I wouldn't have to anyway, as I am used to traveling for up to two weeks with a small carry-on. Maybe someday I will again enjoy flying to distant lands as a visitor, but I think it will take a while to recover from the process of accumulating a surfeit of air miles.

75 OUR MAN IN THE WHITE HOUSE

President Ronald Reagan wanted California wines served in the White House, a major change from the French *crus* of the Kennedy era. His advisor Mike Deaver became the designated wine shopper. With the help of Sacramento wine merchant David Berkley, he purchased wines that were often ferried to Washington on Air Force One.

When the Clintons moved into the White House in 1993, the First Lady decided it was time to replace its rich, dated French menus with more contemporary fare. She wanted healthy American food and American wines. A new chef arrived, and soon afterward the word went out from the Usher's Office that a search was underway to fill the newly created position of food and beverage director.

My friend Bruce Hall, general manager of the historic City Tavern Club in Georgetown, got a call from the Usher's Office asking if he could recommend anyone. Bruce called me.

My thoughts went immediately to Daniel Shanks, who had long been the restaurant manager at Domaine Chandon. Having entertained winery guests there regularly for years, I knew Daniel well and thought he could be the right person for the job.

His military bearing hinted at a desire to serve his country. He was a native of Virginia, unfailingly polite and soft-spoken. He was a commanding presence in the dining room, always on the alert. And he knew fine food and wines, having amassed an amazing cellar for the restaurant over the years.

I called Daniel, having no idea whether he'd be interested. He was. The connection made, I got out of the way.

Three weeks after he'd started his new job, I was in Washington on business and we met for an early breakfast at The Madison. Daniel was not happy with the lax service in the White House, which fell far below his exacting standards. He was distressed by the low quality stemware rented for state dinners. Over time, he was able to retrain and upgrade the staff, but the White House still lacks appropriate stemware.

It's a national embarrassment to serve America's best wines in cheap wineglasses, especially when entertaining visiting heads of state and other dignitaries. At least twice, Women for WineSense attempted to address this problem.

With Daniel's enthusiastic support, we found an American crystal producer, researched costs for five-stem place settings for 250 people, devised a plan to raise funds from American wineries, and enlisted the support of the Smithsonian. We naively thought that, since First Ladies often donate a china pattern of their own choice to the White House collection, one would surely welcome an effort to do the same with stemware.

To date, the decision making of two First Ladies we approached has been political, with the risk of incurring the wrath of potential anti-alcohol forces and media sniffing around for a "gotcha!" outweighing the benefits of this offer to help. Only in Washington could one perceive political risk in accepting a gift of wineglasses to the nation.

With Daniel in the White House, vintners whose wines were selected for state dinners received a letter on White House stationery and one of the gilt-edged menu cards commemorating the occasion with perfect calligraphy and the presidential seal. It was understood that these were not to be used for marketing purposes, and most vintners complied.

When selecting wines, Daniel always tried to find a point of commonality with the guest of honor; for example, when Israel's Prime Minister Netanyahu dined at the White House in the 1990s, he was served St. Supéry's kosher Napa Valley Cabernet bottled under the Mt. Maroma label.

Since Air Force One hadn't been used to transport wine from California for years, Daniel did most of the White House's wine shopping locally in Washington. I had kept him informed about new St. Supéry wines in the hope that someday there would be an appropriate occasion. I was delighted when he called to ask if there was enough St. Supéry Virtù, our white Meritage blend, in the Washington area to serve at an upcoming White House event. I immediately checked with our distributor, who assured me there was.

The day before the dinner, Daniel called me again, this time to tell me that the distributor had come up short of the three dozen bottles of Virtù required. He would have to find a last-minute substitute.

It would be an understatement to say I was sorely disappointed with our distributor. As longtime operators in the capital, they should have been highly aware of the White House wine program, and ready to address such prized requests with the careful attention they deserved. I was also chagrined at inconveniencing my friend in the White House. I hope the calligrapher hadn't yet started work on the menu cards.

Daniel is currently serving his third presidential family.

76 BANKS I HAVE KNOWN

From the beginning, all the funding for the new enterprise that would become St. Supéry came from the owners in France. With the purchase of the Dollarhide ranch in 1982, the Skallis had begun pouring millions into land acquisition and vineyard development. In 1986 came the purchase and redevelopment of the Rutherford vineyard, along with winery construction.

These millions of former francs arrived in Napa through Bank of America (BofA). When I arrived late in 1988, I discovered that BofA was taking seven to ten days to process the incoming funds before releasing the cash to the winery's account. A float of this magnitude struck me as, shall we say, inefficient.

One of my first official acts as the new CEO was to move our business to a locally owned commercial bank, Napa National. The capital coming from France flowed more readily, and we had access to the few banking services we needed.

During the 1990s, phylloxera resurged in California vineyards one hundred years after its first devastating attack. The cost to replant all the affected Napa Valley acreage was estimated at half a billion (yes, that's a B) dollars to nearly twice that much. Most of the usual agriculture lenders were frightened off by the magnitude of the loans that would be required, dubious about the vintners' and growers' ability to repay them.

In walked an unlikely savior: Silicon Valley Bank (SVB) was looking for new niche markets to diversify its very successful business funding tech startups, and fine wine was a target.

The founder of SVB's wine division, Rob McMillan, and its CEO John Dean were making the rounds of Napa wineries in 1994 and came by to get acquainted. St. Supéry may be the only winery in the U.S. that didn't need to borrow money, thanks to the Skalli family's investment strategy, but as owners of a 25-acre, dying vineyard, my husband and I were acutely aware of the dearth of replant financing. I spent two fascinating hours talking with Rob and John, who saw opportunity where other bankers saw only hard luck and trouble, and thereafter recommended SVB to a number of my industry colleagues.

In 2000 Wells Fargo acquired Napa National. By this time Silicon Valley Bank had developed a strong presence in the fine wine industry in Napa, Sonoma, and the Pacific Northwest. It was an easy decision to seize the opportunity created by the absorption of Napa National into Wells Fargo to move our operating accounts to winery-focused SVB. The Skallis wanted to keep St. Supéry's serious dollars at UBS because of a longstanding relationship with their pasta, rice, and wine enterprises in France.

By 2007, St. Supéry was piling up cash. The shareholders did not want to reinvest in the still relatively young winery, and there were tax issues limiting how much could be returned to France in the form of dividends.

Our CFO did some research and came up with a proposal to place the funds in auction rate securities, a financial instrument offered by the broker-dealer arm of UBS and other investment banks that promised slightly higher interest rates coupled with unusually good liquidity. The Dutch auctions that reset interest rates weekly were considered safe because the investment banks were willing to be bidders of last resort if needed. This sounded like a good deal, and safe because of the Skallis' confidence in UBS, so St. Supéry's board of directors voted to proceed.

Early in 2008 these auctions started failing. This led to the revelation that from the start the investment banks had not been the bidders of last resort, they'd been the only bidders. With the promised liquidity blocked, the banks started marking down the value of these securities and then, unbelievably, froze their own clients' accounts. The clients howled. Regulators opened investigations. The media smelled blood.

I was astonished at the banks' brazen behavior, but Robert Skalli was infuriated at having his invested cash frozen by UBS. He wanted to know why I, as a bank director, hadn't seen this coming. (Silicon Valley Bank's management had not been tempted by auction rate securities, so the topic never came up in our board meetings.)

Robert demanded a meeting at the UBS office in San Francisco, where he frostily read the riot act to a team of perspiring bank vice presidents. St. Supéry was a relatively small client with only a few million dollars invested in auction rate securities, but the Skalli enterprises in France were quite the opposite.

It was inconceivable to me that the money would be lost. Although the bankers could offer no immediate solution, they had reputations to save, lawsuits to avoid, and the possibility of jail time to incent remediation.

Bigger investors than St. Supéry soon filed class action suits to compel the investment banks to repurchase the misleadingly marketed auction rate securities. Under pressure from regulators, politicians, and the media, the banks and the underlying funds slowly did so. It took a year to unblock St. Supery's UBS investment account, but we recovered all the money, with interest.

77 WHO HAS TIME TO COOK?

We eat well in the fine wine business, supporting the restaurants and hotels that offer our vintages to an appreciative public. Some of us are also excellent cooks, but I'm not among them. Perhaps it was seeing Margrit Mondavi prepare simple, delicious lunches for distributors visiting the winery in the 1970s that warned me off the hospitality side of vintner life, where I was unlikely to shine.

In spite of spending all day figuratively immersed in wine early in my career, alone at home my husband and I rarely drank it. Our thinking was: wine is meant to accompany a real meal, not the hastily assembled salad or popcorn we scrounged after a long day at work.

Given the preparation time needed, and fully occupied by all the excitement of starting up Domaine Chandon, I saved cooking for dinner parties. We entertained frequently on weekends, and even asked architect Andrew Batey to design our house around that purpose.

Never a creative cook, I relied on recipes. A dinner party is meant to honor the guests, and one feels compelled to raise the level of the food to match that of the wines. In the 1970s it was impossible to find flavorful fruits and vegetables, imported cheeses, or good bread in Napa Valley—except at the Oakville Grocery.

I plunged fearlessly into complicated recipes, usually managing to produce a reasonable facsimile of one of Julia Childs' multi-course menus from *Mastering the Art of French Cooking* without poisoning anyone. Except for the time I forgot, when asked, whether there were mushrooms in the minestrone, causing an allergic guest a wretched evening.

We washed down all this rich food—Julia wasn't afraid of butter—with an average of one bottle of wine per person over the course of a long, convivial evening. We typically began with bubbles and ended with first growth Sauternes, the latter quite affordable in the 1970s with half-bottles available for six dollars. These gatherings were as much about exploring wines as enjoying good food and conversation, and guests always brought a bottle to share. We invariably ended up with more wine than we'd started with, a welcome wine country custom that endures today.

The arrival of children changed that. The parties became considerably less frequent once there were little ones to mind, but having children also marked the turning point when we finally developed a lifelong habit of enjoying wine on a daily basis.

A fine way to lose weight involuntarily is to try to feed oneself while holding an infant. Cutting meat with one hand just isn't possible. It is, however, quite easy to hold a glass of wine and a baby simultaneously.

There is a cultural imperative to sit down to dinner with one's children as a means of passing along news, values, manners, and history. Providing balanced nutrition for growing young bodies unable to sit quietly in restaurants meant cooking, so we did.

Instead of staying late at the office, I now made a point of getting home from work by 6:00 p.m. to prepare dinner when I wasn't traveling. Children get hungry early, so our family dinners were quickly prepared, simple but tasty meals, with tomato-basil pasta and "special chicken" everyone's favorites. We developed quite a repertoire of pasta dishes, as do many parents.

Our observant children understood early that wine was an integral part of dinner and conversation. As soon as their hands were strong and steady enough, Kate and John became our wine waiters, proudly replenishing glasses without spilling a drop. They became proficient with corkscrews and wine etiquette. If they expressed interest, they were invited to smell and taste the wine. After they finished their dinner and galloped off to play, Gregory and I would have a few quiet moments to talk while savoring our last glass.

When the children reached adolescence and were no longer interested in spending time around us, we resumed our paused social life and have enjoyed old and new friends with increased relish ever since. It's much easier to shop for dinner parties today, with many choices of locally produced fruit and vegetables, excellent bread, cheeses, fish, and other goodies. I have an edible garden, too. We really do eat well, and healthily, in Napa Valley.

One of the most frustrating phrases voiced to wine writers and vintners is "I'm saving this wine for a special occasion." It's hard to convince some people there's already too much good wine withering away in cellars across America, waiting in vain for an occasion special enough to pull the cork.

So in the mid-1990s we were eager to comply when Dorothy Gaiter and John Brecher, wine columnists for the *Wall Street Journal* (*WSJ*), encouraged readers to "open that special bottle" on the last Saturday in February and report back to them.

With five other couples, we organized a high-level potluck dinner with aged wines as the evening's focus. Twice the *WSJ* published excerpts from my slightly garbled notes on our OTSB dinners (Appendix C), where bottles and magnums unearthed from our and our friends' cellars easily outnumbered the diners. It was great fun, and I hope this fine tradition continues.

Many people can't visualize a sitting CEO stirring a pot, at least in the kitchen. Apart from close friends, few knew that I had come to enjoy cooking when time allowed it to be a leisure activity. It was also oddly satisfying since, unlike the never-ending responsibilities of the job, cooking a meal had a finite end point.

Robert Skalli was a considerate boss who almost never called me outside work hours, in spite of the eight or nine hour time difference between Paris and Napa. But one day he did. I was taking a few days off, and happened to be at home when the phone rang. His image of me apparently didn't include domesticity, because he laughed out loud on hearing that I was entertaining myself by cooking something special for our family dinner.

On another occasion I had invited Robert, his cousins, and St. Supéry's management team for dinner at our home at the conclusion of two days of board meetings that had, as usual, been preceded by intense preparation. The only way to carry this off was to hire a caterer. That evening I overheard Robert admiringly pointing out to his cousins that in the hour since the end of our meetings, I had miraculously produced a multi-course dinner for a dozen guests.

78 THE THINGS WE DO TO SELL WINE

This is a story of pigs and people.

St. Supéry's hard charging, entrepreneurial young vineyard manager Josh Anstey was easily bored. The considerable challenge of managing a 475-acre vineyard with a wild diversity of soil types, elevations, aspects, drainage, rootstocks, and wine grape varieties wasn't enough to keep him entertained.

So he planted several kinds of olive trees on parts of the thousand acres of Dollarhide Ranch that were unsuitable for wine grapes, with an eye to olive oil production. Olive trees grow too slowly for Josh, so he expanded into fruit trees: heirloom apples, peaches, pluots, and apricots all thrived and were soon yielding bumper crops.

Next, our UC Davis graduate with a master's degree in Agronomy went into animal husbandry with a dozen head of cattle, most of which he personally helped convert to steerdom, yielding plentiful Rocky Mountain oysters. Then a couple of paint horses arrived. His purebred German shorthairs loved to harass a growing flock of turkeys, ducks, and chickens, even after putting in many happy miles chasing the vineyard foreman's dogs all over the ranch. A farmer's paradise, but still...not enough.

Fortunately I had warned Josh about the pumpkin project we had undertaken four years before his arrival in 1999, so he wasn't tempted to try that again. The idea had been to strengthen relationships by enticing visitors to Dollarhide, where they could gather as many free pumpkins as they liked. And if they happened to stop by the winery in Rutherford on the way home to pick up some wine, well, that was fine too.

Our vineyard manager in 1995 had a very different idea from mine what "a few pumpkins" could mean. Thinking big, as usual, he planted five thousand pumpkins. Each would have to be individually upended to assure a classic round shape, not to mention nurturing and harvesting.

Walking through the pumpkin patch just before they were ready to harvest, I was flattered to discover a splendid five-foot long (someone had neglected to upend it) specimen into which some wag had carved my initials early in its development. By harvest time, that "MKR" had grown to marquee size.

This personalized prize soon arrived on my doorstep along with a few dozen large, classically round pumpkins. Hundreds more soon decorated the winery entrance, an idea quickly adopted by other wineries and now something of a Napa Valley winery tradition at Halloween. We begged winery visitors to "steal" the pumpkins at will, and they obliged. We replenished the display daily from our bountiful stores.

By mid-December the pumpkins on my front porch had begun to rot, so I heaved them into our family vineyard to enrich the soil. I had forgotten about the seeds; volunteer pumpkins sprouted amid our Sauvignon Blanc vines annually thereafter. And at Dollarhide. But I digress.

As with the pumpkins, eventually there was a problem of surplus produce from Josh's orchard. His solution was a wine marketing *tour de force*: he would offer tree-ripened, hand-picked-that-day Dollarhide peaches to local restaurateurs in the hope they would in turn look favorably on carrying St. Supéry wines. This worked well, as Josh was the first to think of it and the peaches were superb; it also helped that the "locavore" phenomenon was well under way.

While I was enjoying lunch one day at Cindy's Back Street Kitchen in St. Helena, including an irresistible dessert made with luscious Dollarhide peaches created by pastry chef Annie Baker (really! that's her name), chef/owner Cindy Pawlcyn stopped by the table to chat.

I asked what else she had in mind for locally sourced foodstuffs, and she promptly responded "heirloom pork." Clearly having done her homework, she further specified Berkshire or Red Wattle. This was beyond my ken, but I offered to talk to Josh about raising designer pigs at Dollarhide.

The next thing I knew, Josh had dispatched assistant vineyard manager Geoff Gatto to Iowa to pick up a pregnant Berkshire. She was large, lean, and pink; we enchanted non-farmers naturally named her Petunia. Lonely in her shady pen, personable Petunia loved company, grunting happily at visitors and arching her back to be scratched.

I made the mistake of introducing Robert Skalli to our porcine charmer on one of his regular visits to Napa Valley. That introduction was to have disastrous results for our budding heirloom pig program.

In time Petunia gave birth to an impressive passel of piglets, about half of which did not survive. Of the seven remaining, six were male, useless for breeding but excellent for meat production. The sole female was destined to carry on the line. Two weeks after giving birth, exhausted Petunia expired during a brief but intense heat wave, leaving Josh to bottle-feed seven ravenous piglets. This was not in the playbook of this former All-American defensive end, but he did it and they all thrived.

The USDA has something to say about meat processing. Petunia's baby boys grew apace and soon needed to be converted. This required a six-hour drive to Eureka, site of the nearest USDA approved *abbatoir*.

Cindy was thrilled with Josh's first delivery, and promptly put Berkshire pork chops on the menu. To keep supplies flowing to Cindy while awaiting Petunia's grandchildren, Josh acquired a few pre-teen Berkshires. He even godfathered the not exactly in vitro fertilization of Petunia's virgin daughter. Oh, the things we do to sell wine.

At the height of the H1N1 (Swine Flu) virus crisis in the spring of 2009, Mr. Skalli again returned to Napa Valley. Alarmed by the American media's characterization of the potential pandemic, his thoughts turned to Josh's Berkshires. What if some of Petunia's offsprings' delicious pork were to be linked to swine flu? It would be a public relations disaster for St. Supéry! The pigs must go.

Mr. Skalli knew me well enough to understand that I would probably wait for the whole thing to blow over rather than act on his concern, so he called Josh upon landing in Paris and issued a direct order to eliminate the pigs. Good citizen Josh sadly complied.

The media eventually got around to publishing the uninteresting update that pigs do not spread swine flu, people do.

79 WINE TOURISM

When my young attorney husband and I arrived in the Napa Valley in 1972, the locals were quick to tell us "it takes a long time to be accepted here." We found that not to be the case. We made friends easily and have enjoyed welcoming newcomers ourselves. The wine business is all about sharing.

Nonetheless, there existed among the natives a certain grumpiness about tourists. Although there were relatively few wineries open to the public and therefore few visitors to Napa Valley in the early 1970s, the blue-collar community in the city of Napa and even some of the vintners had mixed feelings about sharing this little paradise.

Upper Napa Valley Associates, the group led by Jack Davies and others that had successfully fought off a Caltrans proposal to widen Highway 29 north of Yountville to four lanes, was not about to concede to any growth-inducing activities.

In St. Helena, where Highway 29 slows to a crawl when it becomes Main Street for three miles, residents trying to cross to the other side of town resented the increasing traffic they were quick to blame on tourists. (Surveys consistently show that, on the contrary, people who commute to work in Napa Valley are a much larger percentage of the cars on Highway 29 than visitors.) The weekly *St. Helena Star's* standard front-page headline in the early 1970s, "Accident at the Traffic Light," would soon apply to multiple stoplights on Main Street.

I found this negative attitude remarkable. Could not those who benefit directly or indirectly from tourism comprehend its importance to the health of the local economy? There is only one way to develop a lasting customer base for fine (read: expensive) wine and that is to build a relationship with the interested parties who present themselves as buyers. In short, visitors.

Some vintners got it, of course. Charles Krug, Beaulieu, Inglenook and, above all, Robert Mondavi, were all wineries that had historically worked hard to attract visitors, and welcomed them with open arms. Without their leadership, one wonders what might have become of Napa Valley in spite of its extraordinary wines.

For decades, Napa County's efforts to support tourism development were half-hearted, at best. Funding was minimal, leading one frustrated executive director with more ideas than budget to use his personal credit cards in support of the cause. The board fired him.

Lacking any sense of urgency, Napa Valley risked losing its preeminent position during the 1980s and 1990s as newer appellations like Paso Robles and Monterey were spending millions to establish themselves as wine destinations. In spite of its complacency, Napa's natural beauty, sense of place, fine wines, and proximity to San Francisco preserved its historic status as America's premier winegrowing region.

There were periodic wake-up calls. When the dot.com implosion occurred in 2001, destroying techies' stock options, those bands of free-spending day trippers (they worked too hard to take vacations) disappeared from the Napa Valley overnight. Winery profits plunged.

Then Sonoma started using its five million dollar tourism development budget to redefine Napa as snobby and overcrowded, and Napa failed to respond. It gradually gained a mostly undeserved reputation for elitism that turned off potential visitors.

It took the major recession of 2007-2009, when visitors not only stayed home but economized by dropping out of wine clubs, to bring into sharp focus the value of tourism to Napa Valley wineries and indeed to all of Napa County.

Feeling the pain of the Great Recession, Napa's hotels, restaurants, and wineries were receptive when a solution appeared.

Clay Gregory, a former Robert Mondavi and Kendall-Jackson executive, took on the leadership of the somnolent Napa Valley Destination Council (NVDC), formerly the moribund Napa Valley Conference and Visitor Bureau. He discovered an existing California law that allowed businesses to create self-funded development districts, provided at least half of the affected businesses voted in favor of the assessment. Once passed, the assessment would become mandatory for all similar businesses in the new district.

Clay and Napa County's lodging community undertook a campaign to create a Napa Valley Tourism Improvement District, which received an overwhelmingly positive 70 percent vote from the county's hoteliers. With the funds raised from the new, mandatory surcharge on lodging in Napa County, the NVDC rapidly evolved into Visit Napa Valley (VNV). The new organization forged partnerships with the Napa Valley Vintners, Visit

San Francisco, and Visit California, and started proactively and strategically marketing the Napa Valley experience to visitors.

Napa's fragile infrastructure cannot accommodate more visitors at peak periods, so VNV encouraged people to come during the quieter times: weekdays and "Cabernet season," defined as November through April. VNV also reached out to the community to create a better understanding of the economic benefits to Napa County of welcoming visitors. I was delighted when Clay asked me to join the Visit Napa Valley board of directors, and served as chair in 2012-2013.

By 2014 there were more than 500 Napa Valley Vintners member wineries and about the same numer of non-members, usually smaller or virtual wineries; hundreds of restaurants of all types; and approximately 5,000 hotel rooms with more planned. This was quite a change from 1977 when Domaine Chandon opened the first fine dining restaurant in Napa Valley. The only lodging available then was the El Bonita motel in St. Helena and a couple more not as nice in Napa.

Forgive me for interjecting here my ususal rejoinder to the urban legend that Napa Valley is "second only to Disneland" as a California tourism destination. That has never been true, and never will be. With the strong pull of San Francisco, San Diego, Yosemite, Santa Barabara, Tahoe, and probably the beaches in southern California, Napa Valley is nowhere close to the top of that list.

Nonetheless, in that context, by 2014 tourism's economic impact in Napa County had grown to $1.6 billion, with hospitality second only to the wine sold directly by wineries, in stores, and in restaurants (nearly 50% of total visitor spending).

Even downtown Napa, which my husband and I remember as a newly redeveloped wasteland of empty storefronts in 1972, is coming back to life. New shops, hotels, restaurants and cafés, tasting rooms, and live entertainment venues like the restored Opera House (now City Winery), Silo's, and the Uptown Theatre attract residents and visitors alike.

The Napa Valley has found a path to economic survival, without sacrificing its natural beauty and prized agriculture.

The natives are less grumpy today, but an undertone of concern remains. There is fear that what has become almost a monoculture—wine grapes—is risky, ironically in a place where some people remember the 1950s when cattle represented 99 percent of the much-smaller economic output of Napa County. Others complain there is too much focus on pleasing visitors and not enough on the locals' quality of life: affordable restaurants and housing, practical shopping, ease of movement. The issues are well understood, and remain at the top of local leadership's agenda.

80 SELF-AWARENESS

It took me aback when Philippe Jeanty, then chef de cuisine of the restaurant at Domaine Chandon, sidled up to me a few weeks after our daughter Kate was born and said, "You know, Michaela, I don't want you to take this the wrong way, but you're much nicer since you had the baby."

My reaction was similar 25 years later when several people remarked shortly after I'd retired from my day job as CEO of St. Supéry, "You look so relaxed, Michaela."

I never thought of myself as not nice (even after sales manager Stu Harrison gave me a T-shirt customized for a Domaine Chandon volleyball game emblazoned "Merciless Michaela"), or stressed out as a CEO. Clearly, I was kidding myself.

Philippe had a point. Children teach you patience. I needed to learn that, according to him, and he was right: not everyone is in as much of a hurry as I was. I became more aware of my tendency to finish other people's sentences and tried to curb that behavior. My husband, who used to make me crazy with his admonition to "slow down and go faster," started to make sense.

Children teach you to be sensitive to others. It is useful, for example, to have an understanding of sibling rivalry when taking charge of a group of high-powered managers vying for the CEO's attention. Any hint of favoritism can undermine an otherwise cohesive team.

In 1994 the CEO of Silicon Valley Bank introduced me to Myers-Briggs, a personality test that reveals naturally occurring differences in people's decision making. After spending two hours together touring St. Supéry, John Dean proclaimed me an ENTJ extraverted type like himself. He then sent me a copy of the book.

It was an eye-opener to find that people have very different ways of experiencing the world, a revelation that helped me accommodate the various ways in which one arrives at conclusions or makes recommendations. I no longer expected everyone to understand what I was thinking. I took time to explain my reasoning, and to appreciate theirs. I tried, anyway.

A major problem CEOs face is the lack of constructive feedback from those with whom they work. It is rare that even a direct report will risk being completely frank with the boss. I have been lucky to work with a few, like Lesley Russell, who were willing to tell me things I needed to hear.

This is why I welcomed the suggestion to do a 360 review of St. Supéry's six-member management team. The consulting firm we engaged provided an online questionnaire to complete on ourselves and on one another, and then sent each of us our results. As CEO, I also received my team's individual reports with instructions to share as I saw fit.

I discussed each manager's report in private with him or her, and shared my own results. Everyone had a few surprises, so it was a good exercise and strengthened the team's bonds. The only shortcoming was the limitation inherent in checking boxes on a questionnaire; the responses would have been richer in professionally guided, open-ended interviews.

If only there were a useful mechanism for dealing with the stresses that come with CEO responsibilities. I had become acclimated to using my only truly private time, the hours when I should have been sleeping, to unravel work problems. No one ever suggested I looked stressed until after I'd stepped down.

Even early in my career at Domaine Chandon, *bon vivant*, grape grower, art collector, and friend René di Rosa would occasionally stand behind me and knead my shoulder and neck muscles to loosen the tension he'd noticed. Annual visits to the Esalen Institute in Big Sur had taught him to recognize and deal with stress.

Immediately after retiring from my CEO job I found myself sleeping more and better, helping me understand at last that my body had been sleep-deprived for years. I was also moving my body more, now that I was no longer confined to airplane seats, conference rooms, and a computer screen. The lesson here may be: don't wait for retirement to get adequate sleep and exercise.

I hope future CEOs will have better guidance to becoming more self-aware and ways to make their lives less stressful, because this rewarding work comes at a cost to oneself, one's family, and one's colleagues.

81 TIME FOR CHANGE, AGAIN

Former ambassador to Austria and vintner Kathryn Hall puts on a wonderful holiday luncheon every year for dozens of her women friends and colleagues from all over the country, with delicious wines and entertainment. One of the perennial favorites is an astute psychic she invites in from Texas, whose back-to-back, five-minute private sessions are claimed before all the guests have even arrived.

I was shocked when, laying her hand on mine and thinking hard, she pronounced me a workaholic. What did she see/feel/surmise that made her think my life consisted of nothing but work?

But her remark prodded me to reflect. As the children had grown older and increasingly independent, through inattention I had let work gradually creep into that vacated space in my life, time that I had intended to guard for myself and my husband.

Then I came across a wonderful word that helped me decide how to respond. I wanted to be a workafrolic! In fact, I did have a lot of fun at work. The lure of fine wine attracts interesting people from all walks of life, from all over the world, people I otherwise would never have met.

Work took me to stimulating places like Paris and Shanghai that others only dream about. I stayed in top hotels and enjoyed fine restaurants as part of my job—these were our wine buyers. I had opportunities to be creative, especially in marketing. I liked and admired the people on my team. I enjoyed challenges, especially those we overcame. How much more fun can one hope to have in one's career?

Nonetheless, I decided it was time to reclaim some time for myself. It wasn't hard to do: just be attentive, work efficiently, and delegate more. I started playing tennis, sneaking in a weekly 7:00 a.m. lesson when I wasn't traveling in order to miss only one hour of work.

Tennis was a way of connecting with my father, 2,000 miles away in St. Louis. He was a very good player – he won the singles championship at

NAS Alameda in 1961 -- but when he finally retired in his early 70s and had time to play as often as he liked, his knees gave out. That planted an idea: how could I find more time for friends, family, even myself, and tennis, before *my* knees went?

I deliberately started reserving time for neglected friends and scattered family members. I joined an annual adventure with my middle and high school girlfriends, who proved as much fun as ever even after a multi-decade hiatus. Several had already retired from teaching, and were having a fine time. That planted another seed. Retirement started sounding pretty good.

My service as a corporate director for publicly traded Silicon Valley Bank had taught me that succession planning is a major responsibility. I first brought the topic up to Robert Skalli in 2004, fifteen years into my tenure as CEO. He shrugged it off. I tried again the following year. He changed the subject. And again the next year, with similar results. Either he didn't want to believe I was serious about planning for St. Supéry's future leadership, or he thought I didn't understand myself well enough to know that people like me (like him?) don't retire because I/we would surely expire from boredom.

It wasn't until we were on a New York media tour to promote his French wines in 2007 that I finally succeeded in getting Robert's undivided attention. I seized the opportunity while we were waiting for a flight. The discussion, once engaged, lasted 45 minutes and was so intense that we missed our plane despite standing right in front of the departure gate. He finally understood, and accepted, that I was serious about stepping aside. This launched my next major project: finding a successor for irreplaceable me.

82 FINDING ONE'S SUCCESSOR

Robert Skalli and I agreed early in 2008 that I should launch the search for my successor. From that moment on, every time the word "retirement" came up in conversation, a huge grin lighted up my face. It was definitely the right decision for me.

My first thought was to look internally, given the well-understood reasons for promoting from within. All but the newest member of St. Supéry's management team responded in the affirmative when I asked if any of them would like to be considered.

Recognizing that these specialists in their fields of finance, winemaking, sales, viticulture, and marketing would need additional preparation for the CEO job, I helped each create an individual development program. Some needed more finance training; others felt they didn't know enough about production and wanted to learn about vineyards and winemaking; others felt deficient in marketing skills; all wanted to know more about leadership.

While this was going on at the winery, the directors agreed at the July board meeting in Marseille that we should concurrently be looking at outside candidates. Selecting the next CEO for St. Supéry warranted professional assistance to assure the best candidates were found and considered.

And so I went looking for an appropriate executive recruiter. Previously I had used one only when looking for national sales managers, an exceptionally challenging job to fill and keep filled. I was pleased to find a greatly expanded field of recruiters serving the wine industry, many of them escapees from the tech world where executive search is highly professional and competitive.

Systematically working my way through the list, I found that the best had conflicts, being already engaged for CEO searches, but two of them referred me to a third firm. That is how Julie Chuharski, a former Diageo marketer who had launched Wine & Spirits Recruiting eight years earlier, joined the quest to find my successor.

If we ultimately decided to hire from the outside, the original plan was to create a new COO position for the person who would, after a reasonable time to prove him or herself, succeed me as CEO. I was determined to have a smooth transition, and offered to stay as long as 18 months to give the future chief executive time to get up to speed.

Fortunately for everyone, including me, the shareholders recognized that lengthy transitions are not optimal. After abandoning the COO concept, we settled on a three-month transition period of near joint tenancy with the incumbent CEO (me) and a new president. Thereafter I would continue to serve on the board of directors and act occasionally as a brand ambassador.

Before we could start the outside search, we needed job descriptions for the CEO and the president. I wrote a very simple, 30,000-foot version for the CEO, and a detailed list of responsibilities for the newly created role of president. We also had to develop a compensation package. With Julie's help and my own resources we assembled a set of recruiting documents to launch the search.

Then we drew up a preliminary list of candidates. I contributed several names, she added others, and St. Supéry's management team candidates filled out the list. Julie started reviewing resumes, making calls to assess interest, and checking experience and reputations. Our goal was to have three or four finalists to present to the shareholders in October. We would have to move fast.

All but one of my management team candidates eventually dropped out, having decided either they didn't really want to be CEO or believing they hadn't time to develop the needed skills. Shame on me for not starting earlier. At the October board meeting, our sole internal candidate presented an excellent pitch and answered the directors' questions well, but ultimately was not selected as a finalist.

This left us with the best of the outside candidates vetted by Julie. By the end of the three-day meeting, I believed we had a winner. Just before Robert flew back to Paris, we met with her again over dinner in San Francisco to discuss the offer.

Since wine industry CEO jobs like mine rarely become available, I was surprised when shortly thereafter she withdrew her candidacy. It was hard to believe this opportunity wasn't compelling, so it was something of a relief to learn years later that she hadn't been as ready to make the change as she'd thought. I know that feeling, having agonized myself for nearly two years whether to leave Domaine Chandon.

It was then mid-October 2008 and I found myself in a severe time crunch. The next opportunity to present a candidate would be in six weeks, at the December board meeting in Paris, and Julie and I had just spent months thoroughly canvassing the field. I feared we'd already found all the candidates we would find, but this time the surprise was a happy one.

There were more top candidates available on the second pass; they simply hadn't been looking or available during our first search. I ended up taking excellent candidates with me to Paris in December, both highly qualified and very different from one another in terms of background and management style.

In spite of considerable teasing from my boss, I steadfastly refused to tell him which I thought would be the better choice to succeed me. It seemed more appropriate for him and the other directors to decide their preferences without being guided. Following individual interviews with the board, the directors split up to take each candidate out to dinner to get better acquainted—an interesting exception to the French rule of not conducting business during meals.

Robert Skalli could hardly wait to reconvene after dinner to let me know the shareholders' consensus. I then found myself in the interesting position of disagreeing with their choice, and told him why. I believed they would be happier with a CEO less like me, one with a strong financial background who would aggressively drive ROI. They changed their minds, and so it was done.

Emma Swain joined St. Supéry in March of 2009 as president, and took over as CEO when I officially retired after a happy celebration at the end of May. I continued to work throughout most of June anyway, thanks to Auction Napa Valley and VinExpo, before finally reducing my involvement with St. Supéry to continued service on the board of directors.

83 THE MARKETING WIZ

You'd think, after years of wine marketing, that I'd know what makes a good story. And mostly, I do—except when it comes to me.

In April of 2009, we decided to hold an intimate media dinner at St. Supéry in honor of the winery's twenty years of public operation, and to give a glimpse into its future. The date was chosen to accommodate Robert Skalli's travel schedule, and happened to coincide with my antepenultimate month on the job as St. Supery's CEO before I handed over the reins to my successor.

In attendance were the other two vintners, both French-speaking, whose advice Robert had sought in the early 1980s as he was formulating the vision for his Napa Valley Winery: Bernard Portet of Clos du Val and

Margrit Mondavi, shown on the previous page with Robert Skalli and the author. This event may have been the first time all four of us were together since St. Supéry's opening celebration in 1989.

I was surprised to find that the planned twentieth anniversary story on offer was hijacked by a casual mention that I would be retiring from my day job in a few short weeks. Our media guests instantly decided that was the news story.

84 FULL CIRCLE

If the wine business in Napa Valley ever goes south, the Rodeno family will be in serious trouble. For more than four decades all our eggs have been in one vinous basket: my career, Gregory's law practice, our family vineyard in Oakville, and our Villa Ragazzi micro-winery. Son John is building a career in wine marketing.

Daughter Kate, three thousand miles away in the corporate world, would be the only one unaffected—inheritance issues aside—if Prohibition returns to bring down the wine business one more time. We can only be grateful that the country is unlikely to risk another such spectacular failure of social engineering.

We Rodenos have been growing Sangiovese in the Napa Valley since 1985, and bottling fewer than a hundred cases every year or two under our Villa Ragazzi label since 1989. This was Gregory's idea for honoring his Italian ancestry, and Villa Ragazzi was all his. Between work, kids, and business travel I had no time to help.

Phylloxera killed our Sangiovese vines shortly after the dot.com implosion, and replanting was delayed for several years by Napa County's stringent hillside regulations.

As I was retiring from St. Supéry in mid-2009, our replanted Rodeno clone Sangiovese was just coming back into production. The Villa Ragazzi project had outgrown our barn years earlier, so we were fortunate to outsource winemaking of our 2-3 tons of Sangiovese to Antica Napa Valley, the Antinori family's winery managed by good friend Glenn Salva.

It occurred to me that at last I would have time to work on Villa Ragazzi. In fact, it sounded enticing—the siren song of another startup or, in this case, a restart after a ten-year hiatus.

There's a big difference between being a winery chief executive and a one-woman band (not to take anything away from Gregory). I had grown accustomed to having resources: staff, money, equipment, consultants.

Villa Ragazzi had none of that. I would have to reinvent myself as a tech savvy, problem-solving worker bee to reintroduce our Sangiovese after its nearly ten year absence from the market. The good news was that the internet makes marketing communications (and research) affordable for even the tiniest of micro-wineries.

VILLA RAGAZZI

1 9 8 9

Sangiovese

N A P A V A L L E Y

Rodeno Vineyards

13% Alcohol by Volume.
Grown, produced and bottled by Rodeno Vineyards, Oakville, California. Contains Sulfites.

The die-cut spikes that made the original Villa Ragazzi label memorable also made it impossible to apply to bottles—except achingly slowly, by hand. It took us a year and a week to label the 1989 vintage, our first.

With practice, I could label a case in an hour (the back label was easy, but those spikey fronts were not). Twenty-plus years later, I reluctantly ceded to practicality and agreed to add a black rectangular background to maintain the appearance of spikes without the production challenges of spikes.

Melanie Doherty had created the original artwork prior to the digital era, and I lacked the necessary software and skills to recreate it for printing. I was grateful when Tina Cao, one of my marketing protégées, volunteered to apply her graphic skills to the challenge. Thanks to her, the updated 2009 labels could now be printed as pressure-sensitive and easily applied on a mobile bottling line. Step One.

Step Two was to obtain label approval. In the old days the Bureau of Alcohol, Tobacco & Firearms provided this service, but with firearms and explosives drawing all the resources, label approvals were shifted to the new Alcohol and Tobacco Tax and Trade Bureau (TTB). The emphasis, as usual, was on tax collection.

The big breakthrough since my long-ago last encounter with label approval applications was that final printed labels were no longer required; a jpeg file of the artwork sufficed. It took several tries to get the label into a format that TTB would accept in its new online application process. After final revisions to satisfy the usual nitpicking, Villa Ragazzi Sangiovese had its COLA (Certificate of Label Approval).

As the bottling date for the 2009 Sangiovese drew near, it was time to develop a go-to-market plan—one that I would be able to execute. I dutifully created a timeline of necessary activities, and never looked at it again. Armed with my MacBook Pro, I set out to create a website for Villa Ragazzi.

This is where knowledgeable friends come in handy. John Milliken, a tech consultant whose wife Beth is the president of Spottswoode Winery, steered me toward a simple website template company engagingly named FatCow. I spent long days figuring out how it worked, eventually realizing I needed to buy an upgrade to accommodate all the information I wanted to include. I then spent more long days struggling with the shopping cart provider iCal before switching to FatCow's equally frustrating second choice, PayPal.

Throughout the process I spent hours on the phone with tech support asking newbie questions. After a while their jargon started making sense. Conversations with the help desk grew more productive for me, and probably less irritating for the incredibly patient techies answering FatCow's phones.

I was lucky to have good advice from friends and family. Karen Jess-Lindsley, an ace marketer, read my first content draft and made several suggestions that improved the flow and made the entire website more engaging. Millennial son John unmercifully announced that no one would read so much text. I conceded his point and applied old-fashioned newspaper techniques to the website: lead with the important information, adding details of decreasing importance as you move toward the bottom of the page. These days only the truly fascinated will give anything more than a few nanoseconds of attention.

Daughter Kate was the first to think of googling Villa Ragazzi. She called me, dismayed that the search results were headed by the website of a gay bed-and-breakfast in the south of France sporting photos of bare-chested young men with abs of steel. I quickly added "wine" to our domain name and began trying to learn something about SEO.

When the time came to release the 2009 Sangiovese, in the fall of 2011, I combed through the 2,000 names in my personal address book for potential clients. Three-quarters were colleagues in the wine business. Theorizing they had plenty of wine of their own to deal with, I set most of them aside. (I reserve the right to change my mind about this.)

Armed with my list of 500 friends, family, and connections, I spent days figuring out how to send group emails through Mail, an Apple product not designed for this purpose. Somewhere in the fine print I discovered the trick: keep the batches under 100 names or Mail will refuse to send out the message—without bothering to notify the sender. I still haven't managed to keep the Villa Ragazzi logo from disappearing when an email goes out, but I'm working on it.

Two years later I took some good advice from another generous friend, and started using MailChimp for email blasts. This was another steep learning curve for me, but at least the program was purpose-designed.

When the first orders for 2009 Sangiovese started coming in, PayPal revealed its deficiencies. The shopping cart template asks for a shipping address, but if the address provided doesn't match the credit card holder's billing address, which is not requested, PayPal rejects the payment without explanation. I found this out only by spending hours on the phone with PayPal's help desk.

At first, PayPal didn't like American Express, but that changed. Magically, those cards started being accepted.

PayPal says it can link sales tax rates to zip codes. That may be technically true, but you soon learn that you, not PayPal, will have to research the local tax rates in every zip code you might ship to, and input the information to your PayPal profile. Imagine thousands of PayPal shopping cart administrators doing a monumental data collection task that PayPal could easily provide, and keep updated, for all its customers. Hello?

Worse, PayPal Here's smart phone card reader unpredictably refuses credit cards used for "liquor" sales. Buyers and producers of Napa Valley wines discover this the hard way when a buyer's valid credit card inexplicably bounces.

The last straw: if PayPal sends me one more supremely annoying customer satisfaction survey, I'm going to take another look at iCal.

Since I can't trust PayPal to automate anything, and I can't afford CRM (customer relationship management) software for Villa Ragazzi, I keep all the sales, inventory, and contact information in spreadsheets and my Mac's address book. In the first year I lost track of only four cases of wine, which I consider not bad for a beginner. My excuse? I'm admin, bookkeeper, webmaster, marketer, order taker, shipping clerk, tour guide, delivery driver, social media maven, and warehouse supervisor. I'm doing the best I can.

As you know, I'm not really a one-man band. Gregory – Villa Ragzzi was his idea, remember? – took on the transport division, among other responsibilities. His ancient half-ton pickup had to be reinforced to move a half-pallet at a time of taxpaid case goods from Antica's bottling line to our warehouse. He and occasionally our son John are the only ones brave enough to drive the loaded truck down that steep mountain road.

Unloading requires a cadre of strong legs, as our naturally cool basement is the Villa Ragazzi warehouse. Gregory, John, and I carry every case from the truck — no forklifts for us — up five steps to the front door and down 15 steps to the basement. John can heft two cases at a time, so he does twice as much work as Gregory and me combined. Whenever an order comes in, one of us heads to the basement to schlep box(es) upstairs to load onto the pickup for delivery. It helps to think of all this activity as a fitness program.

When the CEO of the new M Restaurants group in London came to Napa Valley in the spring of 2014 looking for some good wine, he and Gregory hit it off. Our Sangiovese and Faraona would be featured on the inaugural, very international wine list in M's swank new eatery near the Bank of England, the first of several restaurants planned for London.

This bit of good fortune launched an effort to relearn the intricacies of international trade, as it had been decades since I obtained an importer permit for M & H Vineyards to allow us to bring in Moët champagne for parties on the mountain. A major issue was resolved when M Restaurants found a willing UK importer for Villa Ragazzi who patiently walked me through export documentation. Creating UK-compliant import stickers on my computer wasn't too difficult, but hand applying them to each of 420 bottles is best described as tedious. We made the deadline to deliver to the freight forwarder, after cautiously dividing the shipment into two smaller truckloads, and the wine got to the ship in time.

But there's more! Gregory is also in charge of acquiring barrels for each new vintage, a task where his personal contacts proved invaluable. Once-used Limousin oak barrels from Quintessa are pretty special. As a lawyer, he was the natural candidate to handle most compliance issues (export is mine). These include but are not limited to regular state and federal production and tax reporting. To round out his regular duties, Gregory deals with bulk wine brokers as needed, and is the Villa Ragazzi point man for the vineyards.

One of the entertaining things that often happens in the wine business is the unplanned expansion of product lines. Since its inception, Villa Ragazzi offered a fine example of focus on a single product. On my watch, Villa Ragazzi has taken one short year to wander off its designated Sangiovese path.

The 2010 harvest proved generous and good, giving us twice as much Sangiovese as the 2009 vintage. The same was true of Cabernet; we had forty extra tons of excellent fruit without a buyer. So we took the plunge and decided to have the unsold Cabernet grapes custom crushed for sale on the bulk market. That normally risky behavior seemed a good bet, given the Cabernet shortage that had developed while demand continued to grow but replanting halted during the Great Recession. St. Supéry's winemaker Michael Scholz worked his usual magic, producing a delicious Cabernet from our fruit that sold well on the bulk market.

Concerned about my ability to double our 70-80 cases of Sangiovese sales in one year, we decided to bottle a normal amount, then another smaller amount of the 2010 vintage as Riserva to be released after several more years of bottle age. (I overthought that one, since we ran out of 2010 Sangiovese quickly and had to release the Riserva instead of holding it back. But the wine does age beautifully, thanks to Sangiovese's naturally high acidity.)

After tasting the 2010 Cabernet, we decided to add a super-Tuscan blend dominated by Sangiovese and deepened by a little Cabernet. I named it Faraona, inspired by a memorable guinea fowl dinner at Il Giardin da Felicin in Monforte d'Alba. Our blending team – Gregory, John (an excellent palate), me, and winemaker Nate Weis – ultimately decided to add 25% Cabernet to the Sangiovese. This was a surprise, as we'd expected more than 10% to overpower the desired Sangiovese character. We also decided to save and bottle a barrel of the Cabernet Sauvignon as 100 percent Cabernet because it was so tasty.

We skipped the 2011 vintage for reasons too complex to discuss here. More serendipity, as it proved to be a challenging vintage for many in Napa Valley.

In 2012, Nate recommended a *saignée*, resulting in more concentrated Sangiovese and a bonus of 14 cases of delicious Rosato di Sangiovese. Dry rosé is a contrarian product whose time has finally come in the U.S., though many Americans remain convinced that rosé is a sickly sweet wine they wouldn't consider drinking.

If you've been counting, you've witnessed Villa Ragazzi offerings mushroom from one wine to five in short order. Plans and strategy don't have much of a chance in the face of reality and opportunity.

We continue to produce the well-received Rosato, and are debating in 2015 whether to bottle a few cases of Cabernet again. Sangiovese and Faraona are keepers. If anyone dares suggest adding a Syrah, I will be firm. Villa Ragazzi will stay on its Sangiovese course. It makes no sense to confuse those who think of Villa Ragazzi as the producer of "perhaps the best Sangiovese in the U.S./California/Napa Valley," according to a number of highly regarded wine writers.

So ... anyone still want to start a small winery?

EPILOGUE

Long ago I realized I would be horrified to depart this life with nothing to show for it on my headstone but "She Worked."

I have been blessed with a fulfilling career, a wonderful family, good friends, rare flashes of brilliance on the tennis court, and occasionally a soul-satisfying compliment, as when Liz Fitrakis Mercer said, as we arrived at St. Supéry for a wine auction meeting in 2012, "this is the house that Michaela built." But work took much of my time, and still does.

My long career in wine was filled with interesting people, stimulating things to do, and challenges to meet. Serving on corporate boards is a different kind of work, even more stimulating. Writing books and helping run a small family business further contribute to a life of learning. There is little I would change, even if that were possible.

It would have been helpful to live in an era of more advanced technology allowing me to attend meetings in holograph form, or transport myself instantly ("Beam me up, Scotty") to distant places instead of accumulating two million frequent flier miles. When he was six years old, I half-seriously asked our son John if he could invent a transporter so I could be home more. The young *Star Trek* aficionado thought hard for a moment, then sadly admitted he could not.

I hope that you who read this book find encouragement to believe in yourselves, and that you will pay attention to opportunity when it crosses your path. Above all, I urge you to embrace change. Transporters may not be that far in the future.

AUTHOR'S NOTE

"I am not one of those who in expressing opinions confine themselves to facts."

Mark Twain (1835–1910)

Andrée Abecassis is a photographer friend who also works in her ageless mother's New York literary agency. In 2002, Andrée suggested I write a book about the wine industry.

I enjoy writing so the idea appealed, but then she mentioned that it normally takes about 18 months to write a book. After she'd explained how to go about getting published, it was clear that a book would have to wait. For the next decade I would be fully occupied with leading St. Supéry, serving on the board of directors of Silicon Valley Bank, and raising two children—thankfully, not alone. But I started thinking about a book, and saving random notes in a file.

I didn't want to write a book about the wine industry. That would require research, fact checking, and other onerous tasks sure to be rendered obsolete by a dynamically changing business before the final manuscript could be published. But I did like the idea of sharing what I had learned in my forty years of working in Napa Valley as a grower, producer, marketer, and winery CEO. Such a book could be a way of giving back, or maybe just helping others see the "aha!" moments we all encounter.

So my musings turned to a memoir. That seemed a fine idea until my journalist friend Kathleen Buckley ominously warned, "You realize you'll have to name names, don't you?" I usually forget stories as soon as I hear them, especially gossipy ones, and am even worse at remembering jokes, so that wasn't much of a concern. The bigger problem was recalling who did what, when, and to or with whom; I envisioned an avalanche of indignant corrections from those who did remember, or thought they did.

My next notion was to write a *roman à clé* where I could tell my stories but assign fictitious names to the protagonists. No, that wouldn't work either. It would be nearly impossible to disguise some of the Napa Valley's highly colorful characters, and the ruse would tempt people to play guessing games instead of unearthing the embedded lessons.

In 2010 I discovered a workable approach in the Mark Twain Papers, a series of his private papers newly published by the University of California Press. Not only are they a highly recommended read, they lay out Mr. Clemens' methodology. For years he struggled with false starts at an autobiography, eventually settling on an episodic walk through parts of his life that held his interest, writing (dictating, actually) bits as they occurred to him in no particular order.

He insisted that the 210,000 plus words he produced in this manner not be published until 100 years after his death, freeing him to name names at will and providing excellent cover from complaints and lawsuits. The Bancroft Library scholars worked for years to organize his jumbled papers.

Unlike Mr. Clemens, who created headaches for the scholars by not dating his writings, I ultimately decided it would save confusion to organize my randomly written stories in roughly chronological order. So, with gratitude and apologies to Mark Twain, ten years after Andrée had planted the idea, I began to write.

The first part, Startups Are Such Fun, covers the early, transformative years from 1973 to 1988 when I was privileged to learn about business while helping build Domaine Chandon. The second part, Becoming a CEO, covers my years of continuing education as the first chief executive officer of St. Supéry (1988-2009). It ends with my so-called retirement as a corporate board member, entrepreneur, author, and vintner.

My focus is not on the evolution of the wine business over the past four decades, though the significant changes brought by globalization and technology provide context. Rather, my intent is to share what struck me from observing and working with and for the people who've built inspiring enterprises in California. The best of them made it fun, and I can think of no better reason—certainly not money—to be engaged in business. It is to these leaders and above all the support of my family that I owe a successful career.

GLOSSARY

Abbatoir – slaughterhouse

Adjointe: assistant

Année scolaire – academic year

Appellation d'origine contrôlée: delimited, codified, and sometimes classified wine growing region with rules governing wine production and identification

Auberge: elegant hotel in the country

Baguette – long slim loaf of crusty white bread, a household staple in France purchased fresh daily

Bec fin: someone with a refined palate who appreciates fine food

Boeuf à la ficelle: beef filet on a string, cooked in broth

Boiseries: intricate woodwork

Bon vivant: man about town

Bordelais – a resident of Bordeaux (fem: bordelaise); also an adjective

Boulangerie – bread shop

Brix: a measure of sugar in grapes indicating degree of ripeness

Brut: a measure of dryness in champagne indicating absence of sweetness

Café crème – strong coffee with hot milk, also known as café au lait

Carbonnade de boeuf – beef stew made with beer

Centre ville – the center of town

Champenois: originating in Champagne, France

Charmat: a process for making sparkling wine where the second fermentation takes place in a tank

Châtelaine: lady of the house/château

Chef de caves: head winemaker

Chef de cuisine: head chef

Chef d'oeuvre: masterpiece

Chef saucier: chef responsible for making sauces

Champagne viticole (la): the delimited area in France where champagne is grown

Confrère: colleague

Cuvée: blend of wines

Danseuse – Dancing girl, often a kept woman

Demi – colloquial term for a half-liter of beer

En croûte: a dish topped with or wrapped in baked puff pastry

Entrée: main course in a French meal

En tirage: champagne or sparkling wine undergoing second fermentation and aging in the bottle

Estomac: literally a stomach, meaning a mouth to feed

Etoile: star

Faculté – school or college within a university

Faux amis – literally, false friends; words that seem similar in English and French but have different meanings

Faux pas – a mistake, or a social error

Fleur de lis – the lily, symbol of the French monarchy

Flics: French cops

Foie gras: literally "fat liver," a delicacy usually from geese and ducks

Free run: the first juice from a press load of grapes, the highest quality because it is pressed only or principally by the grapes' own weight

Gauloises – very strong French cigarettes

Gendarmes: French police

Grande toque: renowned chef (a toque is a French chef's traditional tall white hat)

Idée reçue – preconceived notion

Imbuvable: undrinkable

Joie de vivre: zest for life

Laissez-faire – leaving people to do as they please

Méthode champenoise: traditional method of making champagne by fermenting wine a second time in a closed container (bottle) to capture the resulting effervescence. The wine is clarified through riddling and disgorging, and goes to market in this same bottle.

Muselet: the wire cage that holds a champagne cork in place

Négociant – a wine producer who buys, blends and bottles wines purchased in bulk rather than growing and/or processing wine grapes

Oeil de perdrix: partridge eye, a term used to describe a pale salmon color in wine

Orangerie: elaborate greenhouse where citrus trees overwinter

Parisienne – a native of Paris (f.)

Père de famille - father

Pelure d'oignon: the color of onionskin

Pot-au-feu: French beef stew

Premier plat: first course in a French meal

Première tailles: the first light pressing (after free run) of grapes or wine;

depending on quality, this may or may not be included in a sparkling wine cuvée

Prix fixe: a set menu at a set price

Régisseur: manager

Raconteur: storyteller

Raison d'être – reason for existing

Renfermé – closed in, unwelcoming

Saignée – literally "bleeding" off some juice early in a fermentation to concentrate the color and aroma of the remainder fermenting on the dark skins; the wine removed early makes fine rosé from certain varieties, notably Grenache and Sangiovese

Savoir faire – knowing what to do; wise in the ways of the world

Sekt: German sparkling wine

Soirée: party

Soldes – fashion sale; the big ones take place in France in June and December.

Stagiaire: an intern or trainee

Terroir – a term indicating grapes or wine having a sense of place, a distinctive personality derived from a vineyard's location

Tête de cuvée: a producer's best sparkling wine or champagne (e.g., Moët's Dom Pérignon or Roederer's Cristal)

Tour de force – master stroke

Transfer: a process for making sparkling wine where the second fermentation takes place in a sealed bottle, and the wine is then transferred via a filter to a different bottle in contrast to *méthode champenoise* where the sparkling wine stays in its original bottle (fermented in *this* bottle vs. fermented in *a* bottle).

Très fin: a high compliment meaning very refined

Verboten: German for forbidden

Vigneron – winegrower

Vrai(e) – true

APPENDIX A

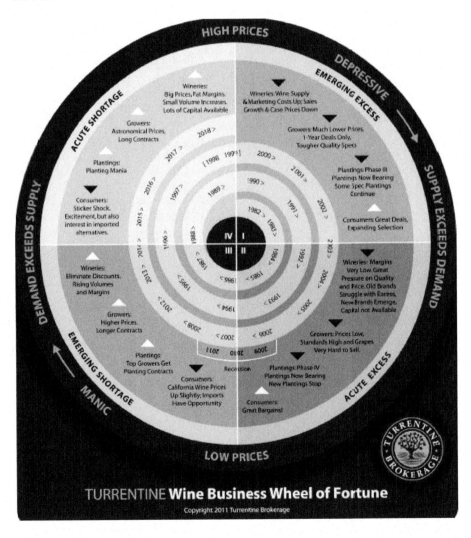

APPENDIX B

A case study on wine public relations written by the author and included here with permission of the publishers of *Spin the Bottle,* a compendium in which it was first published in 2003.

St. Supéry's Smellavision, aka The Liberator

Everyone in the U.S. wine business knows that until recently, Americans were, with few exceptions, terrified by wine. Fear of *faux pas,* aversion to humiliation by snobby sommeliers, lack of "required" knowledge... all conspired to keep potential wine drinkers from exploring any nascent interest in wine.

When I arrived at St. Supéry late in 1988 after 15 very consumer-oriented years at Domaine Chandon, plans for an elaborate gallery of museum-quality, educational wine exhibits were already in place. Some were wonderfully instructive, like the 5 foot tall, 2 foot thick block of Rutherford soil showing its strata and the root system of an ancient vine. I barely had time to deep-six the final exhibit, which sternly suggested that hapless visitors use only the glasses designed for hock, bordeaux, and burgundy with those wines. The penalty for using the wrong glass is too awful to contemplate.

What I proposed in lieu of an intimidating etiquette lesson was some sort of interactive exhibit with which visitors could play. That brought to mind something I'd seen several years earlier: a wine aroma kit produced in France entitled "Le Nez du Vin," which linked hundreds of individual aromas of fruits, flowers, and spices, captured in tiny vials, to the wines where they are commonly found. Add that to my longstanding conviction that we humans all come with the same basic equipment (noses, taste buds, memories) that enable us to appreciate and enjoy wine without formal instruction, and you have the genesis of what I thought of as the "sniffer exhibit."

As we worked with the exhibit fabricator to start drawing up plans, another aspect emerged: a visual component to demonstrate that there is no single "right" color for wine. Cabernet can range from brick to ruby to purple; Sauvignon Blanc can be pale green or deep gold or nearly transparent.

The theme of this wine exhibit was fast becoming "with wine, there is no single 'right' answer." It took us a while longer, and some visitor feedback, to understand that we had stumbled onto something important.

From the moment St. Supéry opened in late 1989, visitors happily pushed the levers that released a whiff of one of four concentrated aromas found in Cabernet (wild cherry, black pepper, green pepper, cedar) or in Sauvignon Blanc (new mown hay, dried wildflowers, grapefruit, green olive). They were delighted to find that they easily recognized the aromas. What kid [of a certain age] doesn't have Proustian total recall of Luden's Wild Cherry cough drops?

But the best was yet to come. Leaving that final exhibit, visitors headed for the tasting room. Instead of the usual shyly mumbled "yes," "no," or "I don't know" in response to "Do you like this wine?" these newly confident tasters started sniffing and swirling and seeking out the varied aromas that they had just discovered. Then they started discussing with some excitement what they were finding in their glass, and *voilà*—a few more new wine consumers were hooked, uh, born.

As we've traveled the country since, we keep meeting people who have visited St. Supéry eager to tell us that their fondest memory is Smellavision. They not only remember playing with the exhibit and identifying the aromas, Smellavision is indelibly linked in their minds with a happy experience at St. Supéry. They may not even realize that the real probable cause of this powerful memory is their own breakthrough into wine enjoyment. Nonetheless, of all the wineries they visited, St. Supéry stands out because of Smellavision (and a few other things that merit individual case studies of their own). That's a public relations success.

APPENDIX C

THE WALL STREET JOURNAL.
ONLINE

March 16, 2007

TASTINGS
By DOROTHY J. GAITER AND JOHN BRECHER

A Toast to Memories

You tasted the family winery's last bottle, shared a six-liter Bordeaux, grilled steak in Russia's wilds. Readers tell our columnists their tales from Open That Bottle Night.
March 16, 2007; Page W1

Michaela Rodeno is the widely respected chief executive of St. Supéry winery in Napa Valley and a leader of her industry. But rarely have the industry's history and traditions been celebrated quite as they were Saturday, Feb. 24.

Ms. Rodeno, her lawyer husband, Gregory, and a large group of friends opened a virtual cellar full of wines, including "the 1980 Chalone Pinot Noir that Bobby got a discount on by purchasing her husband, Dave, 100 shares of Chalone stock in the early '80s"; a 1970 Louis Martini Cabernet Sauvignon ("I have always had a special place in my heart for Louis P. Martini, a wonderfully wise and kind man"); and a rare 1995 Lokoya wild-yeast "Sauvage" Chardonnay "made by Greg Upton, who died in his 30s of cancer on Thanksgiving Day in 1997." Added Ms. Rodeno: "It's now after 10 p.m., and several people are singing 'Werewolves of London.' Amazing how many of us know the lyrics."

MORE FROM OTBN 8

· Read about some bottles[1] that were opened, along with a few tasting notes.

· Read about a few of the dishes[2] prepared by OTBN celebrants along with one of the wines they paired with the meal.

· Take a look at some photos[3] from Opening Night.

Ah-ooooo! From Oakville, Calif., to Russia to Tokyo, it was Open That Bottle Night 8, when thousands of people all over the world -- sometimes in romantic couples, sometimes as part of giant parties, often at restaurants and even at big fund-raisers in Vail, Colo., and Rochester, N.Y. -- finally uncorked that wine that has always been too precious to open. Some of the wines were special because of their age — like a 1900 Moscatel de Setúbal from Portugal -- but others were priceless for other reasons.

Just ask Jake Kaufman of Chambersburg, Pa. At a charity event in 2002, he bought a bottle of 1999 Sangiovese made for the Thomas Jefferson Foundation from the replanted vineyard at Jefferson's Monticello estate in Virginia. Two years later, Mr. Kaufman's house burned to the ground. When the salvage crew removed the debris, they found five bottles of wine; the last remaining bottle was the Sangiovese, which he opened with friends on OTBN. "The label was brown, but the wine was still good!" marveled the host, Patricia Mathews.

APPENDIX D

survey..

SPRING 1987

Who *Are* You, Anyway?

Our ad agency, skeptical New Yorkers all, asked us for a profile of a typical Chandon Club member. Well, that was a thinker. We ended up telling them that you appear to be a diverse group (who may have little in common besides your enthusiasm for Chandon sparkling wine and the winery and restaurant), that you like to have fun, that you are mostly professionals ranging from 25-54 in age, well-travelled, open-minded, independent thinkers, actively participatory, wine knowledgable and, above all, confident of your own judgment. OK, they said, prove it.

So we devised this questionnaire to test our theory. The ad agency revised it to make it more complicated. We revised their revision. The ad agency said no more than 10% of you would take the time to fill it out. We said, nonsense ... Chandon Club members like to communicate with us. We can hardly wait to see who's right. Please. We want to win.

Please don't be put off by the complexity of questions 1 and 2. The rest are *much* easier.

1. Rank the following sparkling wines and champagnes from 1 to 5 (with 1 low, 5 high) in each category according to your own perception, real or presumed (if you have no relevant perception, check "don't know"):

	Prestige	Quality	Popularity	Value	Don't Know
(Domaine) Chandon					
Krug					
Korbel					
Cristal					
Schramsberg					
Freixenet					
Moët & Chandon					
Piper-Sonoma					
Dom Pérignon					
Taittinger					

2. Rate the following attributes of Chandon sparkling wine according to their importance to you, from 0 to 5, with 0 being totally unimportant and 5 being very important:

American _____	Product quality _____	Flavor _____
Bubbles' _____	Prestige _____	Price _____
Reliability _____	Value _____	French heritage _____
Napa Valley _____	Compatibility with food _____	Méthode champenoise _____
Availability _____	Brut _____	Product consistency _____
Festive _____	Status _____	California _____

3. Which of the following sources do you use to obtain information about wines and champagne/sparkling wine?

	Check those that apply	Check those that apply for champagne/sparkling wine
Wine writers' columns	☐	☐
Wine newsletters	☐	☐
TV advertisements	☐	☐
Magazine ads	☐	☐
Newspaper	☐	☐
Friends	☐	☐
Store displays	☐	☐
Knowledgable wine merchants	☐	☐

(continued inside)

ABOUT THE AUTHOR

Michaela Kane Rodeno is a business leader, entrepreneur, corporate director, consultant, grape grower, wife, and mother. Her successful 40-year career in the wine industry, more than half of it as a CEO, has made her a role model for young people who want to excel. She has a BA and MA from the University of California, Davis, in French Literature, and an MBA from Berkeley/Haas.

The Rodeno family lives on a 25-acre vineyard in the Napa Valley where they grow Cabernet Sauvignon for Robert Mondavi Winery, and from which they bottle 100-200 cases annually of Sangiovese and Cabernet Sauvignon under their Villa Ragazzi label.

CPSIA information can be obtained
at www.ICGtesting.com
Printed in the USA
FSOW04n1637061015
11849FS